C0-ADX-685

AMERICA'S REVOLUTIONARY SPIRIT

BOOKS BY JOHN R. TERRY

America's Revolutionary Spirit
Speak English from the Heart, 3 Vols.
Cannery Row (Japanese Translation)
English Research and Methodology

America's Revolutionary Spirit

The Evangelical Religious Heritage of the Nation

John R. Terry

An *Exposition-University Book*

Exposition Press   Hicksville, New York

First Edition

©1977 by John R. Terry

All rights reserved, including the right of reproduction in
whole or in part, in any form or by any means, electronic or
mechanical, including photocopying, recording, or by any information storage and retrieval system. No part of this book
may be reproduced without permission in writing from the
publisher. Inquiries should be addressed to Exposition Press,
Inc., 900 South Oyster Bay Road, Hicksville, N.Y. 11801

Library of Congress Catalog Card Number: 77-086730

ISBN 0-682-48888-7

Printed in the United States of America

To the Lord Jesus
who not only brings
individual salvation
but heart revolution as well

CONTENTS

PREFACE

I have lived abroad well over half of my adult years. Living in another land, especially one in the Orient, is an adventure in itself. Sitting cross-legged, eating raw fish or spearing something with chopsticks can be very challenging. The new atmosphere filled with new ideas and surrounded by strange customs makes one ponder about many of life's problems.

The Westerner cannot help compare his past life to the new one he is immersing himself in day by day. The limbs grow numb as he sits on tatami floors. His ears try to sort out the babbling conversation about him. But most of all he is surprised by how much the religious faith of the country seeps into every action and most thoughts.

Looking at America from Japan is helpful. One finds new customs that are even better than those in the United States. An individual may even grow homesick for a hot dog or a

nice piece of apple pie. But he realizes that America is more
than the Statue of Liberty or the Golden Gate Bridge.

Japan is so much older than the United States that it
seemed almost laughable to take the latter's Bicentennial
seriously; yet, I found myself wondering why America could
rise in such a short time to become the strongest nation on
earth. The best way to find out was to begin at the beginning.

In my college days I received many impressions about the
Puritans, the Revolution, and the nation that was formed. When
I thought of the New Englanders I thought of prudish people
who found no joy in life and who only heard sermons like
Sinners in the Hand of an Angry God. I also learned that the
rebels in rags had many things going for them and the victory
over the redcoats was a rather natural result.

I decided to dig into some volumes in my 8,000-book library.
The results were amazing. There were my ancestors, warts and
all, becoming as familiar to me as my modern-day neighbors.
Instead of finding prudes, I found a people who liked to play
and who enjoyed puns. Instead of a ready fighting force to
shove the foreigners from their shores, I found an army that
lacked money, materials, and manpower. But most surprisingly,
I discovered a nation immersed in religious atmosphere.

I dug these nuggets from more than 200 volumes, and I
am deeply indebted to what the other scholars have done to
supply me with such a wealth of information. At times I did
not like what I found, particularly when it dealt with the
treatment of Blacks in the new colonies. But the results of my
studies did convince me that our forefathers came to these
shores to form colonies on religious principles, and with this
foundation they built a society where there was respect for
the individual, a lack of rigid class lines, and freedom of
worship. The most important thing was the living religion
they practiced. Their savior was real and dear to their souls.
No dead formalism there, but a land where the Bible was
the book for instruction, for faith, and for the basis of a
democratic government.

AMERICA'S REVOLUTIONARY SPIRIT

I PUBLIC PREJUDICE AGAINST THE PURITANS

*Perhaps I do not go too far when I say, next to the intro-
duction of Christianity among mankind, the American
revolution may prove the most important step in the progressive course of human improvement.*

DR. RICHARD PRICE

Christianity caused the greatest revolution in the history
of the universe. It not only toppled the religion of the greatest
empire of its day, it revolutionized the heart of each individual
it touched. No political philosophy makes new men, only
old men in new clothing. Only God, whose own personal touch
brought this earth into existence, can create entirely new men
where "old things are passed away; behold, all things become
new."

This was the central belief of those hardy individuals who braved a hostile world to make the long journey to a new land. In 1587, 117 women were put ashore on Roanoke Island to be the first settlers to enter Virginia. They all disappeared without a trace. In 1607, a new settlement was begun at Jamestown under the auspices of the Virginia Company, which had used many clergymen to encourage settlers to leave England for a life unknown. Of the 500 men and women living in this town in 1609 only 60 would be alive one year later. The company seriously considered calling the colonists home, and when they voted about staying at that spot on the James River, only one man voted in favor of the proposal. Without a deep faith in God, very few of the Pilgrims would have dared risk their lives in the wilderness of America.

The spark of faith that ignited in the human heart by faith in Jesus Christ is the chief cause of revolution in the world according to Pearl Buck. It creates independent individuals who will bow before no man and only hold their trust in God. The Virginia Company itself was dedicated to "expanding the religion, power and glory of England" in that order. The Pilgrims came to advance "the Gospel of the kingdom of Christ in these remote parts of the world." The Quakers expected to build their own utopia where freedom of religion would undergird the spirit of the community as a whole.

The thoughts of Dr. Richard Price, a liberal Englishman, were echoed by the Frenchman de Tocqueville when he said that this experiment was "interesting not only to the United States, but to the whole world; it concerns not a nation, but all mankind." The Americans felt the very same way and believed they had wrought a new type of civilization that others might wish to copy in the future. Tom Paine said, "America made a stand, not for herself only, but the world, and looked beyond the advantages which she could receive."

At Gettysburg—Lincoln emphasized the fact that our forefathers had "brought forth a new nation" that was in marked contrast to the European states which had been developed by century-long historical processes. In the Declaration of Independence, we read these words by Thomas Jefferson: "We hold these truths to be self-evident, that all men are created equal, that they are endowed by their Creator with certain unalienable Rights, that among these are Life, Liberty, and the pursuit of Happiness." Fifty years later the author of this world-shaking document would say, "May it be to the world, what I believe it will be, the signal for arousing men to burst the chains under which monkish ignorance and superstition had persuaded them to bind themselves. . . ." Two centuries later, in the middle of the Watergate scandal that shook the very foundations of the national community, a political scientist was to remind America of an essential point—the United States was "a nation only by faith."[1]

This should not blind us to the flaws in our journey through history. Perhaps violence is not as American as apple pie, as Rap Brown claimed; but we should not overlook the shortcomings of the men who managed our checkered past. The Loyalists looked back to pre-Revolutionary America as a "Golden Age" when all was right with the world. Even Cromwell had once considered the idea of moving to that new territory that promised so much. Lincoln believed that the Fathers of America had set up "a standard maxim for free society, which should be familiar to all, and revered by all; constantly looked to, constantly labored for, and even though never perfectly attained, constantly approximated, and thereby constantly spreading and deepening its influence and augmenting the happiness and value of life to all people of all colors everywhere. . . ."

It would probably startle Americans to know that the brilliant students of a famous French university could only vaguely recognize Jefferson as an American politician. India's Jawaharlal Nehru gave the Virginian one line in his monumental book, *Glimpses of World History*, and he even misquoted the Dec-

laration of Independence on top of that.[2] The names of men
who have become household words in America are often
unknown abroad.

Even though the first group to settle at Jamestown had to
live on the charity of the Indians, the Massachusetts Bay Colony grew rapidly. Within ten years, the population rose to
almost twenty thousand. By the time the 1770s arrived, the
country was a nation of young people. Half the population
was under the age of sixteen and three-quarters were below
twenty-five. Most of the signatories of the Declaration of Independence were very young, considering the average age of
politicians today. Franklin was seventy and Rutledge of South
Carolina was only twenty-six, but the average age was not
much over thirty years. The colonies had more than a fourth
of the population of her mother country and was larger than
many of the independent nations and principalities of Europe
at that time. In 1759, there were 1,250,000 whites and 340,000
Blacks in the thirteen original colonies.

A historian writes: "Any inventory of the elements that
have gone into the making of the 'American mind' would have
to commence with Puritanism." Whereas some British citizens
seem to have had no knowledge about the American Revolution
today, the Loyalists of that period were quick to blame it all
on those nasty Puritans. The Tory historians of the last quarter of the eighteenth century said that the ideas of Separatists
and Puritans were based on "principles of ecclesiastical polity
[which were] directly repugnant to those of the Established
Church, as their ideas of civil government were to those of a
mixed monarchy." Loyalist Joseph Galloway stated, "The charter of Massachusetts Bay was manifestly calculated to efface
all the laws, habits, manners, and opinions which it ought to
support and to level all orders, arrangements, checks, and bal-
ances, wisely graduated and tempered, of a mixed monarchy,
to the lowest and most imperfect of all political systems, a
tumultuous, seditious, and inert democracy."

The word *Puritanism* causes people to sneer and shake their heads. D. H. Lawrence bitterly attacked Benjamin Franklin as "typical of the hypocritical and bankrupt morality of the do-gooder American, with his stress upon an old-fashioned Puritan ethic that glorified work, frugality, and temperance—in short, a 'snuff-coloured little man' of whom 'the immortal soul part was a sort of cheap insurance policy.' " Lawrence resented being shoved into "a barbed wire paddock" and made to "grow potatoes or Chicagoes." He continued his tirade by stating how much he hated "clever America" lying "on her muck-heaps of gold." This liberal's acid comments were made even though Franklin had fathered only one child, an illegitimate son, who became a Tory royal governor of New Jersey and finally left for England never to return.

Writers of fiction are not the only ones to level their weapons at men of another age. One of their prime targets was Rev. Cotton Mather, but he was one of the most enlightened men of his time with a healthy interest in science and medicine. He pressed the people to be vaccinated over the objections of the medical establishment in Boston. Daniel J. Boorstin wrote, "The unlikely hero of the story was none other than Cotton Mather (1663-1728), on whom has been focused the ill-informed hatred of generations of liberal historians." Another historian agrees with Boorstin, but in relation to a different event in the cleric's life. "History has not been fair to Cotton Mather. Indeed the majority of historians have, in complete defiance of the facts, presented him as a man who instigated witchcraft trials to satisfy his own lust for fame and power," says Chadwick Hansen. He continues, "If Cotton Mather was never a witch hunter he was always a witchcraft scholar. His scholarship was thoroughly impervious to shifts in popular opinions."

No person, much less a true believer in Jesus Christ, can find anything to glorify in the witch-hunts and trials by their ancestors. But the traditional interpretation of what happened

at Salem is "as much the product of casual journalism and
imaginative literature as it is of historical scholarship."[3] Execution for witchcraft was not limited to one denomination
nor to any one nation. In fact, it continued in Europe for
more than one hundred years after the people of Massachusetts had called for a day of prayer and fasting in repentance
over what had happened in their colony.

Witchcraft trials were far from usual and surely not simply
the result of Puritanism. George Lyman Kittredge tells us:

> The Salem outbreak was not due to Puritanism; it is not assign-
> able to any peculiar temper on the part of our New England
> ancestors; it is no sign of exceptional bigotry or abnormal super-
> stition. Our forefathers believed in witchcraft, not because they
> were Puritans, not because they were colonials, not because they
> were New Englanders—but because they were men of their
> time. They shared the feelings and beliefs of the best hearts
> and wisest heads of the seventeenth century. What more can
> be asked of them? It is hard to satisfy modern writers on
> witchcraft, who insist on censuring the sixteenth and seventeenth
> century on a basis of modern rationalism. It is quite certain
> that if some of those who now sit in judgment on the witch-
> prosecutors had been witch judges, no defendant would ever
> have escaped.[4]

One of the worst problems for these types of authors is
that they could not possibly understand the problems under
discussion about those things dealing with the Scriptures because of "the incapacity of these historians to understand a
culture whose central concerns were religious." The Puritans
themselves had lived in this kind of atmosphere before they
left England. One of their historians writes: "When, by the
travail and diligence of some godly and zealous preachers,
and God's blessing on their labors, as in other places of the
land, so in the north parts, many became enlightened by the
word of God, and their ignorance and sins discovered by the
word of God's grace, and began, by his grace, to reform their

lives and make conscience of their ways, the work of God was by his grace, to reform their lives and make conscience of their ways, the work of God was no sooner manifest in them, but presently they were both scoffed and scorned by the profane multitude, and the ministers urged with the yoke of subscription [to follow the rites and literature of the Anglican Church], or else must be silenced."[5]

Even though Puritan punishment for crime was in many ways less severe than in other countries of the world, the authors of American history have for most part overlooked this. They only have been interested in all the dirt they can dig up about those who practiced a piety they both detested and misunderstood. Kai T. Erikson says, "Students of American history have long been attracted by this grisly subject, not only the school children who learn something about Roger Williams and the witchcraft frenzy but whole generations of serious scholars as well. Until later in the nineteenth century [and even well into the twentieth] historians of Massachusetts wrote so much about Puritan severity that one might have thought they were postponing other relevant topics until they could come to terms with at least this one compelling chapter of the past."[6]

Religious personages are often criticized for their warped interpretation of the facts. But here we find a few honest historians slapping the wrists of the members of their own brotherhood and warning them that they cannot understand our New England ancestors unless they cast aside preconceived misconceptions. Bernard Mayo called his brethren to task when he exploded, "Admittedly the line between myth and reality, thought often very broad, is sometimes narrow, and symbols in varying degree do have a basis in actualities. But this does not excuse the historian from his responsibility to separate fact from overblown fancy to the utmost of his fallible abilities. Alas, while history does not repeat itself, historians often repeat one another."[7]

The building of tall tales is not simply involved in the events that took place two hundred years ago. Theodore Sorensen was fearful that John F. Kennedy's "martyrdom would make a myth of the mortal man." We should expect enlightened critics of the modern world to be above criticism as they have had the opportunity to judge things without passion or prejudice.

Dr. Chomsky was a harsh censor of America's adventures in Southeast Asia. He not only wrote with feeling, he pled his case with a deep sense of moral indignation and well he might. He led a "moral elite" who chomped on any rich morsel that fell from the government presses. But Arthur M. Schlesinger, Jr., questions his writing. "Somewhere in the book Dr. Chomsky writes with his usual sententiousness, 'It is the responsibility of intellectuals to speak the truth and to expose lies.' Chomsky must be putting us on. His argument contradicts the first half of this responsibility and his practice the second. Judging by *American Power and the New Mandarins,* one can only conclude that Dr. Chomsky's idea of the responsibility of intellectuals is to forswear reasoned analysis, indulge in moralistic declamation, fabricate evidence when necessary and shout always at the top of one's voice."

Christians have often been frightened by the name of some authority on the front of secular books. Even in the field of science men have been fearful of questioning some important individual simply because he is held to be an expert in his field. This weakness is compounded when birds of a political feather flock together. During the early history of the prestigious *New York Book Review,* Richard Hofstadter, a noted historian, called it *The New York Review of Each Other's Books.* Consistently, they only tossed around the same ideas among themselves and were cheered when everyone ended up patting his brother on the back.

Hofstadter has never liked the mixing of moral precepts and historical analysis, but he knew where this secular commitment came from. He writes:

To understand the reform mentality, we must consider the vigor with which the Progressives attacked not only such social questions as the powers of trusts and bosses, but also such objects of reform as the liquor traffic and prostitution. The Progressive mind, I have said, was preeminently a Protestant mind; and even though much of the strength was in the cities, it inherited the moral traditions of rural evangelical Protestantism. . . . Here it was that a most important aspect of the Protestant personality came into play; its ethos of personal responsibility. . . . The more the muckrakers acquainted the Protestant Yankee with what was going on around him, the more guilty and troubled he felt. The religious institutions of Protestantism provided no mechanism to process, drain off, and externalize the sense of guilt.[8]

The guilt, as any evangelical could have told him, was an internal problem, not an external one. Having to battle with his guilt, and hating the Puritan mores passed down from generation to generation, the New Left has not only attacked American diplomacy, it has questioned the validity of society as a whole. They have vented their spleen about everything the population held dear and warped their own preconceived conceptions in the process. "What bothers me most," wrote Richard W. Leopold, "is the assumption that, somehow, taking a position is more important than the documentary foundation on which the position rests and the thoroughness of the research. . . . What is important to the New Left is to expose and to say something new. . . . A second attitude of the New Left that bothers me is its intolerance—the assumption that these matters are not susceptible to doubt." Herbert Feis could not stomach the obviously slanted opinions that were of more importance to the new revisionists than an objectivity toward a given subject.

Historian Thomas A. Bailey complained about the new generation as he wrote, "All this means is that they start with a built-in bias, which is the very thing we were all warned against in graduate school." But perhaps the older generation has missed the more positive points of the New Left. They were questioning some things that needed to be questioned. It stirs up fires of controversy and makes one assess one's viewpoint again. Dr. Divine praises the New Left-wingers for that.

Coming back to the Puritans and their shortcomings, we now will have to judge them by the same principles applied to other groups in the same period. One of the questions we all would have put to the judges of that day was whether or not they were punishing demented individuals. In the case of Goodwife Glover, she was led before a committee of physicians, not clerics, to see if she were sane. They all agreed that she was in her right mind, although a genuine witch in their opinion. Almost all the doctors of that day were convinced, like the above, that witches did exist. "In fact, the seventeenth-century physician was apt to attribute everything he could not explain organically to witchcraft, just as the twentieth-century physician is apt to call whatever he cannot understand as psychosomatic," writes an expert on the subject of witches.

Even though approximately nine hundred witches were burned in the city of Bamberg, Germany, and approximately five thousand in the single French province of Alsace, we see no great wave of indignation on the part of the scientists of the seventeenth century. This was the age when most of the seminal ideas of modern science were developed, so it was entitled "the century of genius" by Whitehead. Bacon, who saw the possibilities of an inductive scientific method, believed that you could cure warts by rubbing them with a rind of bacon and hanging it out of a window that faced south, and, more importantly, that witchcraft may take place "by a tacit operation of malign spirits." Robert Boyle, author of *The Skeptical Chemist,* believed in using stewed earthworms for healing; that a worsted stocking that was worn close to the skin would aid an individual's health; and that human urine was efficacious and could be taken internally or used externally. He also suggested that miners be interviewed to see if they met any demons under the earth. Newton spent more of his time in occult studies than he did in the study of physics. John Locke argued, "If this notion of immaterial spirit may have, perhaps, some difficulties in it not easily to be explained, we have therefore no more reason to deny or doubt the existence of such spirits, than we have to deny or doubt the existence of a body. . . ." Thomas Hobbes wrote, "As for witches I think not that their witchcraft is of any real power; but yet that they are justly punished, for the false belief they have that they can do such mischief, joined with their purpose to do it if they can; their trade being nearer to a new religion than a craft or science."

We don't see any intellectuals burning the books of Bacon, Boyle, or Locke. Even though they were quick to accept the testimony of a known liar, who criticized Puritans of the same period, few have acknowledged their own bias in dealing with this religious group. One wonders if these intellectuals judge the scientists listed above with the same strictness.

Twenty years after the last trial in Salem, there was a woman condemned to death in England for witchcraft, and in Scotland, in 1722, there were executions. On the continent, we see witches sent to the next world as late as 1745 in France; in Germany in 1775; in Spain in 1781; in Switzerland in 1782; and in Poland in 1793. In South America, executions continued well into this century, and in 1929, three Pennsylvania-Germans were convicted of murdering a "pow-wow" doctor. The first serious medical study into witchcraft in this century was in 1942 under the title of *Voodoo Death*.

Perry Miller tells us, "There are some respects in which Puritans writing about their own history are amazingly impartial; since they viewed whatever had happened as God's doing, they could suppress or twist facts only by running the danger of blaspheming God's work."[9] Those who put their faith in Marxism are entirely different. Bertram Wolfe writes, "All Party histories and memoirs written while Lenin was alive, or indeed throughout the twenties, give the above four names [Kamenev, Tshakaya, Japaridze, Nevsky (or Lehmann)], differing only as to whether the fourth man was Lehmann or Nevsky. All histories written in the first half of the thirties, as weapons in Stalin's faction war on his associates, are purposely evasive on the make-up of the Transcaucasian Delegation to the Congress."[10]

Too much has been written of a negative nature about the Puritans. One of the keys to understanding the power of their precepts, which have been handed down to us today, is to realize that they viewed Christianity as a personal, not a collective, religion. Each person was responsible not to a priest or a bishop, but directly to God for his salvation and blessings.

Increase Mather ceremonially burned a copy of his book, *More Wonders,* in Harvard Yard to show his repentance about any part he had in the witch scares in Massachusetts. John Winthrop confessed, "Lusts were so masterly as no good could fasten upon mee." Sin was not something to be giggled about; it was to be confessed to God with deep repentance.

The applicants for church membership had to satisfy the Elders and then the whole congregation of "the worke of grace upon their soules, of how God hath beene dealing with them about their conversion . . . that they are true believers, that they have beene wounded in their hearts for their originall sinne, and actuall transgressions, and can pitch upon some promise of free grace in the Scripture, for the ground of their faith, and that they finde their hearts drawne to beleeve in Christ Jesus, for their justification and salvation . . . and that they know completely the summe of Christian faith."

One of the major problems for secular authors is to understand the relationship between the Puritans and Calvinists. They almost always feel that the Church of God in Massachusetts predestined individuals to hell and that there was no way of salvation for a major part of society. This definitely was not true. Whosoever wished to find Christ and would bow their knee in real repentance would become a child of God no matter what their station in life. This equality in Christianity was one of the main tenets of the Puritans. This is why historians point out that it was "religion and education" that brought true democracy to New England.

Not only were the Puritans interested in universal education, based on their view of the Scriptures, but they were definitely not antiintellectual. Daniel Boorstin wrote, "Cotton Mather's interest in diseases was probably sharpened by his Puritan theology." Since he followed the basic teachings of the word of God he would agree with science historian D. T. Atkinson, who tells us that the "science of public health" was developed from the Old Testament and that it "formed the basis of sanitation in the more advanced countries of the world for over two thousand years." Not only did he look backwards at the blessed teachings of God about hygiene, etc., but he took an active part in pressing for smallpox vaccination while he was opposed by Dr. William Douglass, who was the only gentleman in Boston to possess his M.D. degree. Luckily for the people of the colony, Mather was more persuasive and through his efforts the community was protected from a dangerous disease.

So whether or not the Puritans were active in church government, education or in science, they were first thinking of the people under their tutelage. Even so they were ever worried about their relationship with God. Just because they had come to America with pure motives did not mean that their Creator would sanction their colony because of patriotic pulsations. Far different from the zealous patriots of the modern era, they supported their government not because it was of their own making, but only on the grounds that it would continue to follow the basic teachings of God and rest in his guidance.

The Puritans were not the only religious folk in America. The Quakers had a far more enlightened approach to the problems of life, whether it dealt with freedom of religion or the prison system. Even though they were very liberal, they interpreted the Bible in a very conservative manner. William Penn not only wrote *No Cross, No Crown,* he insisted that man needed salvation to find the true meaning to man's existence. But the history of the Quaker church, according to a secular scholar, was much less compromising than the Puritans in the long run. The Congregational churches of the Bay Colony gradually widened their views, but the Quakers became proud in their own practices, so they began to lose ground.[11]

As the nation moved toward war, it was evident that the British were most upset with the colony of Massachusetts. Connecticut was more generous to outsiders and liberal in her laws, so she did not feel the initial wrath of the king. Vermont, although later to boast of having seen the first battle of the war, was not powerful enough to cause much anxiety in England. New York State often bothered the governor, so he dissolved the legislature; but they had many Tories in that colony whom the London officials were more lenient with than the Bostonians. Virginia would recall the fiery speeches of Patrick Henry, but the Church of England was strong in the Old Dominion.

There were a good number of firsts in relationship to the Puritan province:

1. The British believed that the quarrel was largely with Boston.
2. The crown believed that Boston and the colony were leading the other colonies into rebellion.
3. The British believed that Boston should be punished like Edinburgh.
4. Even though Boston was unpopular with the other colonies, she was the first colony to win the joint sympathy and aid from the others.

5. Massachusetts was the first place where Loyalists signed pledges to support the king.
6. Massachusetts would be the initial spot where Tories actually organized to try to stem the tide of independence.
7. Massachusetts was the center of the Revolution.
8. Gen. William Howe believed that the organized resistance was localized in Massachusetts.
9. Massachusetts would be the first area to have a battle against the British.
10. Massachusetts had been so impressed with the views on liberty that she was the first colony to try to abolish slavery within her borders.

The war was being fought not only to win liberty for the secular world, but to make sure that there was no establishment of a church from abroad. Richard A. Bartlett describes the feeling of those people:

> The type of Christianity that was so successful in the new country, at least east of the Mississippi, was pietistic and highly individualistic. A man or woman could make peace with God without a mediator. This has been called the Universal Priesthood of All Believers, and although it had been practiced by certain persecuted peoples in Europe—the dissenters of the Rhine Valley in particular—it achieved its greatest acceptance in America, where the formal priesthood of established churches was missing. Moreover it was a faith of the heart, of the emotions, rather than of reason and intellect. It was an optimistic faith in spite of the numberless sermons that stressed hellfire and brimstone, for its theme was redemption. The individual had the power within him to suffer personal repentance for his sins, and thus gain redemption.[12]

The simple reasoning of the people of that day was much like what Pascal had to say: "To be mistaken in believing that the Christian religion is true is no great loss to any one; but how dreadful to be mistaken in believing it to be false."

The Americans were just awakening from their slumber. Just as the fire in the soul of the first-century Christians had grown to such proportions that it toppled the mighty empire of Rome, the population now armed themselves to defend their freedom against the most powerful government in the world. Jonathan Edwards tells us that during the days of the Great Awakening, in the Connecticut Valley, men would shout, "What shall I do to be saved?" Now these same people were calling on God to save them, not from their sins, but from the wrath of another king, the one who ruled in London but not in their hearts.

NOTES

1. Theodore H. White, *Breach of Faith* (New York: Atheneum Publishers, 1975), p. 138.
2. Lawrence H. Leder, *The Meaning of the American Revolution* (Chicago: Quadrangle Books, 1969), p. 73.
3. Chadwick Hansen, *Witchcraft at Salem* (New York: George Braziller, 1969), p. 1.
4. George Lyman Kittredge, *Witchcraft in Old and New England* (Cambridge, Mass., 1929), p. 338.
5. Alexander Young, *Chronicles of the Pilgrim Fathers of the Colony of Plymouth, 1602-1625* (New York: Da Capo Press, 1971), p. 19.
6. T. Kai Erickson, *Wayward Puritans* (New York: John Wiley & Sons, 1966), p. 188.*
7. Bernard Mayo, *Myths & Men,* The Academy Library (New York: Harper & Row, Publishers, Harper Torchbooks, 1959), p. 53.*
8. Richard Hofstadter, *The Age of Reform* (New York: Random House, Vintage Books, 1955), pp. 204-205.*

*Denotes paperback edition

9. Perry Miller and Thomas Johnson, *The Puritans,* 2 vols., The Academy Library (revised ed., New York: Harper & Row, Publishers, Harper Torchbooks, 1938), 1: 86-87.*

10. Bertram D. Wolfe, *Three Who Made a Revolution* (1948; reprint ed., Middlesex, England: Penguin Books, 1966), p. 510.*

11. Daniel J. Boorstin, *The Americans: The Colonial Experience* (1958; reprint ed., Middlesex, England: Penguin Books, 1965), pp. 54-55.*

12. Richard A. Bartlett, *The New Country* (New York: Oxford University Press, 1974), pp. 368-69.

II THE RELIGIOUS BACKGROUND OF AMERICA

Upon my arrival in the United States, the religious aspect of the country was the first thing that struck my attention; and the longer I stayed there, the more did I perceive the great political consequences resulting from this state of things, to which I was unaccustomed. In France I had almost always seen the spirit of religion and the spirit of freedom pursuing courses diametrically opposed to each other; but in America I found that they were intimately united, and that they reigned in common over the same country. My desire to discover the cause of this phenomenon increased from day to day.

ALEXIS DE TOCQUEVILLE

In 1650, the eyes of the world were on Europe. Every European nation had a royal personage on the throne. Even in the midst of splendor and educational triumphs, the ideas about the rights of men were completely forgotten. There was almost no political activity made on the part of the people. There were very few pieces of literature written on democracy and many of the upper classes looked down on anything that supported the spirit of liberty in the poorer classes. But at this time in the New World, people were so active in the interests of the common man that some have said that almost every American thought like a lawyer and took an active interest in political matters.

Europe was beginning to look around for areas to conquer. In 1418, Prince Henry established himself at the southern tip of Portugal where he lived in a residence that resembled a monastery more than a palace, and where this ascetic bachelor, who gave up drinking wine with his meals, could devote his life to the promotion of voyages to discover the riches of the outside world. His first hope was to find sources of gold in Africa and secondly to bring untold heathen to Christian salvation as he understood it. The Order of Christ paid the expenses for these adventures and was delighted when the ships brought back a hold full of black gold in the shape of African slaves. They rationalized this traffic in human flesh by noting that "though their bodies were now brought into subjection, that was a small matter in comparison of their souls, which would now possess true freedom for evermore."

Even Columbus was imbued with a deep sense of piety, and he not only wished to bring riches back from distant isles, but also to aid in the number of spiritual victories of his church. Bartolome de Las Casas, in speaking about the Italian, said, "He was especially affected and devoted to the idea that God should deem him worthy of aiding somewhat in recovering the Holy Sepulchre." He also hoped to drive the Moslem infidels from overseas areas. There was a mixing of the secular and spiritual in these European adventures.

King Manuel is an excellent example of this double vision.

Vasco da Gama was given bombards, crossbows, fire bombs, and lances so that the Portuguese could make a deeper penetration into India. The king issued the following orders: "In those places, even though they be situated far distant from the Church of Rome, I hope in the mercy of God that not only may the faith of our Lord Jesus Christ His son be proclaimed and received through these efforts and that we may obtain the reward thereof—fame and praise among men—but in addition kingdoms and new states with much riches, wrested by force of arms from the hands of barbarians."[1]

It will be interesting to contrast the differences between the religious reasoning of these monarchs and that of the various parties who populated America. Perhaps the following words of a Roman Catholic believer will help us understand why. He wrote: "The greatest part of British America was peopled by men who, after having shaken off the authority of the Pope, acknowledged no other religious supremacy: they brought with them into the New World a form of Christianity, which I cannot better describe, than by styling it a democratic and republican religion."

Not all of the adventurers who came ashore at Jamestown, Plymouth Rock, or in Georgia had an abiding faith in Christ, but the atmosphere of the colonies definitely was a religious one. They had not come to find gold or glory but basically to spread the Gospel. One historian noted the importance of religion in the coming revolt in this way: "Yet if we realize that the eighteenth century, for all its enlightened rationalism, remained an age of faith, the religious background of the Revolution becomes instructive. This is not to say, of course, that religious grievances or religious ideology CAUSED the Revolution, but that the subterranean forces which motivate political behavior can be found within the more general atmosphere of the times. On the eve of the Revolution, the Protestant religion constituted a fundamental aspect of American culture."[2]

De Tocqueville said, "It must never be forgotten that religion gave birth to Anglo-American society." This Frenchman saw that religion was commingled with the political habits of the nation, but he did not find that one tried to dominate the other. It was a natural union, although the religious doctrine remained the same and the legal aspects of American life were altered from time to time. He continues by saying, "Religion in America takes no direct part in the government of society, but it must nevertheless be regarded as the foremost of the political institutions of that country; for if it does not impart a taste of freedom, it facilitates the use of free institutions." He quickened to add that he was not sure if all the people who called themselves Americans had a sincere faith, as he couldn't search each heart, but he was certain that they hold it to be indispensable to the maintenance of republican government and in daily life.

Dean Acheson penned the following words: "We Americans are, for the most part, a pretty moral people, as these things go; certainly we set great store by morality. Our traditions are deeply rooted in the Puritan theocratic state of the seventeenth century and in the evangelical revival of the nineteenth. They are both Cromwellian and Wesleyan." The former secretary of state did not wish to present a picture of unrestrained holiness within the state we call America, as he added that "we fall from grace often and far"; but he questioned those who called us hypocrites for our failings. Our very weaknesses bring us to acknowledge our need of God's mercy and his wish for us to live more uprightly. Each humbling experience casts us upon God and his leadership in our lives.

John Richard Green, the popular nineteenth-century historian in England, said that the English were a people of a book and that book was the Bible. If this was true of the British, it was doubly true of the Americans. Whereas the faithful Anglican rested his faith on two volumes—the Bible

and the *Book of Common Prayer*—most evangelical denominations lived by one "book," the Word of God. One of the
greatest complaints on the parts of religious sufferers in England
was the demands put upon them by the Anglican church to
recognize their pronouncements and literature as necessary for
the Christian walk. The conservative theologians resisted this
pressure and backed themselves with scriptural arguments.

This spirit of evangelical Christianity continued on into the
war. When the redcoats were marching on Philadelphia, the
Congress did two things. First it called on the citizens to
repent and reform themselves and ordered a "day of solemn
Fasting and Humiliation." Second, they urged the army under
Washington to refrain from "profane swearing and all other
immoralities." Later, when it looked like Cornwallis had trapped
Washington and his forces not far from Princeton, a young
soldier asked his officer how they were going to escape. The
officer answered cheerfully, "I don't know, the Lord will help
us."

This was not simply a foxhole religion. The magistrates in
Massachusetts often used the Bible to increase their own wisdom in dealing with the problems that confronted them. The
highest glory of the American Revolution, according to President John Quincy Adams, was that "it connected, in one in-
dissoluble bond, the principles of civil government with the
principles of Christianity." Samuel Adams was so interested
in public worship "that he constantly attended divine services
in the German church in York town [Pennsylvania] while the
Congress sat there, when there was no service in their chapel,
although he was ignorant of the German language." James
Madison saw the hand of God in the Revolution, and the
future president said, "It is impossible for the man of pious
reflection not to perceive in it a finger of that Almighty hand
which has so frequently and signally extended to our relief
in the critical stages of revolution." But his faith was not of
the blind type. America would have to behave herself if she

was to be blessed by God. "Our Country, if it does justice to itself, will be the workshop of liberty to the Civilized World, and do more than any other for the uncivilized." Almost two hundred years later, when America's name had been blackened by the Watergate scandal, Senator Ervin turned back to the basic foundation of American life. He spoke as follows: "I do want to take this occasion to amplify the legal discussion and I want to mention a little of the Bible, a little of history and a little of the law."

Philosophical questions please the mind and stimulate debates, but the religion planted in American soil was of the individual variety. It takes no commitment in the heart to choose between two political parties as has been proven by the 1964 and 1972 presidential races, when people crossed party lines in droves. But during the Revolution, the choice was much different. The New York Convention declared that "every individual must one day answer for the part he now acts"—either as a Tory or patriot.

Peter Van Schaack, facing this dilemma, stated, "The question whether a government is dissolved [breaking ties with England] and the people released from their allegiance is a question of morality as well as religion, in which EVERY MAN must judge, as he must answer for himself. . . . No majority, however respectable, can decide it for him. . . ." It seems strange today that an American would call this a moral and religious question. But in the atmosphere of that day the spiritual was so strong in the philosophy developed in America that decisions were made before God rather than man. "No one can fully understand the American Revolution and the American constitutional system," states A. M. Baldwin, a recent commentator, "without a realization of the long history and religious association which lied back of [them] . . . without realizing that for a hundred years before the Revolution men were taught that these rights were protected by divine, inviolable law."

General Greene made this decision and believed that the Declaration of Independence would "call upon the world, and the great God who governs it, to witness to the necessity, propriety and rectitude thereof." A British historian disagreed with the "Fighting Quaker." He shouted that the Declaration of Independence was not only a mistake but "a great impediment to the highest Christian and Anglo-Saxon civilization among the nations of the world." Peter Oliver, another Tory pen wielder, granted that the Puritans had left England because of persecution; but he didn't like the fact that they turned their backs on their mother—the Church of England—once they landed in America. He was also bitter at these nonconformist clergymen for making their people believe that God was now on their side in the conflict. It had all begun because these righteous rectors encouraged the people to riot against the authority of the king. This made these "New England Clergy [an] everlasting Monuments of Disgrace." Oliver went even further, stating that they had made "a League with the Devil, and a Covenant with Hell."

The Loyalists were very upset that the radical pastors began to call on God for protection against Lord North and King George. Those who did not follow the king and the Established church became known as the "Black Clergy" for the following reasons:

1. They listened to the radicals who had said that it was important for the men who loved liberty to get the support of the clergy in Massachusetts.
2. It all went back to their own rebellion against the king's desire that they have Anglican bishops in each colony to control things. Their present-day treason could be traced back to this spiritual resistance against England and her church.
3. The clergymen in Massachusetts had encouraged the women of the colony to make American goods that would

compete with English imports; so as the females spun garments during the week, "the Parsons took their Turns, & spun out Their Prayers & Sermons to a long Thread of Politicks . . ." on the Lord's Day.

King George III was not worried about the power of the "Black Clergy" or the Spanish fleet that might hook up with the French and Americans to cause the British navy to run for cover. The king said, "I trust Divine Providence, the justice of our cause, the bravery and activity of my navy; I wish Lord North could review it in the same light for the ease of his mind." His political hacks got on their stumps and branded "American courage, American religion, and American intellect as cowardice, hypocrisy, and dullness." In their backhanded way they were acknowledging the religious character and faith of the American civilization. This had driven Benjamin Franklin, after he had heard such vindictive words in a House of Lords debate, to quote from the Bible: "Even so the tongue is a little member, and boasteth great things. Behold, how great matter a little fire kindleth! And the tongue is a fire, a world of iniquity: so is the tongue among our members, that it defieth the whole body, and setteth on fire the course of nature; and it is set on fire of hell" (James 3:5-6).

The basis of the struggle and the argument about the Revolution, then, went back to the relationship between man and God. The British were putting their faith in the verses that called for obedience to government and the king, whose rule was authorized by God. The Americans were saying that they had to answer to God directly and they were happily willing to do just that thing. Also, God had emphasized the fact that kings were to glorify him and to live for his people instead of suppressing them. Nowhere in Scripture is man called on for blind obedience to anyone. They had but one true king—King Jesus—who they prayed would rule in their hearts.

A secular historian was thoroughly convinced that God was no abstraction to the Puritans. They completely believed in God and his Son, and they were determined to make their New Jerusalem a place where his principles were first in the hearts of the people, thus forming the very foundation for democracy and the laws of the colony.

The Puritans believed that they were God's children who had accepted the Great Commission from above, and they went to America to fulfill their part in "propagating and advancing the Gospel of the kingdom of Christ in these remote parts of the world." They had to walk for God for two reasons: one, to have rich fellowship with him each day; and two, to bring the infidels to the Savior. They took literally the words of the Bible which stated, "By faith Abraham . . . sojourned in the land of promise," and they thought of America as their spot of testing God in prayer to see if he really fulfilled his promises given to them from the Bible. Both John Winthrop and Roger Williams testified to their practical experiences with God. The latter wrote: "Thus the Heavenly Son-Dial is one and constant in its guidance and direction to us poor Travellers."

William Penn was not simply an individual interested in the greater teachings of religion while having no time for personal conversion himself. He heard an evangelist who emphasized that all should be like the Bereans who received the Word with all readiness of mind. He was so struck by the messages of this evangelist that he wished everyone could hear the message of life. It is said that evangelist Loe's preaching was so forceful that William's father and their Black servant broke into tears. Even his secular biographer admired his ideas and admitted that William Penn, Jr., based them on the Bible and very little on profane history. George Fox, Quaker

leader, returned from America with fire in his veins; he wanted
to build an overseas utopia for his followers and Penn led the
way for these pilgrims of Pennsylvania. Penn felt that his
followers should evangelize and not stagnate in the new land,
and they worked to win souls for Jesus Christ.

As we pass below the Mason-Dixon line, we think that we
are moving into an area where religion was of little interest
to the population. Why do we have this feeling? Daniel J.
Boorstin tells us, "The identification of the great Virginians
with French 'atheism' and 'rationalism' was mostly accom-
plished long after the fact, by theological enthusiasts like
Timothy Dwight who could not imagine a decent society sur-
viving doctrinal diversity. But the life of Virginia had given
the lie to library distinctions. Just as the faith of many Virginians in republican government stemmed from their happy
experience with gentlemen freeholders in planting aristocracy,
so men raised under the broad Virginia Church could not be
horrified by diversity of religious belief. They had seen diversity
in their own well-ordered community."

Capt. John Smith testified to God's goodness. "But now
was all our provisions spent, the sturgeons gone, all helps
abandoned, each hour expecting the fury of the savages; when
God the patron of all good endeavors, in that desperate ex-
tremity so changed the hearts of the savages, that they brought
such plenty of their fruits, and provision, as no man wanted."
In 1609, Governor Gates was told by the council to Christian-
ize the Indians, and he even was advised to seize the medicine
men in order to destroy the heathen ceremonies. But they
didn't stop there. He was to maintain the worship of the Established church in Virginia and require regular attendance at
church meetings.

John Smith tells us that each day was begun with prayer
and the reading of the Bible. This surprised the Indians very
much, and soon they were also folding their hands and pre-

tending to be worshipping the Creator. These early settlers had a marked interest in the things of God. This was the starting point of the spirit of religious faith in the Old Dominion. Religion occupied a conspicuous part in the acts of the first Assembly in 1619. A certain number of Indian children were to be educated and trained in Christianity, "for laying a surer foundation of the conversion of the Indians to the Christian Religion." They also called on their ministers to read the divine service each Sunday and "to Catechize such as are not yet ripe to come to the Communion."

One of the founders of the Georgia colony was greatly upset about "the spiritlessness of religion" in his day. General Oglethorpe also emphasized the need for pure motives such as "charity and humanity" when he wrote to Bishop Berkeley in 1731. All the twenty-one trustees named in the Georgia Charter had been active in purely charitable ventures previously. Some had been associated with Dr. Thomas Bray and his effort to convert Blacks in the British plantations. Others had been active in supporting Protestant missionary societies of their generation.

The more practical members were not keen on having active Christians as members of the new colony, as they feared they would have more interest in spiritual things than in following a fruitful career. But all over England, sermons were given to encourage their members to give money for Georgia and her settlers. In the end it failed, not because of a lack of interest on the part of Christians, but because the founders did not have the grand vision of the Massachusetts Puritans or the "call" the Quakers felt to form their own province in Penn's woods. But, as we can see, the initial vision for Georgia was a Christian one, even though many of the settlers sent to her shores were common criminals.

People in the Carolinas were also very interested in the Bible and God's teachings. This proved to be a sore spot with the Anglicans as they looked down upon the Baptists and Presbyterians who were very strong, particularly in the rural areas. It was from this section of the states where the drive for independence was the strongest, and the folk wanted freedom of faith and freedom in political philosophy.

The Congregationalists, Presbyterians, Baptists, Lutherans, the Reformed church and the Roman Catholics all supported the War of Independence. The Quakers, Mennonites, Moravians and Amish refused to fight, but certain members helped out the Americans on an individual basis. Of the 3,105 congregations, there were 480 Anglican parishes, or a little more than 10 percent of the churches in the colonies. They, of course, were the main body to support the king while the Congregationalists (658 churches), Presbyterians (545 houses of God), and Baptists (498 parishes) were the main denominations that backed the forces of Washington and provided him with chaplains for his fighting men.

In the world today, America has the highest percentage of churchgoers, the highest amount of people who believe in God (98 percent), and those who are certain that there is life after death (73 percent). The first item is 22 percent higher than Great Britain, and the U.S. tops her old mother country in the second category by a whopping 45 percent! Also, 63 percent said that they pray frequently and only 6 percent said they seldom did so, with another 6 percent saying that they never pray or bend their knee before Almighty God.

Perhaps a more interesting story in relationship to religious feeling in the United States of America is the surge of evangelical or conservative denominations in recent years. While the more liberal denominations were losing members, those who followed the Bible were blossoming.

This seems to prove that America is seeking a real answer to the chief quiestions in life. How can I go to heaven? How can I find peace in my heart? How can I live an active and dedicated life for God?

NOTES

1. Louis B. Wright, *Gold Glory and the Gospel* (New York: Atheneum Publishers, 1970), pp. 86-87.
2. Peter N. Carrol, ed., *Religion and the Coming of the American Revolution* (Waltham, Mass.: Ginn-Blaisdell, 1970), p. xi.

III WERE EARLY AMERICANS PRUDISH?

It was the habit of proponents for the repeal of the Eighteenth Amendment during the 1920's to dub Prohibitionist "Puritans," and cartoonists made the nation familiar with an image of the Puritan: a gaunt, lank-haired killjoy, wearing a black steeple hat and compounding for sins he was inclined to by damning those to which he had no mind.

PERRY MILLER

There has been an open season on Puritans since the turn of this century. Even the word itself brings smiles to the lips of those who have never cracked open a book about their forgotten ancestors. Hating both prudes and patriots, they endeavor to smear those they disagree with by using simple

45

explanations that would be hooted at if they simply realized that these sturdy citizens of the northern colonies neither dressed in such outlandish headwear nor lived joyless lives as depicted in popular literature.

Puritans are held to be responsible for witch-hunting and terror tactics against helpless old ladies or tiny tots. In the dim, dark past, you will see that Lutherans, Anglicans, and Catholics believed the same tales about goblins and witches as did the people in Massachusetts. As a historian asked, "If Puritanism was responsible for the hanging of nineteen people in Salem, what was responsible for the burning of nine hundred people in Bamberg?"

This is not to make light of what went on in the name of Christianity around the Boston area; it is only to make an in-depth study of what these people were really like and to compare them with other people of their time. If the outbreak of witchcraft was the result of sexual repression, as some have said, then we should find a people so depressed in spirit and fearful of every gray shadow, that we would end up praising our God that we have been delivered from such a hell on earth.

The Puritans were men of the Book, but in its covers they found reason for joy as well as severity. The Anglicans might believe that every word in the *Book of Common Prayer* was infallible, but there was only one love letter from the Creator in the eyes of these hardy Pilgrims. Daniel J. Boorstin, an outstanding historian, underscores the belief that their lives were ruled by the Word of God and that it alone was their guide for faith and practice; but some interesting facts can be found within its pages that support the fact that God is interested in all-around men as his children.

Continually they sought fellowship with God. He was not simply a Sunday guest in their hearts but a companion in their pilgrim progress. They were sure that human goodness would not bring them salvation, because the Scriptures pointed out that "all had sinned and come short of the glory of God." They might respect the honest citizen, who lived just down the street, but without repentance, confession of sin, and faith in the redemption purchased on the cross by Christ (John 3:16, 36), this individual was lost and undone.

Their personal relationship with their Heavenly Father was of prime importance. John Winthrop was very troubled about his attachment for things that had only limited importance in his uphill climb toward the pearly gate. He asked himself an important biblical question: "For what shall it profit a man if he shall gain the whole world, and lose his own soul" (Mark 8:36)? Edwards breathed the same sentiments in his quest for a closer walk with God: "I had vehement longings of soul after God and Christ, and after more holiness, wherewith my heart seemed to be full, and ready to break; which often brought to my mind the words of the Psalmist, 'My soul breaketh for the longing it hath.'"

The whole community was ever thoughtful about God. In 1639, there were nineteen Fast and Thanksgiving Days in the Massachusetts Bay Colony, but they were upped to fifty, one hundred years before Lexington and Concord. They expected people to work for the community and had as their goal the public welfare of all the citizens. This meant that each one of them did not spare himself.

Was New England the only place for pious platitudes and prudish programs? Queen Philippa of Spain set out to reform both King Joao and the court. "She became the scourge of the philandering courtiers and complaisant ladies. Hundreds were literally dragged to the altar and married. When she caught the King kissing a lady-in-waiting in the palace at Cintra, even Joao was speechless before the frown of his wife and could only point in excuse to a motto [she had] painted on the ceiling, FOR GOOD."[1]

A liberal British historian around the time of the American Revolution attacked the baseness of the theater and mentioned that a Solon "struck the ground with his staff, not without indignation, crying out, that he foresaw that these trifling amusements would come to be a matter of great importance in life." The love of frivolity had once destroyed a great empire as "a Roman wanted nothing but bread and the Circensian games." Even in France, Henry IV "had a great passion for play, which had terrible consequences, as it rendered this destructive vice fashionable, which is alone sufficient to throw a kingdom into confusion." His countrymen realized this, and in 1735, the British Parliament passed a motion for "restraining the number of playhouses."

This very same historian condemns the looseness of morals in his homeland. "Jane Shore did penance at St. Paul's in a sheet, and a wax taper in her hand. A good and wholesome discipline, and would be useful in our times. When it was proposed to punish adultery with death, a gentleman observed, that such a law would only make people commit the crime with greater secrecy. But even with this view, such a law would be useful."

In jolly old England, the Parliament officially abolished Christmas in 1644. Whereas, a little over one hundred years later, in America, the British soldiers organized "Loyal Association Clubs" that held cricket matches and cockfights in sedate Philadelphia. From January to April, they had weekly balls and much gaiety, but one Tory looked down her nose at such antics. Mrs. Henry Drinker commented, "The day may be remembered by many for the scenes of folly and vanity. . . . How insensible do these people appear, while our land is so greatly desolated, and death and sore destruction have overtaken and impends over so many."

When one thinks of fox hunts, splendid balls, and magnificent dinners, one immediately recalls Virginia. Virginians took pride in Southern hospitality. "Planters often posted Negro slaves along the road with instructions to invite travelers to stop for refreshment." Washington and others were surprised when they realized how much of their monthly earnings went to entertaining guests who suddenly popped up at their plantations.

But in Old Virginia, one could be put to death for criticizing any article of faith of Christianity, and even until the Revolution, children could be taken from their parents if the latter denied the Trinity. Governor Argall decreed, "That every Person should go to church, Sundays and Holidays, or lye Neck and Heels that Night, and be a Slave to the Colony the following Week; for the second Offence, he should be a Slave for a Month; and for the third, a Year and a Day." A dozen years later the Assembly passed a Sabbath-observance act that provided a fine of fifty pounds for a month's absence from church. We think of the glorification of the Southern Belle, but in the early days of this province, 90 young women were put up for auction for 120 pounds of tobacco apiece The spirit of moral teachings continued right on into the middle of the Revolution as the Virginia Convention of 1776 sought to outlaw gaming and swearing in the Old Dominion. When the Puritans entered the colony, they preached to good crowds but were driven out because the colony required that all preachers have orders from the Church of England. But the Puritan revolution actually had a broadening effect in this great state. Henning tells us, "That at no former period were the civil and religious rights of the people so well secured or justice and humanity towards our neighbors, the Indians, so sacredly regarded."

The leadership and population of the Massachusetts area were generally pessimistic and doubtful about the generosity of mankind. But William Penn and his people were just the opposite. Even when he looked at the Indians in America, he could only see their good points, although he must have known their attacks had caused a terrible loss of life in his province and in other colonies. He simply was the most liberal of all the great men who founded colonies in the New World.

Still, Penn's personal views were much stricter than many

would believe. In his book, *No Cross, No Crown,* he leveled his preaching at the whole of England, and he spared neither the non-Quaker churches nor the government. He said his homeland was "invested with cheating mountebanks, savage morris dancers, pickpockets, profane players and stagers." He shouted that England was bound to suffer the wrath of God unless she changed her ways. The fire of his words meant that men read his works and listened to his preaching while more mannered ministers put them to sleep in their soft pews. He called the priests "pretended servants of the Lord," but really "the agents of Satan."

Whereas the Puritans didn't wear tall black hats but prettied themselves up in all the colors of the rainbow, Sir William attacked the worldliness of the dress of his day. He asked, "How many pieces of ribbon, feathers, lace bands and the like had Adam and Eve in Paradise or out of it? . . . Did Eve, Sarah, Susanna, Elizabeth and the Virgin Mary use to curl, powder, patch, paint, wear false locks of strange colors, rich points, trimmings, laced gowns, embroidered petticoats, shoes and slip-slaps [slippers] laced with silk or silver lace and ruffled like pigeon's feet, with several yards, if not pieces of ribbons?"

If William was bothered by the buttons and bows of lads and lassies, he was even more disappointed in the cream of the college crop at Oxford. He found them to be much more intent on having fun than in scholarly pursuits. Penn said, "Oxford is a signal place for idleness, loose living, profaneness, prodigality and gross ignorance." He was not attached to the books at the Christ Church College either. With the exception of books on law, theology, history, and science, he found works like Shakespeare, Spenser, and Fletcher as almost worthless. They were "an oppression of the mind and extinguished the natural candle" and produced "many senseless scholars."

The Quakers in their policy of liberalism in the new colony set up model penal institutions that were later copied by all

the states and by European governments as well. But in practice this denomination had all kinds of trouble. They would
not doff their hats or swear to oaths because they interpreted
the Scriptures very narrowly. Once it might have set them
apart and brought in new believers, but now it could easily
develop into dead formalism and a false pride in something
that had nothing to do with the heart of salvation matters.
Even to get around oath taking they used various devices so
they could accomplish the same thing under another title.
They also refused to allow their members to marry anyone
outside of their denomination, so they were even more strict
than the men of the Plymouth Bay Colony.

The civil liberties of the people were guaranteed, but the
general laws were very strict in Pennsylvania. "All such offenses
against God as swearing, cursing, lying, prophane talking,
drunkenness, drinking of healths, obscene words, incest, sod-
omy, rapes, whoredoms, fornications, uncleanness . . . all
treasons, misprisons, murders, duels, felonies, seditions, maims,
forcible entries and other violences to persons and estates,
all prizes, stage playes, cards, dice, may-games, masques, revels,
bull-baitings, cock-fightings, bear-baitings and the like, which
excite the people to rudeness, cruelty, looseness, and un-religion,
shall be respectively discouraged and severely punished."

Even after just a rough glance at the surface of other
colonies and their beliefs, we have to agree with historians
that the Puritans were not the oddballs of their generation.
They felt basically the same as others about the problems of
the day. They were proud of their English heritage. They hated
those nations who threatened Great Britain's supremacy. They
were not overly disturbed by the relationship between themselves and the mother country. Like other Protestant groups
they feared the Catholic church and the pope in Rome. Finally,
they held the same views on morals as did other denominations,
even in England. They could have shouted amen to the words
of John Donne, Dean of Saint Paul's in London. The Reverend

Mr. Donne said, "All knowledge that begins not, and ends not with his [God's] glory, is but giddy, but a vertiginous circle, but an elaborate and exquisite ignorance."

De Tocqueville would not buy the notion that the Puritans were simply interested in the next life. "Puritanism was scarcely less a political than a religious doctrine." To prove his point he quotes the first act passed once they had landed on the barren coast. "In THE NAME OF GOD. AMEN. We whose names are underwritten, the loyal subjects of our dread Sovereign Lord King James, etc., Having undertaken for the glory of God, and advancement of the Christian Faith, and the honour of our King and country, a voyage to plant the first colony in the northern parts of Virginia [their original destination]; Do by these presents solemnly and mutually, in the presence of God and one another, covenant and combine ourselves together into a civil body politick. . . ."

Not only were they interested in a political union, but the Frenchman believes that they were interested in the whole man. "The energy . . . with which they strove for the acquirement of wealth, moral enjoyment, and the comforts as well as liberties of the world, is scarcely inferior to that with which they devoted themselves to Heaven."

This visitor to America's shores in the early nineteenth century was quite surprised by what he found, as he was a Roman Catholic believer. "I have seen no country in which Christianity is clothed with fewer forms, figures, and observances than in the United States; or where it presents more distinct, more simple, or more general notions to the mind." But even with all its simplicity, he felt that all the denominations were distinctly interested in all the needs of men. "The American ministers of the Gospel do not attempt to draw or fix all the thoughts of man upon the life to come; they are willing to surrender a portion of his heart to the cares of the present, seeming to consider the goods of this world as important, although as secondary objects."

Robert Cushman preached a sermon at Plymouth on the dangers of self interest based on I Cor. 10:24: "Let no man seek his own, but every man another's wealth." He emphasized the need to form a community that would bring benefits to all. "Now, brethren, I pray you, remember yourselves, and know that you are not in a retired, monastical course, but have given your names and promises one to another, and covenanted her to cleave together in the service of God and the King. What then must you do? May you live as retired hermits, and look after nobody? Nay, you must seek still the wealth of one another, and inquire, as David, How liveth such a man? How is he clad? How is he fed?"

Cotton Mather appealed to his people to look outward and think positively. "Awake, Shake off thy Shackles, lay no longer fettered in a Base confinement unto nothing but a Meaner Sort of Business. Assume and Assert the Liberty of now and then Thinking on the Noblest Question in the World; What Good may I do in the World?"

We have not only the testimony of saints of another century, but Edmund S. Morgan, a popular historian, found that the Puritan family was much more interested in the enjoyment of life than most critics would like to believe. "Contrary to popular impression the Puritan was no ascetic. If he continually warned against the vanity of the creatures as misused by fallen man, he never praised hair shirts or dry crusts. He liked good food, good drink, and homely comforts. . . . In using the good things of this world, however, he kept in mind the order which God had ordained; he sought God's glory in eating and drinking, sleeping and recreating."[2]

How many people realize that the aim of God is to make individuals joyous? We immediately identify the man humming a tune or the lass singing a new ditty as a happy person. God puts a song in the heart of the believer and gives him a smile that lasts through trial and storm. Job tells us (20:5) that the joy of the hypocrite is but for a moment, but Nehemiah says (8:10) the joy of the Lord is our strength. Christ wanted all the believers to have a permanent and complete joy as he said, "These things have I spoken unto you, that my joy might remain in you, and that your joy might be full" (John 15:11).

This joy was not simply the earthly variety with crude jokes and gay parties. In preaching a Thanksgiving sermon, a Puritan pastor made this very clear. "Though our civil joy has been expressed in a decent, orderly way, it would be but a poor, pitiful thing should we rest here, and not make our religious grateful acknowledgments to the Supreme Ruler of the world, to whose superintending providence it is principally to be ascribed that we have had 'given us so great deliverance.'"

Jonathan Edwards, whose famous sermon, *Sinners in the Hands of an Angry God*, is often quoted in works of literature to impress the world with the narrowness of Puritan preaching, also was interested in the joy and sweetness in life. In his brief *Personal Narrative*, he used the word *sweet* or *sweetness* forty-eight times. He said, "I walked abroad alone, and looked up on the Sky and Clouds; there came in my Mind, a *sweet* Sense of the glorious Majesty and Grace of GOD, that I know not how to express."

Puritans were not the only people to find joy in salvation and dedication to God. Quaker John Woolman recalled the "sweetness" of his conversion when he testified, "That Word which is as a Fire and a Hammer, broke and dissolved my rebellious Heart, and then my Cries were put up in Contrition; and in the multitude of his Mercies I found inward Relief . . . I was often sad . . . and . . . sought Desarts and lonely Places, and there, with Tears, did confess my Sins to God. . . . While I silently ponder on that Change wrought in me, I find no Language equal to it. . . . This white Stone and new Name is known rightly by such only as have it."

The Puritans were a very warm and affectionate people. The love letters were not the torrid type of the modern generation, but they were as soft and endearing as most of those our Founding Fathers wrote to their devoted spouses. John Winthrop enjoyed the sweet letters from his wife, but he put her comfort before his loneliness as he penned, "I will not looke for any longe letters this terme because I pitty your poore hands; if I had it here I would make more of it than ever I did, and bynde it up very softly for fear of hurting it."

They were not nearly as prudish as their neighbors. They were told of the evils of drunkenness but even at church parties liquor was served. In relationships between the sexes they were not blind to the beauty of the human body, as we can see in a funny note from a young man who purchased a pair of garters for another Puritan, who desired it for his fiancée. He teased his friend about the debt and his lovely sweetheart. "I do not say I am fond of the happyness to kiss her hands, but her feet, having interest in her legs till my Garters be payd for, which I adjure you to be carefull of as you would be glad to have a Lady leggs and all."

When it came to marriage itself, they felt it was a joyful occasion and wished the couple to be one in both spirit and flesh. John Cotton in preaching a wedding sermon told the new pair that he had known of those who had married but never consummated their contract in becoming truly one after marriage. He pointed out the Scriptures taught it was not good for men to live alone and that God wished them to know the full joy of matrimony. The Puritans believed in having a big wedding feast and making a joyful celebration when two of their own became man and wife. But when the man was found to be impotent, the marriage could be annulled and there are several cases where this happened in the Pilgrim state. The man was supposed to cherish and honor his bride and be a witness to her of God's faithfulness in bringing them together.

Modern left-wing movements have often tried to tamper with the family system in advanced countries. In Japan, one of these groups demanded that all ties be broken, but when

men began to act like capitalist husbands, by being possessive
of a specific gal, they were put to death. The children produced by such affairs were taken away from the mothers and
given to other members of the group for upbringing. De
Tocqueville, of course, did not find such practices in the new
land of America, but he did feel that the children in that
budding nation were given much more freedom than in Europe.

Hessians who came to Canada were pleasantly surprised
that the lassies kissed them directly on the lips rather than
on the cheeks as they had been led to expect. Otherwise,
the women in the cold north were careful in doling out affection to strangers. Tories were disturbed that rebel females
took an active part in tarring and feathering Loyalists in the
states to the south. Women, such as Molly Pitcher, even
manned guns during the hot days of the Revolution.

Modern young people swear they are following the act
of Samson when they choose to allow their lovely long locks
to grow, but Puritans frowned upon such practices. The parents of the pre-Revolutionary period did try to control their
children. An English historian gives us his view of the different
denominations and their relationship to child upbringing: "The
difference between the behaviour of the grave and regular
Quakers, even in youth, and that of all other sects among us,
which is brought about chiefly by the management of parents,
shews what is in the power of parents. The Quakers hold
frugality and industry for religious duties. They accordingly
thrive better, and people more than other sects."

One would assume that the Yankees were always interested
in making an extra buck. They did bring up their children to
be frugal, but the saints were not about to deny the child an
enjoyable childhood. John Cotton did not think it was evil
for youngsters to "spend much time in pastime and play, for
their bodyes are too weak to labour, and their minds to study
are too shallow . . . even the first seven years are spent in
pastime, and God looks not much at it." The Puritan preachers

put a heavy burden on the parents to live a joyous life before the children and not to emphasize the making of money or force-feed them with the manna of materialism.

Instead of looking at riches, the parents were to remind their children of the blessings of the Lord and to witness the fact that he had watched over their settlement year after year. They were also to be honest with the children and warn them of the final long journey that led to the grave and beyond. Cotton Mather preached to the little ones about the necessity of being prepared for eternity.

Mather was convinced that it was very important to teach the children while they were young and flexible about the claims of Christ. But Pastor Peter Bulkeley pointed out that "children whiles they are young are like narrow mouth'd vessels, which can receive that which is poured into them, but by drops." Both would have agreed that simple rote memorization of all the answers was an inherent danger in a society that was so deeply religious, so they told the teachers that they must question them by the catechism very carefully.

The last sermon Cotton Mather preached was at the funeral of a pastor friend, and he took as his text Isa. 26:20, which was "an invitation to die readily and cheerfully." The believer in those days had a wonderful peace about his last journey. Their loved ones were not "to weep as others who have no hope." But it would be wrong to assume that they had no interest in keeping the body alive or trying to ease the pain of someone who became ill. Like Rev. Nicholas Collin, of the Swedish Churches of Pennsylvania, they believed that God had provided herbs to remedy the illnesses of his children.

These men of the cloth had a great interest in medicine and they often did better than the doctors of their day. Dr. Oliver Wendell Holmes, though hostile to the Puritans, left the following testimony about the clergymen-physicians of his home state:

What has come down to us of the first century of medical practice, in the hands of Winthrop and Oliver, is comparatively simple and reasonable. I suspect that the conditions of rude, stern life, in which the colonists found themselves in the wilderness, took the nonsense out of them, as the exigencies of a campaign did out of our physicians and surgeons in the late [Civil] war. Good food and enough of it, pure air and water, cleanliness, good attendance, and anaesthetic, an opiate, a stimulant, quinine, and two or three common drugs, proved to be the marrow of medical treatment; and the fopperies of the pharmacopoeia went the way of the embroidered shirts and white kid gloves and malacca joints, in their time of need. "Good wine is the best cordiall for her," said Governor John Winthrop, Junior, to Samuel Symonds, speaking of that gentleman's wife, just as Sudenham, instead of physic, once ordered a roast chicken and a pint of canary for his patient in male hysterics.[3]

Probably the most famous crime in New England was that of adultery because authors have used it for famous tales to spice up their literature. It is true that Massachusetts and Connecticut made that crime a capital offense, because they wished to comply with the laws of God. But it is amazing to find that this was carried out only three times although other methods of punishment were used, such as symbolical executions, where the guilty party stood on the gallows with a rope about her neck. In trying to follow Bible teachings, they were against the use of lawyers, as they assumed Christians would use biblical principles and not take each other to court. But in the long run the laws of New England were less severe than those of Old England, where theft was a capital crime.

The laws of Scripture took precedent over the laws of Great Britain, because the first allegiance in the hearts of the Pilgrims was to God and not to the king or homeland. In Pennsylvania, only treason and murder required the use of the death penalty, where as their mother country had numerous laws on the book that required the taking of the life of the offender. But back in the Massachusetts colony they had a deep interest in the soul of the sinner. At an execution they called on the criminal to repent and three sermons were preached that day with even the murderer taking part in "begging the congregation to profit from his example" and saying that he had gotten right with God before his final departure into the great beyond.

William Penn was much like the Puritans in that he lived a very disciplined home life, but like all people, he may have broken the principles he preached about. The man who attacked ribbons and rubies wore a wig to make himself look handsome. Winthrop believed that the Roman Catholic church was in error, but among his close friends was a man he brought to the colonies who thought that believers in that denomination were redeemed. The leader of the Plymouth Rock Colony also welcomed a bigamist to his home, even though he professed to believe that man to be in error and a breaker of the laws of man and God. Even the strictest, then, were not alien to those who lived round about them.

Historian Perry Miller tells us that the average "Puritan was a radical and a revolutionary, but not an anarchist." The evangelical groups in the United States were the ones who fought against the status quo and for liberal policies in dealing with both church and state. George Whitefield himself emphasized that believers were not required to obey any law if it was found to run counter to the teachings of God. Instead of standing up for masters in relationship between them and their servants and slaves, the Puritans demanded that the former treat their workers with honor and dignity and by their own lives bring their slaves to God. Being opposed to simple emotionalism in the pulpit, they came down on the side of charity instead of legalism in the church of God and demanded that Christians practice good works to glorify God in Heaven (Matt. 5:16) and not themselves. They left their minds open and searched all things to prove if the thoughts or legislation was of God or of man. Finally, they did not seek to work through a dictatorship, as no resolution could be passed in a Congregational assembly unless a working concensus was reached, thus providing a basis for unity of the population.

The Puritans were no more prudish than their neighbors. They enjoyed the good life and looked to religious practices to provide them with a firm foundation for a joyous existence on earth. The balance of their life and practice should point to one thing—they were far from cruel or unfeeling, they only sought to serve God for his glorification.

NOTES

1. Louis B. Wright, *Gold Glory and the Gospel* (New York: Atheneum Publishers, 1970), p. 4.
2. Edmund S. Morgan, *The Puritan Family,* The Academy Library (New York: Harper & Row, Publishers, Harper Torchbooks, 1944), p. 16.*
3. Daniel J. Boorstin, *The Americans: The Colonial Experience* (1958; reprint ed., Middlesex, England: Penguin Books, 1965), pp. 242-43.*

IV MORALS, MANNERS, AND MEN

The Presbyterians live in great charity with them and with one another; their minister, as a true pastor of the gospel, inculcate to them the doctrines it contains, the rewards it promises, the punishments it holds out to those who shall commit injustice. . . . As fellow Christians, obeying the same legislator, they love and mutually assist each other in all their wants. . . .

J. HECTOR ST. JOHN DE CRÈVECOEUR

The Anglicans painted these Presbyterians in the worst hues they could think of. They were troublemakers, loud and insincere, as well as unlearned. The author above was a French Catholic who lived among these individuals in early America. The preacher had a deep responsibility to teach his people the whole truth about man's lost condition, his need for personal salvation, his responsibility to glorify God secretly by good

61

works because of his gratefulness, and his calling to follow the positive program laid out for believers by the Word of God.

The British governors in Massachusetts were thoroughly confused by the attitude of the Puritans. They were terrified if they knew they had lied and men lost their lives when they refused to say they had dabbled in witchcraft, when they actually hadn't. Men of modern machinations cannot possibly understand this state of mind. It was based on the true teachings of God. "But the fearful, and unbelieving, and the abominable, and murderers, and whoremongers, and sorcerers, and idolators, AND ALL LIARS, shall have their part in the lake which burneth with fire and brimstone, which is the second death" (Rev. 21:8).

Their preachers warned about the faithful citizen who was obedient to the powers that be but was on his way to hell. Nothing bothers those outside of God more than to be told they cannot be admitted into the glories of heaven by their own good works. And yet, it is perfectly clear that if man could get to the glory land by a "bootstrap religion," then there would have been no need for Christ's death on the cross. The Bible was very clear about this point. Jesus had not come into the world simply to set a good example for future generations. Paul wrote: "This is a faithful saying, and worthy of all acceptation, that Christ Jesus came into the world to save sinners; of whom I am chief." This is the testimony of the saint who traveled over 15,000 miles preaching the Gospel as a missionary. Titus underscored Paul's teaching: "For we ourselves also were sometimes foolish, disobedient, deceived, serving divers lusts and pleasures, living in malice and envy, hateful, and hating one another. But after that kindness and love of God our Saviour toward man appeared, Not by works of righteousness which we have done, but according to his mercy he saved us, by the washing of regeneration, and renewing of the Holy Ghost."

The Puritan doctrinal position was as follows:

I. *Man was sinful and needed salvation*: "For all have sinned and come short of the glory of God" (Rom. 3:23). "The heart is deceitful above all things, and desperately wicked, who can know it" (Jer. 17:9)? "Let the wicked forsake his way, and the unrighteous man his thoughts: and let him return unto the Lord, and he will have mercy upon him; and to our God, for he will abundantly pardon" (Isa. 55:7).

II. *There would be no balance-sheet salvation as man was too far in debt to bail himself out*: "Now to him that worketh is the reward not reckoned of grace, but of debt. But to him that worketh not, but believeth in him that justifieth the ungodly, his faith is counted for righteousness. Even as David also describeth the blessedness of man, unto whom God imputeth righteousness without works, Saying, Blessed are they whose iniquities are forgiven, and whose sins are covered" (Rom. 4:4-7). "For by grace are ye saved through faith; and that not of yourselves: it is the gift of God: Not of works, lest any many should boast" (Eph. 2:8-9). "And be found in him, not having mine own righteousness, which is of the law, but that which is through the faith of Christ, the righteousness which is of God by faith" (Phil. 3:9).

III. *The works of man are to bring him praise; works should glorify God only*: "The Pharisee stood and prayed thus with himself, God, I thank thee, that I am not as other men are, extortioners, unjust, adulterers, or even as this publican; I fast twice in the week, I give tithes of all that I possess. And the publican, standing afar off, would not lift up so much as his eyes unto heaven, but smote his breast, saying, God be merciful to me a sinner. I tell you, this man went down to his house justified rather than the other: for every one that exalteth himself shall be abased; and he that humbleth himself shall be exalted" (Luke 18:11-14). "Woe unto you, scribes and Pharisees, hypo-

crites! for ye make clean the outside of the cup and of the
platter, but within they are full of extortion and excess.
Thou blind Pharisee, cleanse first that which is within
the cup and platter, that the outside of them be clean
also" (Matt. 23:25-26). "Moreover when ye fast, be not,
as the hypocrites of a sad countenance: for they disfigure
their faces, that they may appear unto men to fast. Verily
I say unto you, They have their reward. But thou, when
thou fasteth, anoint thine head, and wash thy face; That
thou appeareth not unto men to fast, but unto thy Father
which seeth in secret, shall reward openly" (Matt. 6:16-18).

IV. *Man needs salvation and this is provided by God, not by
human strength*: "All we like sheep have gone astray; we
have turned every one to his own way; and the Lord hath
laid on him the iniquity of us all." (Isa. 53:6) "For Christ
also hath once suffered for sins, the just for the unjust,
that he might bring us to God, being put to death in the
flesh, but quickened by the Spirit" (I Pet. 3:18). "For
God so loved the world, that he gave his only begotten
Son, that whosoever believeth in him should not perish,
but have everlasting life" (John 3:16).

V. *Good works of the believer are to glorify God, not the
believer himself*: "Let your light so shine before men, that
they may see your good works, and glorify your Father
which is heaven" (Matt. 5:16). "For we are his workman-
ship, created in Christ Jesus unto good works, which God
hath before ordained that we should walk in them"
(Eph. 2:10). "Now our Lord Jesus Christ himself, and
God, even our Father which hath loved us, and hath
given us everlasting consolation and good hope through
grace. Comfort your hearts, and establish you in every
good word and work" (II Thess. 2:16-17).

These doctrines swept across denominational lines. Every
evangelical group held to these basic tenets, although they

might have differed on the mode of baptism or church polity. Good works were an essential part of the believer's life, but he was so far in debt that he could never pull himself out of the sinful quagmire without God's help. Thus, he could never boast of his own righteousness as he had none.

Love was not some mystical sign painted on a T-shirt. They knew the love of God through salvation (John 3:16; 5:24) and in their personal experience with him each day. It was the love of God that brought them to America in the first place, not an adventure to find the fountain of youth or the gold of far-off islands. Rev. Increase Mather preached, "It was love to God and to Jesus Christ which brought our fathers into this wilderness. . . . There never was a generation that did so perfectly shake off the dust of Babylon, BOTH AS TO ECCLESIASTICAL and CIVIL CONSTITUTION, as the first generation of Christians that came into this land for the gospel's sake."

A British historian in the 1770s was very upset about the morals of his age. He pointed out that Aristotle laid down many strict rules for the youth of his time. And he continued, "We Christians let our youth loose to all encounters, and hardly teach them anything thoroughly, but the necessity of getting money, in order to make a figure in life." Penn held to the same idea when he tried to improve the morals of his people from afar. He said, "Till morals and corrupt manners be impartially rebuked and punished and until virtue and sobriety be cherished, the wrath of God will hang over nations."

But William Penn was not simply interested in hollow words. He wrote his wife, "My love, which neither sea nor land nor death itself can extinguish or lessen toward you, most with you forever. . . . My dear wife, remember thou wast the love of my youth and much the joy of my life; the most beloved as well as the most worthy of all my worldly comforts . . . God knowest, and thou knowest, it was a match of Providence's making."

Then he showered his family with advice. They should always be seeking to do good. They should hold daily meetings for God. They should live frugally until all debts were paid. They should guard against flatterers and friends who encroached on their time. It was better to live in the country than in a town. She (his wife) must teach the children to be obedient, humble, kind and they should love one another. They should be taught to be temperate in all things and speak no evil of others. They should not meddle in the affairs of their friends and neighbors. He believed that there were three supports for their lives: the guidance of the Bible, fellowship with other Christians, and resting on God's righteousness for leadership.

There was a rather practical side to doing good in the days of the Revolution. Ben Franklin decided one day to check and see how many good and bad things he did each day. He remarked, "I was surprised to find myself so much fuller of faults than I had imagined." Next, he decided that he would make up another list. He would ask himself each morning, "What good shall I do this day?" In the evening he would pose another question to himself, "What good have I done to-day?" He was very tidy and hated to see anything go to waste, whether it was time, energy, or resources. Before making decisions he would list the pros and cons and think about them for a few days before choosing which path to take. He surely was an example of the energy just one person can put into life and he was quite different from this age.

The Loyalists looked on their homeland in Britain as the Christians in America looked to their Heavenly Father. The Tories believed that Britain had always taken care of the colonies with tender loving care. She had forsaken her own interest for theirs. She had so indulged the child that the sassy brat was now making life miserable for her. They believed that there was perfection in the way the men of England acted toward their political offspring.

The same author believed that Americans not only were born liars, but that they had decided not to accept any truth which they did not like. He accused the rebels of both sins of commission and omission. He particularly didn't like it when American laws did not exactly copy British ones.

Not only were Americans sinful but they were willing to sell their souls to the lowest bidder. Benedict Arnold, who was experienced in this sort of thing, bragged that each soldier could be purchased at the rate of fifteen guineas per head. He believed that he could buy off the boys in the barracks. He argued that this bargain was much better than the one the crown got from Germany for the Hessians, and King George III had to fork up additional dough for each "Kraut" who lay nestled in an American grave. He wrote to General Clinton, "Money, properly applied in America, may with some have more argument than arms."

The Sons of Liberty were also checking up on the morals of the men dressed in red who came to crush the rebellion. General Clinton wanted to liven up his life in the Fun City. The citizens of New York would see a Hessian soldier flying down the street on a sleek mare pulling a bone on a rope, while the British commanding officer and a host of other men in brass and braid chased after it on fast stallions, as a hound bayed at the greasy object bouncing along the ground. Clinton not only liked to imitate an English foxchase but also to mix with the ladies. He finally took a captain's wife as his mistress to cheer himself up in his off hours.

One of the German princes who sold Hessian souls to the British king had seventy-four children—all illegitimate. The British army also wanted to lift the emotional burdens of its troops in America. The British War Office made a contract with an English colonial trader to transport 3,500 women to become the property of the army quartered in New York

City. When Captain Jackson, the trader, could not get enough ladies off the streets of London, Liverpool, and Lancaster, he sailed to the West Indies to fill his quota with Blacks, who became jocularly known as "Jackson Whites."

New York was filled with more than lovable lassies. The population was only 5,000 people when Howe moved in, but by 1783 the number had gone up almost seven times that. Even in 1778, a refugee described the conditions as "truly deplorable and almost hopeless." Another male who took up his abode in the famous city said that most of the people there had the most "vicious and unfeeling part of human nature." The famous Tory named Galloway observed, "Everyone here thinks of nobody but themselves; and friendship is not to be found."

The king wished to crush the rebellion very quickly. Even though one of his officers had bragged that England could easily put 300,000 troops in the field, they were having problems getting soldiers to fight the lads of liberty. They took three steps to get the necessary cannon fodder. Money in the form of a bounty was offered to each new recruit. Encouragement was to be given to "the Europeans in Washington's army to switch sides and enlist in the King's ranks." Finally, criminals who had not committed capital crimes were given pardons if they would go to America and fight the scum of the earth. These methods still didn't bring in many volunteers.

Even before the clash of arms, the Massachusetts people were disturbed about the morals of the rude guests. In the occupation of the Hub in 1768 and 1769, the English soldiers made a very poor impression on the natives. It was noted that the Britishers had very few Bibles and those they did have gathered dust. They were often drilled on Sunday when the good townspeople thought humans should be in church. One soldier even molested a local female as she was reading her Bible, which aroused the ire of the populous a great deal. The British did not try to win over the people. They even deliberately paraded close to churches on the Lord's Day, making as much noise as possible and disturbing the services of God's children.

The Americans believed that the British would suffer for their immoral actions and that God was going to take revenge upon them. Jefferson believed the biblical teaching that one would reap what one sowed. The handsome Virginian penned, "The seeds of hatred and revenge which present oppressors are now sowing with a large hand, will not fail to produce their fruits in time. Like their brother robbers of the highway, they suppose the escape of the moment a final escape, and deem infamy and future risk countervailed by present gain."

Most people in the colony were God-fearing folk. Even the American soldiers who were on duty during the French and Indian War went to services on Sunday. One of them recalled the message very clearly, the text being John 3:16. During the Revolution, a day of fasting and prayer was held throughout the camps on July 20, 1775, which was not a Sunday but Thursday. The first article dealing with army regulations for the Continental forces read that "all officers and soldiers . . . shall diligently frequent Divine Service and Sermons." The religious spirit creeped into the very life of the soldier no matter where he was stationed.

This is not to say that America was a land of only virtue. The quiet Quakers were ashamed of the worldly ways of the city dwellers in their capital. Those who marched in the ranks of the rebels were not always prayer warriors. Farmers quite often sold their foodstuffs to the British because they would receive hard cash instead of worthless bills printed on paper that the American government designated as money. But this kind of living was condemned from the pulpit and in political pronouncements. Washington wanted his army to follow precepts of the faith, but he knew it would be difficult to enforce such regulations.

A Frenchman believed that the American style of politics

would invite corruption. He pointed out that most of the European governments were run by the wealthy. It seemed very unlikely to him that anyone could influence these politicians with money because they had little need for it. But he felt the American type democracy, where even the poor could be elected to important posts, was weak in that it left men wide open to temptation because, as yet, they had not made their first million.

Europe still thinks this of America. "A state, which raised violence and terror to a basic principle of policy, is paying for this with the lives of its own political leaders. A social and political system that gives birth to political banditry evokes contempt and aversion throughout the world. A rotting society, a degrading society, a decadent society—this is how the present-day United States is being described even by those who not long ago were praising the American way of life." A few years ago these words were published in an American newspaper on the fourth of July. Who spoke these cutting words? They are from the lips of Leonid Brezhnev of the Soviet Union.

Chadwick Hansen, a professor at Penn State University, has written, "Our seventeenth-century ancestors differed from us in most ways, but in nothing did they differ more than in their attitude toward the truth. In this they were closer to the Middle Ages than to us. For them a lie—a breaking of one's faith—was the worst of sins." One of the worst scandals in American political history was based on false statements. "Nixon had been lying, therefore, for more than two years, lying to the public, lying to Congress, lying to his own staff, at times probably lying to himself."

A man of the right of center is not the only one caught with his foot in his crooked mouth. Miss Sontag stressed the responsibility of left-wing intellectuals who have to speak out on the facts because of their "vocational connection with the life of truth and the special integrity of our voices." What did these authors, who spoke in high-flown phrases about morality and Vietnam, do when they had a chance to write about history:

1. Willam Appleman Williams used the technique of constructing imaginary speeches and dialogue by "splicing together phrases uttered at different times and diverse subjects" in his works about the Cold War.
2. D. F. Fleming misquoted a number of important American officials in writing about the relations between the U.S. and Russia on the eve of dropping the atomic bomb on Japan.
3. Gar Alperovitz published *Atomic Diplomacy*, but one of the most common flaws in this book is that he continually cites statements to support his arguments that in context refer to other subjects altogether.
4. David Horowitz, who penned *The Free World Colossus*, continually used secondary sources and repeatedly cited unsupported assertions by others, but more importantly, he neglected to quote people who would disprove his theories.
5. Gabriel Kolko, author of *The Politics of War*, garbled documents—ignoring others and misrepresenting ones he did use.
6. Ms. Dianne Shaver Clemens loaded her case by omitting several significant items plus quoting officials inaccurately when she authored *Yalta*.
7. Lloyd C. Gardner's examples of quotations in *Architects of Illusion* are either taken out of context or placed in the wrong temporal sequence.[1]

Not only do we find fabrications in the work of the New Left, but we find a special type of prejudice against certain individuals. They would be the first group, and rightly so, to

say that there is no room for hatred and a vindictive spirit
in this world; but they have hated Nixon for years and have
openly admitted their own prejudices.

In the race of 1964, President Johnson often showed his
quick temper, but this never hit the newsstands. The same thing
was true about Edward Muskie in his run for the hot seat
eight years later. For months writers had known about the
Maine Senator's tirades and his swearing, but nobody was
worried about such intemperate comments until the Nixon
transcripts hit the streets.

Theodore H. White, in his fine book, *Breach of Faith*, tells
how, in 1952, the press was quick to chastise Senator Nixon
for the funds he had received from Southern California businessmen. White tells us that the fund was commonplace and it
was no secret. In days it had been blown up into a big story.
A few weeks later a story broke about Adali Stevenson, who
had a similar fund. But, as White adds, "It was Nixon who
in the national press was vilified, while Adlai Stevenson was
but gently chided."

This is not to excuse the actions of Richard M. Nixon. He
surely paid a high price for not following the scriptural principles about confession directly to God and then to those he
had injured. John F. Kennedy, after the Bay of Pigs failure,
admitted that the whole show was his fault, and the public
forgave him because of his honesty. It is quite probable they
would have done the same for his 1960 foe, but perhaps not
as willingly. The Puritans would have quoted Prov. 28:13 to
Mr. Nixon: "He that covereth his sins shall not prosper: but
whoso confesseth and forsaketh them shall have mercy."

Men are often inconsistent in their judgment of others as
their personal feelings get in the way. The laws of most of
the colonies were based on the law of God, and they were the
guide for criminal law as well as for moral teachings. Any law
made by men would become inoperative for the Christian if

it ran counter to the teachings of the Bible. This plants the Christian on solid soil.

In London, in 1604, four Puritans were put to death for their belief. Nova Scotia had very strict laws which were more pressing on the public than those in America. But the Puritans were supposed to have compassion when dealing with others who had broken moral laws based on the Scriptures. Critics admit that no coercion was used even in the witch-hunts in Salem. They were very careful about the testimony in their courts when compared to other countries of the same century.

William Penn also was very liberal in making the laws of his province, even though he used the same biblical foundation. No fine, imprisonment, or punishment was to be inflicted except after a fair and open jury trial. Juries were free to interpret the laws and their verdicts were not to be questioned. Even more amazing was the revolutionary treatment given prisoners in Pennsylvania. Criminals were to be taken from the stocks and pillories and placed in private prisons where they could reflect on their misdeeds. This new method of treatment for common criminals was to spread around the globe.

The Christians pressed forward for liberty of the spirit as well as the body. Milton wrote, "Our liberty is not Caesar's; it is a blessing we have received from God himself; it is what we are born to; to lay down this at Caesar's feet, which we derive not from him, which we are not beholders to him for, were an unworthy action, and a degrading of our very nature." Government should have the spirit of Christ too.

Puritans were afraid that corruption might seep into society and make America a laughingstock to other people. Therefore, they decreed everything should be done in consensus with no individual holding all the power, because such would lead to a dictatorship and rob people of their liberty.

But these were necessarily negative measures. The Christians of that period realized that the laws of man would keep their eyes on rules that could never support the good life of helping other humans. They knew that a Christian was simply not a person who did not drink, smoke, or abstain from lust. The believer was to be positive. He was to aid society, as he loved his neighbor as himself. He was to help society, not retreat to a monastery on a holy hill.

Penn had his own program for social betterment. There were campaigns against child labor and for shorter working hours, against exploitation of workers, and the establishment of government-run employment agencies plus mediation offices. He recognized the evils of slavery and wished to see it abolished. He believed in the equality of all races, and minority groups in his colony had the same privileges as his own Quaker brothers. In New England, too, the poor were provided for, and offices were created so that public officials might aid the public in different ways.

Former secretary of state Dean Acheson leaves us with this testimony to the power of the Bible and humanitarian efforts in America: "What was written in the Book was taught also by the life of this country. Never was self-reliance so linked with mutual help as in those early days, when from birth to death neighbor turned to neighbor for help and received it in overflowing measure. No characteristic so marks Americans to this day as this quick and helping hand, a hand offered not only to our fellow citizens but to our fellowmen."[2]

NOTES

1. Robert James Maddox, *The New Left and the Origins of the Cold War* (Princeton, N.J.: Princeton University Press, 1973).

2. Dean Acheson, *Grapes From Thorns* (New York: W. W. Norton & Company, 1972), p. 250.

V EDUCATION NOT FOR AN ELITE BUT FOR EVERYONE

In the New England states this ideal had approached. The Calvinist religion, with its emphasis on the responsibility of every man to read and interpret the Bible for himself, had provided a powerful sanction for universal education which in turn accorded with the democratic organization of society in that region.

LAWRENCE R. CREMIN

Education was a keystone in the foundation for a more informed Christian society. Unless the believer could read the Word of God, it would be impossible for him to understand God's love letter to him. He also would have no way to strengthen his own personal walk with his savior; and it also was essential for the clergy, so that they might feed their sheep. Dr. Stiles, former president of Yale, underscored his feelings about the reason for higher education. He said, "I rejoice that God has hitherto preserved a learned and evangelical ministry in these churches. The theology in general reception comprehends all the excellent things of our common Christianity."

"It being one chief project of Satan to keep men from the knowledge of the Scripture by persuading from the use of tongues, to the end that all learning may not be buried in the graves of our forefathers, in church and commonwealth, the Lord assisting our endeavors . . . we will support universal education in our province." Thus ran the thoughts of the Code of 1650. This law was to establish schools in every township and obliged the citizens to support them or face heavy fines. The historian who read these words from a code written up by New England Puritans almost two hundred years earlier could only say, "In America, religion is the road to knowledge, and the observance of the divine laws leads man to civil freedom."

The Protestant Reformation emphasized the Scriptures. To understand them properly, the clergy would have to understand both Greek and Hebrew. They began to study these difficult languages so they could dig deep into the true meaning of God's teachings. Elder William Brewster, a zealous Pilgrim, even had his own gravestone imprinted with a Hebrew message. Governor Bradford began to study the same tongue in his later years and was refreshed by what he found when he used that knowledge to search the Bible. Learning made these Protestants feel that they did not wish to eat the manna from heaven by second-hand means but rather hoped to find their own sweet food from God by personal study of his Word.

The colonies were not the only places where you could sense the presence of the men in black. You could not walk around the Oxford campus without bumping into several churchmen. In fact, most of the colleges connected with that famous name had been founded by God-loving men. Morison tells us that the generous gifts of Puritan yeomen farmers kept Harvard alive, so that these people might sit in pews to listen to an educated clergy "when our present Ministers shall lie in the Dust."

The man in the street or the farmer who tilled the soil was not without help either. One of the most popular imports from England was hundreds of books, whether one lived in the frigid north or the balmy south. In 1682, an English book supplier sent 800 titles to bookseller John Usher in Boston. About half of them were religious, about one-fifth schoolbooks, and the rest romance or popular themes. But when the book dealer did his own ordering in 1685, he chose the same amount, but half of them were religious volumes and most of the other half were for education, with very little being on romance and like subjects.

About the same time, a clergyman preached about the need of education for the young. The Reverend Mr. Torrey was saddened by the lack of education for the rising generation. Even earlier, Rev. Thomas Shepherd emphasized the same point when he said, "There is a great decay in inferior schools, it would be well if that . . . were examined and the cause thereof removed." While Puritans preached about it, Penn acted. He developed universal education in his province. He also rejoiced that the home government had guaranteed orphans the right to an education with the colony paying the cost.

Back in England, there was interest in the same problems. In relation to moral teaching, the Church of England was supposed to teach the youth about God's plans for man. But they were leaving the younger generation in complete ignorance of the most essential teachings of life. A British historian says that the Dissenters did much better teaching tots, and he acknowledges that they were more capable teachers because of their zeal.

The type of education was quite different from the subjects of today. They were grounded in the Bible, Greek, and Latin. The Europeans, too, believed that the study of Greek and

Latin literature was particularly useful in "democratic communities." In England, the Parliament passed an ordinance in 1644 that all ministerial candidates must be able to read the Hebrew and Greek Testaments. But Patrick Henry didn't think much of the name of the subtitle of his Latin book, which read, *A Delicious Syrup Newly Clarified for Young Scholars Who Thirst for the Sweet Liquor of Latin Speech,* and yet we must admit this type of education produced some wonderful minds and a humanitarian people.

Most of the Founding Fathers were self-educated. John Adams, for example, was an omnivorous reader and built up a library that would keep him well informed on the issues he felt were most important, as he prepared himself "in the service of God, country, clients, fellow men." William Penn never regretted not having formal training, as he had utilized his time with library books for research during his youth. Curiously enough, he advised his children to have only a few books that they should read thoroughly, but he himself could not resist buying every volume he got his hands on. The "Penman of the Revolution," John Dickinson, counted his library as the most valuable part of his estate and rejoiced what his books had done for him in the fields of history, law, and political science. Even in the realm of military arts, few officers were trained for their new occupation. Henry Knox, perhaps typical of such generals, saw his education end at the age of nine, but he built up his own bookshop into the intellectual center of Boston and trained himself to become the foremost authority on the use of artillery, which General Washington eventually put to use in the field.

The British government did not particularly encourage men in the colonies to get a sound education. Royal Governor William Berkeley, one hundred years before the Revolution, wrote to England thusly, "I thank God there are in Virginia no free schools nor printing and hope we shall not have any, for learning hath brought disobedience and heresy into the world." The king backed up this governor by providing orders "that no person be permitted to use any press for printing upon any occasion whatsoever." Up until the war, there was no type made in America that could be purchased by colonial printers, so the British could control this vital import. The same British took a nasty swipe at the freedoms of man when Prime Minister North presented honorary degrees to former Massachusetts Governor Thomas Hutchinson and Deputy Governor Peter Oliver, both torrid Tories, at Oxford on July 4, 1776!

As the Americans grew in knowledge they questioned the ideas they had received from London. If they began to dislike the ideas that swept in from the homeland, they hated the Pope of Rome. The Puritans, and most Protestant clergy, were completely convinced that the Roman Catholic church had stifled true faith in the Lord Jesus Christ and his teachings by keeping their people in ignorance of the Bible. Even the deep suspicion and fears of the Jesuits touched the life of William Penn many times, as he was accused of being a secret friend of the Catholic church. This feeling had such deep roots in America that most citizens opposed the use of public funds for religious schools, as they feared this aid would help Rome and her zealous teachers.

Most residents confined within the shores of the Pacific and Atlantic oceans had felt oppression from the Europeans to the east, which left a bad taste in their mouths for the Old World. Even though most citizens in the New World looked with jaundiced eyes at Europe because of their constant battles, they owed a debt of gratitude to the continent for the educational legacy it left for those far to the west.

Two men of the English Renaissance produced the spark that was to enlighten the minds of millions, as universal education slowly moved ahead. Desiderius Erasmus, an illegitimate son of a Dutch priest, and William Tyndale, a well-to-do

British yeoman, stepped on center stage and contrived ideas that would change the lot of the common man who never was blessed by education.

The thoughts of Erasmus shook the world of that period. He shouted, "To be learned is the lot of only a few; but no one is unable to be a Christian, no one is unable to be pious, and I add this boldly, no one is unable to be a theologian." Tyndale's aim in undertaking the translation of the Bible was so that "he would cause a boy that driveth the plough, to know more of the Scripture than he did." A dozen years after his New Testament was completed at Worms, Edward Fox, bishop of Hereford, could say, "Make not yourselves the laughing-stock of the world; light is sprung up, and is scattering all the clouds. The lay people know the Scriptures better than many of us."

Erasmus substituted the illumination of textual criticism for the obfuscation of scholastic logic, while Tyndale substituted the study of the Bible for the authority of the church. The latter was much more important. Textual criticism comes and goes in its many forms and sizes, while learned men scratch their heads over obscure passages, forgetting the key teachings of the Bible. Tyndale used the language of the laity and fashioned an extraordinarily powerful instrument for popular education. King Henry first sided with Cuthbert Tunstall who wanted to suppress this translation, but about the same time Tyndale was being executed for heresy, his majesty reversed himself and ordered that an English Bible be placed in every English church.

Between 1480 and 1640, over 40 percent of the books printed in England were religious in nature. Those printed in the colonies even reached a higher level, as it is estimated that half the books published in America were about Christ and his kingdom. Helen White observed, "Theology lays the ground for and raises the temple of religion, but devotion takes the hand of the believer and leads him into the presence of the God he has been seeking."

The major books that were being read in America were as follows: John Foxe's *Book of Martyrs* (1563), Lewis Bayly's *The Practice of Pietie* (1612), Richard Allestree's *The Whole Duty of Man* (1658), Richard Baxter's *The Poor Man's Family Book* (1674), and John Bunyan's *Pilgrim's Progress* (1678, 1684). These works were not to glorify man, but to bring him to God. For example, *The Poor Man's Family Book* taught men how to become true Christians, how to live as believers in relationship to God, how to live with others, and how to die as Christians in hope and comfort. Allestree was very specific about the education of children. He said, "As soon therefore as children come to the use of reason, they are to be instructed, and that first in those things which concern their eternal well-being, they are little by little to be taught all those things which God hath commanded them as their duty to perform; as also what grievous and eternal punishment, if they do it not."

There is another thing of interest for us to consider. Even though many of these books of a deeply religious nature were authored by Puritans, they were found in the homes of people of all the Protestant denominations. These books were not written to support a pet theory or to bring people into membership in one sect, but to bring people to God.

The first book on familial education was Thomas Cobbett's *A Fruitful and Usefull Discourse Touching the Honour Due from Children to Parents, and the Duty of Parents Towards Their Children.* The book is full of scriptural quotations. The parents are urged to be good examples for their children and to practice piety while making sure that their offspring go to church where the Gospel is preached. He pressed upon the children to honor their parents and listen to "their graceful counsels."

The origins of British higher education are not completely clear. One school of thought believes that it came about because of an awakening in the religious atmosphere around Oxford in the twelfth century. Other historians believe that it grew out of the recall of English scholars from the University of Paris in 1167 because of the dispute between Thomas à Becket and Henry II.

During the Revolution, when passions ruled, the Loyalists often pointed out that the Americans were of poor stock and were ill-mannered mobsters. It is surprising to find that during the Great Migration of Puritans to New England, there were at least 130 university men who were among them. Of these, 100 had attended Cambridge, 32 had graduated from Oxford, 87 held the B.A. degree, and 63 the M.A.; 98 of these individuals served in the ministry, 27 became public officials, 15 became teachers, 5 ran some business concern, and 3 were doctors. Interestingly enough, almost all of them were part-time tillers of the soil too.

Samuel Eliot Morison is amazed that Harvard College was founded by a legislative body that had been in existence less than eight years. Ten years after the colonists first stepped on shore, they agreed to give four hundred pounds to build a place of higher education. The school was named after Rev. John Harvard who had died shortly before.

Each student was plainly instructed and pressed "to know God and Jesus Christ which is eternal life, John 17:3, and therefore to lay Christ in the bottom, as the only foundation of all sound knowledge and learning." Every student was required to be ready to give such "an account of his proficiency therein, both in theoretical observations of the language, and logic, and in practical and spiritual truths, as his tutor shall require, according to his ability." Each pupil was expected to attend all lectures and to obey the rules of the college. The last rule was that pupils refrain from swearing, and they were to be careful in the friends they made.

One might assume that this college was only producing ministers to fill the pulpits of New England. Such was definitely not the case. Of those who graduated between the years 1642 and 1689, 46 percent became clergymen, 11 percent public servants, and 7 percent doctors.

Oliver Cromwell has been called the most liberal of seventeenth-century Puritan leaders. He tried to be as lenient as possible with all the zealous believers who were carrying out their own schemes in his land. But even he drew the line when the population rose up against the universities. He would not allow antiintellectualism in his kingdom.

There has always been a question in the minds of all believers about how much they should listen to the unredeemed. Increase Mather and the Pilgrims faced the same dilemma. This Puritan pastor wrote: "Some among the Heathen have been notable Moralists, such as Cato, Seneca, Aristides, etc. And although we must not say that their Morality saved them, yet it was not altogether unprofitable to them, for God did therefore reward them with many outward blessings, and they did thereby escape many temporal judgments, which otherwise would have befallen them. . . ."

The Puritan pastors of that generation were not book-burners. They read all the volumes they felt contained any shred of worth for their minds. They were confident that they could weigh each point with the Bible and come away without contamination of their souls. Not only were they protected, but God's wisdom helped them discern what was profitable for them. Rev. John Preston, Master of Emmanuel College at Cambridge, England, said, "Divine grace elevateth reason, and makes it higher, it makes it see further than reason could, it is contrary indeed to corrupt reason, but to reason that is right reason, it is not contrary, only it raiseth it higher; And therefore faith teacheth nothing contrary to sense and reason."

Richard Hofstadter commends the Puritans for their zeal for education. Even though they had suffered from Indian wars, where one of every sixteen males of educational age lost his life, they continued to teach the people. In 1699, Boston still was only a town of 7,000 inhabitants, but they had a college that taught Hesiod, Homer, Sophocles, Aristophanes, and other classical writers besides the Bible; and, more importantly, the degrees given at Harvard were accepted at Oxford and Cambridge.

Hofstadter continues, "The fairest way to assess any intellectual group like the Puritan ministry is not to put them to the test of the most advanced standards of tolerance and enlightenment, but to measure them against their own times, the community in which they lived, and the laymen they served." He didn't make excuses for the witchcraft trials, but "the record of the clergy, though mixed, is better than the lay judges and the public."

After Whitefield's first visit to New England, he was followed by Gilbert Tennent who brought down the house. He attacked the older clergymen by calling them "orthodox, Letter-learned and regular Pharisees." He said that they had no real interest in the souls of the people. Hofstadter adds, "Tennent's approach was hardly ingratiating, but he believed that he was raising a real issue, and it would be hard to deny that what he was advocating could be called religious democracy." If a congregation had a cold unconverted minister, and if it were forbidden to receive an awakened one, except with the consent of the unconverted, how would the congregation ever win access to "a faithful Ministry"?

Gilbert's father established a number of students in his "Log College," and even these could not be pictured as ignorant men of the cloth. Hofstadter says that a more recent evangelist of the same stripe, Charles Finney, "must be reckoned among our great men." But they did spread the fear that they were more interested in emotional changes than in reasoned discussion. That type of shadow rests over the Church of God even today and gives an excuse to the unredeemed for not attending Bible-believing churches.

Getting back to the Protestant Reformation, we find that it underlined the views that took deep root in America. As long as there was a universal priesthood of all true believers, then the idea of a special class of "knowers" vanished. It brought not only a wisp of democratic thought, but it challenged the whole religious establishment because now they would be judged by scriptual teachings.

John Adams was bothered by the affection showered on Thomas Paine for his book, *Common Sense.* He felt that the age he lived in could not be considered to be a very rational one. Others could call it the "Age of Reason," but he would not do so. Perhaps there was a little bias in his reasoning as the seat of education was thought to have been in Europe. The Europeans continually chided Americans for their backwardness. To get back at the English, Harvard College conferred degrees on individuals without getting permission from England. Morison said, "This was almost a declaration of independence from King Charles."

One of the big weaknesses in the American educational system today is the lack of practical results. How many Americans can speak a foreign language with any degree of fluency? But our ancestors were often very good in French. In fact, John Adams had his own system of mastering a foreign tongue in one year. It involved close contact with the people who spoke the language, visits to the law courts and the theater, going to church services, along with diligently working with grammar books, dictionaries, "and reading their best authors."

America didn't have the answers to all of her problems. Princeton was hit hard by the war. William Penn even worried about the population explosion in his day. The colonies probably figured that education would answer these questions.

Well, education has become the biggest business in the

United States today! From 1950 to 1972, the amount of money spent on education in America zoomed from $9 billion to $86 billion. Defense spending only rose $47 billion in the same space of time. In 1940, 55 percent of the high school students in the U.S. dropped out of school. In 1972, it was down to 25 percent. Education is the main hope for most people—even adults. When asked what they would have done differently about their lives, if they could start again, 43 percent said that they would get more education. To make up for lost time, there were 15 million adults taking education classes in the States in 1973.

The Puritans and other dissenting denominations brought a leveling to the American scene. They pressed home the point that everyone was equal under God. They also emphasized the fact that there is a universal body of priests who have become children of God and who need to educate themselves in the plans of God. This evangelical zeal has been mostly lost in Europe. A larger number of American boys and girls are going to college (from families whose income ranges between $3,000 to $5,000) than the TOTAL figure of the students receiving an education for either France, Germany, Italy, or England; but are they educating themselves with the Book of books—the Word of God?

VI THE ALL-AMERICAN DOLLAR

Although the Continental currency was worth no more in Connecticut than elsewhere, one patriot parson owned some to his regret. He was captured by the British at Kingsbridge with some of the "dirty money" in one of his shoes, brought into New York, forced to eat the money and to swear that he would not pray again for Congress "or their doer of dirty work, Mr. Washington."

NORTH CALLAHAN

"They overcharge us mercilessly; everything is enormously dear; in all the dealings we had had with them they have treated us more like enemies than friends. Their greed is unequalled, money is their God."[1] These are the words of French Count Fersen, and he is describing the New Englanders whom he accused of selling goods to the British blockaders while robbing their new allies.

The pope always had economic power; perhaps this French Catholic officer assumed that the Puritan clergy also pushed the prices, too. Cardinal Bentivogolio, who was the papal nuncio in Holland when the English Puritans were there, believed that they had left Great Britain for economic, not political reasons. Samuel Eliot Morison, author of *The Oxford History of the American People*, disagrees with this contention. The famous author writes, "Puritanism was essentially and primarily a religious movement; attempts to prove it to have been a mask for politics or money-making are false as well as unhistorical."

The leaders of the Pilgrims to the rocky shores of New England strongly emphasized that their prime reason for going to the wilderness was religious—profits and popular schemes were necessarily secondary. Increase Mather's brother, Eleazar, who was the first pastor at Northhampton, warned his congregation in 1671, just before he passed away, that "outward prosperity is a worm at the root of godliness, so that Religion dies when the World thrives [Deut. 28:47 and 32:15]. . . . Oh consider, the time when [there was] less of the world, but was there not more of Heaven? less Trading, Buying, Selling, but more Praying, more watching over our own hearts, more closewalking; less plenty, and less iniquity. . . ."

Thomas Jefferson Wertenbaker states that the Puritans were establishing an economic democracy. There was no aristocracy with wealth and the distribution of lots in the new settlements was done in a very democratic manner. Urian Oakes hoped that he'd never see the day when "houses and lands, lots and farms and outward accommodations are of more value than the Gospel and Gospel ordinances. . . . Sure there were other and better things the People of God came hither for than the best spot of ground, the richest soil."[2] A number of years later The Reverend Mr. Higginson continued this theme in his election sermon of 1663, when he preached, "It concerneth New England always to remember that they are originally a plantation religious, not a plantation of trade. . . . Let Merchants, and such as are increasing cent per cent, remember this that world gain was not the end and design of the people of New England, but religion."

The Puritans knew what it was to be frugal. This was drilled into them when they first came to America. They had to pay an interest rate as high as 45 percent on the capital they had borrowed when they shipped over to Plymouth Rock! It took them 23 years to pay off that debt by sending beaver skins and fish to England.

William Penn was always worried about money—both his own use of it and how it would affect his subjects. His father left a trading company and joined the Royal Navy, which was criticized by a friend. His retort was: "Gold to me is dirt; 'tis the goodness of the cause that hath only to put me on, and nothing shall take me off the service." Penn's father continued to rise in the ranks to become an admiral before he retired.

While his son was encouraging people to leave the poverty and pressures of English cities for the rich farm lands of Pennsylvania, other people were peeking over his shoulder. As soon as Penn, Jr., had received his part, his old chums began to ask for special privileges as importers for the colony. Penn rejected these attempts to make money off his friends. He himself was always in fear of imminent poverty and as a financial pessimist he saw dark clouds on the horizon. He once wrote, "I am a crucified man between Injustice and Ingratitude there [Pennsylvania], and Extortion and Oppression here [England]." He believed he lost £64,000 in the first 25 years of his proprietorship.

The idea that the love of money was the root of all evil was not new. The Roman poet, Lucan, said, "The wise ancients thought luxury more dangerous to states, than the attacks of foreign enemies." Charlemagne made laws to restrain the luxury of his nobility and gentry. He even went to such lengths as to tell his people that silk clothing was not fit for men to wear.

Emperor Ching-tsu of China in the thirteenth century ordered that a diamond mine be closed. "The digging of these glittering gems," he said, "fatigues and kills my people, and the stones they find are neither food nor clothing."

In the opening years of this century, John D. Rockefeller decided that he would pass across denominational lines to donate money to missions, not just his Baptist body. The Congregational Board asked for $160,000, and the millionaire handed over $100,000 to help them out. Thirty ministers in that denomination blew their collective tops when they read about this in the *Congregationalist*. They met in Boston and signed a protest demanding that the filthy lucre be handed back to the rich capitalist. Dr. Washington Gladden said, "The money proferred to our board of missions comes out of a colossal estate whose foundations were laid in the most relentless rapacity known to modern commercial history. The success of the business from the beginning to now has been largely due to the unlawful manipulation of railway rates." William Jennings Bryan and Robert M. La Follette took up the attack. "He gives with two hands, but he robs with many," La Follette preached to a Chatauqua audience. "If he should live a thousand years he could not expiate the crimes he has committed. . . . He is the greatest criminal of the age."[3]

It may be true that the ancient philosophers questioned the glitter of gold for their generations and Quakers thought ribbons and ruffles were of the devil, but man must eat—even men of the cloth. The clergy in Virginia were paid in tobacco and this caused later problems. It was obvious that the worth of the 16,000 pounds of weed collected for them would vary each year. In 1753, they were about to make a killing because of the shortage in the Old Dominion. Virginia wanted to make some adjustments and passed a law in 1758 that changed the rate, and immediately these parsons appealed to their Bishop in London because they felt it was unfair as others could take part-time employment when bad times came and they couldn't.

They wanted to make up for it now. The Anglicans aroused bitter resentment when they went over the heads of the House of Burgesses and asked the king to stand up for them. Patrick Henry got his name in the news by defeating this effort. The people were disgusted with the clergy because they tried to live rich lives while others were starving.

The clergy also had some interest in manual work itself. In Massachusetts, we see ladies of various towns assembled at the homes of seven different pastors on each day of one week to spin flax, cotton, and wool. Clergymen differed over English trade and taxes. A Puritan pastor clamored about British restrictions on trade from the pulpit. But the Reverend Mr. Chandler, a Tory, dismissed the tax on tea as no more than "the weight of an atom on the shoulders of a giant," whereas preachers and college teachers showed their patriotism by wearing woolens made in America.

The religious leaders in America devoted part of their time to secular problems. The reason that they were interested in trade and taxes was because they felt this was just the beginning of oppression from England. Rev. John Adams put it this way, "If Parliament could tax us, they could establish the Church of England, with all its creeds, articles, tests, ceremonies, and tithes, and prohibit all other churches, as conventicles and schism-shops." They felt so strongly about it that the day the Port Bill took effect, they resolved to keep the date in "fasting, humiliation, and prayer."

The measures of 1764 were signs of things to come. The British navy was offshore; they were planning on an army for colonial posts; they were revving up the customs service power, and meddling in how justice was done. The mercantilist theory expounded in London meant that the economy of Georgia would be run so as to help the British out, no matter how inconvenient it was for the settlers. They figured they could save £500,000 if silk could be imported from the Peach State yearly. Even though it proved to be a pipe dream, the English weren't about to loosen the chains of these former criminals in Georgia.

The British placed the following restrictions on colonial trade in 1660 and after:

1. The Navigation Act of 1660 prohibited vessels owned by or manned to the extent of more than one-fourth by foreigners to import or export any goods or commodities, and vessels permitted to trade in the colonies were forbidden to export sugar, tobacco, cotton, indigo and dye wood to any place except England, Ireland, or an English colony.
2. The Act of 1663 prohibited the direct importation of most European products to the colonies, as first they had to be shipped into England and then reexported to America.
3. In 1671, the Act of 1660 was amended to prohibit shipment of some colonial products directly into Ireland, and they could ship only enumerated commodities to England itself.
4. In 1673, the Parliament levied duties on shipments of enumerated commodities from one English colony to another so as to discourage intercolonial trade.
5. In 1696, Parliament passed an important act that clarified the prior legislation to plug loopholes and forbid direct export of any colonial products to Ireland. In the same year, they passed legislation that forbade the export from England of knitting frames, so as to protect that industry in the homeland.
6. In 1698, the Parliament passed an act to forbid all English subjects from carrying on trade with the East Indies.
7. In 1704, rice, molasses, tar, turpentine, hemp, masts, and other naval stores were added to the enumerated list.
8. In 1721, Parliament prohibited the importation of any East India products to America.
9. In 1722, an act added fur and copper to the list of enumerated commodities.

10. In 1732, the export of colonial-made felt or hats was prohibited between the colonies and direct shipment of hops from America to Ireland was stopped.
11. In 1733, the Sugar Act was passed.
12. In 1736, Parliament demanded that the initial set of sails for any ship must be made of British-made cloth.
13. In 1750, Parliament prohibited the erection of any new steel mills or furnaces.
14. The American Act of 1764 laid taxes for revenue on the colonies and imposed new restrictions on colonial trade overseas.

King George III rejoiced that the Parliament had worked late into the evening in passing legislation to bring the colonies to their knees. The economy was sickly in Pennsylvania because they were forbidden to trade freely or to manufacture necessities for themselves, so they were on the brink of collapse. Even with all of this, the British were complaining about evasions of their laws. Governors in Rhode Island and Connecticut were elected by the people so they looked the other way when their citizens did not follow the laws made in London; but in Massachusetts the royal governor tried to look out for the king's interests.

The colonies were very quiet even though they suffered many restrictions on their trade and manufacturing. The major acts were yet to come and when that axe fell there would be trouble. Those who began to question the relationship between the two areas separated by the Atlantic Ocean only wanted regulations that would be of benefit to both sides. John Dickinson said, "If Great-Britain can order us to come to her for necessaries we want, and can order us to pay what taxes she pleases before we take them away, or when we land them here, we are as abject slaves as France and Poland can shew in wooden shoes, and with uncombed hair."

We should not think that the British government showed no interest in the economic problems of the colonies. She did have tariff preferences and import bounties that put money into the pockets of the people across the sea. The tariff preferences were on tobacco, pot and pearl ashes, hemp, pig and bar iron, raw silk, white oil, pitch tar, whalebone and various timber products. She placed bounties on naval stores and indigo too.

In 1763, the British decided to enforce the White Pine Acts. After the eighteenth century passed its half-way point, the politicians in London realized that even though they had drawn up many kinds of legislation, it was meaningless to have it down in black and white and not have it followed. The Americans had become experts in evading many of the king's laws by smuggling or simply disregarding them. Provisions to protect the king's woods in America had been made over 40 years earlier and they were very severe. The problem arose because the colonists were bound to interpret the laws loosely. Governor Wentworth of New Hampshire seized over 1,500 logs in Massachusetts in 1758, and in the year this new bill was passed, he took over 2,000 white pine logs in the same state and aroused the ire of the citizens.

One reason the English were starting to squeeze their brothers in America was because their national debt had risen from £72,289,673 in 1755, to £129,586,769 in 1764. Even to pay off the interest on this debt was going to cause many problems and the politicians felt it would be good to make the Americans foot part of the bill, as that would improve their image before the home folk. The annual expenses of maintaining 10,000 troops in America would run to more than £220,000 annually, so they would have to find the money somewhere.

George Grenville assumed the post of prime minister in summer of 1763, and he started to search the books for laws that could be used against the colonists. Like the White Pine

Act, there were several that looked promising—if they could be enforced. Royal customs could be collected under the Acts of Trade, but at this time only £1,800 was dropping into the till, the reason was simple—smuggling. The bosses sat in England drawing handsome salaries while the ill-paid collectors had to accept bribes to stay alive in the land of Yankee traders. If things had tightened up, the king would have been able to smile again.

The Sugar Act of 1733 was on the books. Since that time, they had paid only a small fraction of the prohibitive duty on the import of foreign molasses, but it was hoped that now a heavy duty on Madeira would break the monopoly that that Portuguese product had acquired on the colonial wine market. The duty would have to be high enough to fill the king's coffers but low enough not to stifle the demand of the people. Governor Bernard wrote to London from his hot spot in Boston that "the publication of orders for the strict execution of the Molasses Act has caused a greater alarm in this country than the taking of Fort William Henry did in 1757 and the Merchants say, There is an end of the trade in this Province. . . ."

The Americans tried to talk some sense into their big brothers abroad. The Assembly of Rhode Island showed that their citizens had consumed £120,000 worth of English products while only having £5,000 worth of manufactured goods to sell as exports. Only the profits from the molasses trade had enabled them to pay for the consumption of British goods. The difference between New York's imports and exports was about £470,000 sterling, and this was made up through the trade of French molasses.

The colonies had guessed that the duty on molasses would be about half of what it was. When the news came from abroad, it stirred up the natives to a furor. The merchants boycotted pilots who brought naval vessels into port and offered sailors higher wages to jump ship, then they raised howling mobs when the English tried to impress men to fill out their crews. But most important, they began to question their relationship with the Britishers and began to wonder out loud whether they were constitutionally wronged by such obvious methods to tax them without representation.

The next blow to fall would stamp itself into the minds of all the citizens. Grenville had already been thinking of a Stamp Act, which would basically do its own work. A moderate in America said, "The makers of that act knew full well, that the confusions that would arise from the disuse of writings, would COMPEL the colonies to use the stamped paper, and therefore to pay the taxes imposed. For this reason the STAMP-ACT was said to be a law THAT WOULD EXECUTE IT-SELF. For the very same reason, the last act of Parliament, if it is granted to have any force here, WILL EXECUTE ITSELF, and will be attended with the very same consequences to AMERICAN liberty."

The act provided that a tax stamp appear on every issue of every newspaper, on each legal document, and on every customs paper and ship clearance. Documents relating to tavern licenses and even college diplomas needed a stamp affixed or they would not be legal. Even though Grenville tried to point out that the taxes collected this way would not be a heavy burden, even less than what the average Englishman was paying out in Great Britain, the colonists were furious. John Adams said he was sure that the Puritans would have opposed the Stamp Act.

John Adams realized that the Americans had been paying "indirect" taxes to the crown for many years. But this was the first time they had been asked to pay taxes directly to the British Exchequer without having their own assemblies give consent first. Immediately the Sons of Liberty began to force resignations of the stamp distributors. Augustus Johnson resigned his Rhode Island office on August 29, 1765; James McEvers gave up his position in New York; William Coxe bowed to the mob and resigned his post in New Jersey; Zachariah Hood was so frightened that he fled from his own Maryland; September 10 was the day George Meserve returned from England to New Hampshire and he immediately was forced to toss in the towel; nine days later Jared Ingersoll of Connecticut decided to change his job; on October 5, John Hughes of Pennsylvania promised that he would not act in his post; Inspector George and Distributor Caleb Lloyd of South Carolina relinquished their posts after pressure from the radicals; Col. George Mercer was compelled to resign on the very day he returned from London to his home in Virginia; Georgia's John Parnham signed a declaration that he would not enforce the law; and North Carolina's Dr. William Houston was the final man to give in to the pressure of the day.

This definitely threw a monkey wrench into the English economic machine. William Pitt believed that "Trade is the Wealth of the World." The best thing for England was a strong America. Davenant said, "Generally speaking our colonies, while they have English blood in their veins, and have relations in England, and while they can get by trading with us, the stronger and greater they grow, the more this crown and kingdom will get by them, and nothing but such an arbitrary power as shall make them desperate, can bring them to rebel."

Even with all the restrictions, by 1775 America produced 30,000 tons of crude iron for her mother country—one-seventh of the world's total output. In America, they were building ships at a yearly clip of 140, and by 1775, 30 percent of the British boats had been built in colonial ports. It cost the English only half as much to have their subjects build up their merchant fleet than it would cost in Great Britain. Governor Morris stated that Pennsylvania alone exported enough food to sustain 100,000 people. More than 90,000 barrels of rice were exported from Charleston in 1740. Virginia shipped its surplus wheat, flour, bread, beef, and pork, as well as horses to the West Indies. The fields decked in gold spread from New England to Georgia. If trouble arose, the mother country would be losing out on an excellent chance to prosper along with her rich colonies.

From 1744 to 1748, the northern colonies purchased £3,-486,266 of exports compared to £3,363,333 imported by the West Indies. From 1754 to 1758, the northern colonies' imports more than doubled and reached a figure of £7,414,055, while the West Indies gobbled up £3,767,859 of British products. The opposition to the British government tried to get the merchants to put pressure on the administration by citing figures which showed that 75 percent of the goods manufactured in England found their way into American homes. Pitt took the stand again and reported that even in New England, New York, and Pennsylvania, where smuggling had gone on for years, the legal imports were going to drop if they pressed the radicals too far.

The merchants in the various colonies woke up to the fact that nonimportation was their key to success in breaking the acts they detested so much. Massachusetts, as usual, took the first step to defy the British government and the others followed. In Boston things got rough as various Loyalists thought that they could defy the radicals. Sam Adams first gave a pep talk to the "Loyal and Religious people who are really oppress'd and under a Tyranny." A radical lawyer seconded a proposal with a declaration that "those who dar'd to Import any Goods contrary to the agreement of the Merchants were Guilty of High Treason against the Majesty of the People." New York was the first seaport to resist the Tea Act, and when the text appeared in the local papers, the merchants drafted a letter expressing thanks to those New York ship captains who had refused to load their ships, while docked in London, with the East India Company tea for the "insidious purpose of levying the Duty in America." In Philadelphia, they reacted to the Boston Port Bill by closing up their houses and muffling the church bells while having local ships fly their flags at half mast.

We must remember that the events in America did not hold the attention of the people in London like they did in American cities. In reading the correspondence between King George III and Lord North, one is amazed at how little is written about the colonies and their concerns. Even at the time of the Stamp Act, the king was more angry at his prime minister than he was upset about the news from Boston. George Grenville had drawn up a bill, at the king's request, which would give His Majesty the right to choose a regent in case of serious illness. George III had now just recovered his health after a long bout with a major sickness. But Grenville insisted that the king could not appoint his mother because he believed the rumors that she was the mistress of the Earl of Bute, who was detested by most English politicians.

The king wanted to get rid of his prime minister and in England he had the power to do in his top political commander. He simply had to find a replacement. Even the sentiment of the day helped King George III ease out Grenville. The English merchants were not angry at the businessmen in America who signed nonimportation agreements. They blamed their troubles on Grenville and organized a committee to mobilize mercantile sentiment with the intention of deluging Parliament with petitions for repeal of the hapless act that could not be enforced. These petitions did not mention the rights of American citizens, only that trade was suffering and that it was better to iron things out so exports would be moving again toward ports in America.

Thomas Rockingham took Grenville's place and after a brilliant speech by Pitt decided that the Stamp Act should be repealed; but there had to be a show of reason why it should be done away with. The merchants hinted that there would be 20,000 starving Englishmen and another 100,000 unemployed unless things were put in order. The act was repealed by a vote of 275 to 167, but they let the Americans know where they stood as the Parliament passed other legislation to prove that they were masters of the situation.

Though nonimportation, then, was far from absolute, it had hurt England. Imports from Great Britain dropped from £2,175,218 in 1768, to £1,336,122 one year later. The British lost £232,000 at Philadelphia from 1768 to 1769, and they slid down £65,000 more the next year. The voluntary boycott in New York had remarkable success. In 1774, imports valued at £437,937 were shipped into the Fun City, but it dropped in 1775 to only £1,228! The *Pennsylvania Gazette* said that trade restrictions had cost the British £7,250,000 in lost trade.

Debt and taxes continued to be very important to the people in the provinces. Creditors in England tried to get at a politician in the Parliament who had debts, and some wondered if he should have been protected simply because of his position. Whether that was true or not, two Englishmen stood up for the colonies in England. Lord Camden said, "The British Parliament has no right to tax the Americans. . . . Taxation and representation are coeval with the essential to this constitution." Pitt echoed his sentiments: "The Commons of America, represented in their several assemblies, have ever been in possession of the exercise of this, their constitutional right, of giving and granting their own money. They would have been slaves if they had not enjoyed it."

The problems partially arose in the colonies over taxation because of the instructions given to the royal governors by British officials. They had at times demanded that their men in certain provinces dissolve assemblies to get rid of those who disagreed with the crown. Men of very questionable morals in the Parliament were the ones who wished to tax their brothers and sisters across the sea. A critic stated that they were not men of merit; they held power because the administration was afraid to cross them as it needed their votes on certain occasions. If these men had thought about it, they would have easily understood that taxation of America simply was putting money into foreign pockets, because the colonies were going to seek other ways to import goods that were duty free.

Not everyone criticized British officials for trying to tax the rebels without allowing them representation in Parliament. Galloway, a Tory, concluded that it was only natural that Grenville expected America to pay for her own defense. But Hutchinson thought that the tax bit was only an American excuse. The former royal governor stated, "There were men in each of the principal Colonies, who had Independence in view, before any of those Taxes were laid or proposed." These Tories who left for England after the first guns sounded rejoiced when they received letters of discontent from their friends who remained in rebel land and who were upset because the new governments had imposed their own taxes on the patriots.

Charles M. Andrews noted that Massachusetts taxed non-freemen in the colony before 1684 without allowing them to have representation in the Assembly. Virginia and Maryland taxed Quakers and they had no right to complain. Even the English inhabitants of Saint Christopher taxed the French on the island without giving them the right to vote. But this was much better than being taxed by outsiders. Rhode Island and other colonies saw their finances drained by duties and saw more money taken out of the province than was in general circulation at one time. Connecticut didn't oppose taxation as such—it simply wanted to do the taxing. During the war, Clinton allowed the Carolina legislature to tax its own people, and he honored them by opposing any special taxation from the homeland during the conflict. That would have helped before the clash of arms.

The Americans were gradually weaning themselves away from their mother country. As they flexed their muscles economically, they couldn't help but realize how much better off they would be if they were completely free to trade with all nations of the world. One has to admit that the English kept drawing back from confrontations as they either looked the other way or canceled laws that were products of their own thoughtless leaders.

The Stamp Act was repealed, but the British still had to show the colonies that this was only an act of grace and at any time they might make new amendments that would make the colonies toe the tax line. Duties on glass, paper, and paints were dropped as "contrary to the true principles of commerce." In fact, by only one vote, it was decided to retain the tax on tea and this was "simply for the purpose of vindicating the principles laid down in the Declaratory Act of 1766."

We can see then that both parties wanted to see bad pieces of legislation done away with. But the principles were completely different on each side. The British were doing this not because of humanitarianism or precepts about democracy, but only because they were losing money and it hurt. The Americans were basing most of their arguments on constitutional issues, and these issues made it impossible to back down completely. The English government and king still believed that they had the right to do as they wished with the colonists, and the latter felt that they should be treated as equals just as if they were living in Bristol, England, instead of Bristol, Rhode Island, or Bristol, New York.

This meant that resistance would not be at an end. Tea was still taxed and the Act of Parliament of May 10, 1773, permitted the East India Company to export tea to the colonies and establish a monopoly. As the tea would be cheaper, they believed that no problems would arise, but the principles involved made certain that the patriots would resist again.

Two outstanding historians believe that the act which started the Revolution was the Boston Tea Party. Hutchinson said, "The town is as furious as it was at the time of Stamp Act." Two mass meetings resolved that the ships in the Boston harbor must return to England without payment of duty. Governor Hutchinson refused to permit this and so the patriots took things into their own hands.

Rev. William Gordon, "self-appointed historian of the Revolution," recalls hearing John Adams tell the people that they should not allow the tea to be landed. That night, three groups of men dressed as Mohawk Indians went on the "warpath" and threw overboard 341 chests of tea. This was to push Parliament to action, and they promptly drew up the Boston Port Bill to punish the city.

The Intolerable Acts united the country. A number of states sent food and other things to Boston. George Washington, a moderate, asked a question that must have echoed the feelings of individuals throughout the colonies: "Shall we supinely sit and see one province after another fall prey to despotism?"

NOTES

1. Burke Davis, *The Campaign That Won America* (New York: The Dial Press, 1970), p. 8.
2. Thomas Jefferson Wertenbaker, *The Puritan Oligarchy* (New York: Charles Scribner's Sons, 1947), p. 46.*
3. Daniel J. Boorstin, *The Americans: The Democratic Experience* (New York: Random House, 1973), pp. 566-67.

VII

THE RELATIONSHIP BETWEEN CHURCH AND STATE IN THE LAND OF THE FREE

When confronted with the Puritan demands for the abolition of the episcopacy, James I declared, "No bishop, no king."

CLARENCE B. CARSON

The Established church and the king formed their own mutual admiration society. Both looked to the other for staunch support. But not all other denominations were worried about this. Even the Methodist church stepped in to pat the Anglicans on the back. "We do all in our power to strengthen and support the said Church—And as we conceive that very bad consequences would arise from the abolishment of the establishment—We therefore pray that as the Church of England ever hath been, so it may still continue to be Established." George Shadford scribbled at the bottom, "Signed in Behalf of the whole Body of the people commonly called Methodists in Virginia, consisting of near, if not altogether, 3,000 members."

All Protestants point back to the Reformation for their sectarian birthplace, although God had been saving souls since the creation of man. To them it was a great day when Luther decided to rebel against and not simply reform his church. This was evidence of his faith. They were not disturbed over the fragmentation of the Protestant body. But Tory Peter Oliver believed that this spirit undergirded the atmosphere of anarchy and made it almost impossible for English government and the Established church to reign. He convinced himself that everyone had lost the way and were groping about to find "the regular Path to walk in."

Why did the people turn their backs on the king? Why did the population rise up to tar and feather old friends? Why did they snicker when the Anglican church of America tried to exert her power for good and strong government? Washington's pastor said that it was "the loose principles of the times." Like the Jews of another century, who wished to get rid of Jesus to protect their power in the establishment (John 11:49-52), they could not look at democracy in action without personal forebodings. They said that there was a dangerous notion circulating in America, which was a "deep rooted republicanism, a democratic leveling principle, ever unfriendly to monarchy." "The independent mode of religion," wrote Rev. Samuel Seabury, "is, from its very nature, incompatible with monarchial government." Anglican clergyman Charles Inglis was even more disturbed because he believed they were not simply unfriendly, but that "one of the principal springs" of the rebel conduct was their desire to undermine the Anglican church in America.

Underneath the surface many people were troubled by the

actions of King George when he supported the Quebec Bill, which they felt was bowing the knee to Rome. Edmund Burke said, "By this establishement, said they, the Protestant religion enjoys at best no more than a toleration. The Popish clergy have a legal parliamentary right to a maintenance; the Protest clergy are left at the King's discretion. Why are not both put at least on equal footing, and a legal support provided for both?"

Even though the Anglicans and Dissenters might hold the same opinions about the danger of Catholicism in Canada, they were a mixed breed at best. The dissenting Protestant was jealous of his freedom to think as an individual; no pastor could dictate his thoughts for him from the pulpit or on a political platform. The Catholic believer basically let the Church and the Pope do his thinking for him. But the dissenting believers did not look with much more favor on the Established church in England. They, too, walked too close together with the state—a secular one at that. They called the Church of England "A Rotten foundation—The Liturgy and Discipline— Chaff and Strubble." They accused the Anglicans of messing in politics and with having dead formalism as their foundation.

But just because one feels independent does not mean he will automatically be liberal with others. Prof. William Appleman Williams of Wisconsin University wrote many books that turned on the students of SDS. But these men, who hated the establishment, were not lenient with others. Williams noted, "They say, 'I'm right and you're wrong and you can't talk because you're wrong.'" Simple rebelliousness could not form a democratic basis for the community or religion.

If the Dissenters hurled verbal blasts at the British and their bishops, the Englishmen did much worse. During the Revolution, they turned the Old South Church of Boston into a riding school for British cavalry. They housed horses in the Dutch Reformed Church in New York too. Another Protestant church became a hospital. The Presbyterian Church on Long

Island was used as a prison until it was finally torn down to make huts for English soldiers. The Hessians in Princeton ripped down a church and used the materials to warm themselves. Finally, churches in two towns in New Jersey were deliberately burned by their own people, so that they could not be desecrated by the king's finest. Why this open war on religious buildings? Because the British thought Bible-believing churches must be in cahoots with radicalism.

Part of the Church's political reputation was traceable to the European mentality of the times. As the people and peasants poured their pennies into priestly pockets in the Old World, the property was thought of as the pope's and not as directly owned by the population. They would have been surprised if they knew men willingly gave their tithes to their local church and thought of it as their own possession. In their own countries, no matter how liberal they were, the Europeans couldn't support the spirit of democracy completely. As they burned books in England that made fun of His Majesty, they would destroy churches in the New World that represented rebellion to them.

As the Anglicans only had control of 10 percent of the churches in the colonies, one might assume that they had no power before the Revolution. Nothing could be further from the Gospel truth. In 1696, William III established the Board of Trade and ex officio members of this group included the Bishop of London, who would always be consulted about church matters in America as though he were the pope himself. Then, too, the members of this body, like Lord Halifax, were often as zealous in favoring the establishing of English bishops in each colony as were the Anglicans themselves. The Board of Trade was very eager to do the bidding of the Established church in London and to throw their weight around in America.

The Anglicans always got a sympathetic ear when they complained of persecution, real or imagined, in the colonies. They carefully played down kind gestures, such as when Congregationalists like Thomas Hancock gave donations for a set of bells for Christ Church in Boston.

The Reverend Mr. Rockwell was disturbed that his Episcopalians used a non-Anglican church for services when King's Chapel was being repaired in 1753, as there were two other Anglican churches in the same town. The Reverend Mr. Chandler noted that they prospered more when the other denominations were less friendly, as this new atmosphere caused Anglicans to lose members, there being no reason to defend their particular faith.

When Rev. Thomas Secker, son of a Dissenter, became Archbishop of Canterbury, he was ready to make some adjustments in the strategy. The Reverend Mr. Caner suggested that they open a new mission church in Cambridge, which was the fountainhead of the Congregational ministry for eastern New England. Even though Harvard did not restrict Anglicans from studying at that college, the Englishmen decided to disrupt the peace in that Puritan religious plantation.

In 1762, Caner was writing his boss in London, again complaining about a Massachusetts act that incorporated a new missionary society for work among the Indians that had been organized by Congregationalists and brother churches in the Boston area. He considered this to be an effort to check the progress of the Anglican church instead of rejoicing that the Indians would be hearing the Gospel of Christ. He asked Secker to use his pressure on the Board of Trade to have the act annulled.

The Privy Council disallowed the act without revealing from where the pressure came. Immediately the people of Boston were upset. Rev. Andrew Eliot wrote, "We find by your [Jasper Mauduit, London Agent for Massachusetts] Letter to Mr. Bowdoin that the Act . . . is not likely to have the Royal Approbation. . . . It is strange that Gentlemen who profess Christianity will not send the Gospel to the Heathen themselves nor permit it to be sent by others. . . . We find the Fate of our Charter, that our Enemies are more and greater than we were aware of."

The dearest hope of Secker and his social climbers was to exert their pressure in London to establish colonial bishops. In 1758, he began to apply pressure on the Board of Trade and he was delighted at his reception. Even some men who were not members of the Anglican church, but believers in dissenting denominations, showed no alarm at his suggestion. But once the colonies got wind of the anticipated move, their bitter letters made the Board back down and they never saw British bishops based in Boston.

In Connecticut, the Anglicans were to gain members from the fallout of a quarrel between the "Old Light" and the "New Light" factions of the Congregational church. Many believers were sick of the feud and began to attend Church of England services instead. The Anglicans then tried to have their denomination recognized as the Established church in the colony by applying pressure when the schism was at its height. Their efforts did not prove to be successful.

In Virginia, the Church of England had easier sledding because she was the most powerful religious body in the province, even though she didn't have the strength to appoint pastors in all the churches. The money gathered from the citizens to support her was substantial. In fact, more funds were spent on the churches in Truro and Fairfax counties, than were used for the county budgets!

The evangelical uprising and the war tore at this foundation and practically ruined the Anglicans. When their people were expected to provide funds personally for the pastors of the various parishes, they proved to be very lax in their commitment. Quite a number of Anglican priests left the ministry and churches were begging for men to step out on faith to preach the Gospel.

This spirit surprised the Europeans. They had never thought much on whether or not the churches should rise or fall on the basis of the faith of their followers. This meant that the people considered themselves to control their spiritual future as well as giving them the desire to control their political destiny. It was a faith of rugged individualism and simplicity that emphasized inner peace and not outward frills. As these people dictated their own future, they were not ripe material for despots in government or in the churches.

When Patrick Henry was twenty-seven, he stepped on the stage as a lawyer in the case that nobody could win. The ministers of Virginia had been paid for years in "tobacco-money," which now caused all the trouble. The law required every parish to pay its ministers of the faith a salary of sixteen-thousand pounds of tobacco, no matter how much it would be worth on the open market. When prices dipped, the clergy suffered; when they rocketed, the clergy lived extremely comfortable lives.

One year, the colony had a very poor crop of tobacco, which meant that the clergy was going to be making tons of money. The House of Burgesses saw the dilemma and decided to change the system, so that the pastors would get another rate that would not fluctuate each year but remain the same in purchasing power. The law fixed the new salaries at twopence per pound of tobacco.

The Anglicans went over the heads of the Virginians all the way to the supreme sovereign in London. They asked their bishop to put pressure on the crown in their behalf. The king announced, "I declare the law passed by the Houses of Burgesses to be null and void." The Church of England had wielded its power and the people of Virginia fumed.

Henry decided to take the case, even though he had been named after his uncle, who was a preacher of that same religious denomination. When the clergymen asked to collect their back salaries, he felt someone had to oppose them. Even though he was a believer, he felt that the men of God had stepped beyond the bounds of Christian principles. He knew, as did all the residents of the colony, that many of them were making more money than the ministers of government in Virginia.

As he entered the court, he could see his father, who was one of the judges. As the jury was being chosen, Rev. James Maury, who represented the clergy, called the men being chosen "a vulgar herd." Henry retorted, "Sir, these are honest Virginians and therefore above reproach!"

Patrick's tactics were to show that these men of the cloth lived off the labors of others and that it was inconsistent with their calling to be making more money than the very leaders of the province. He accused them of being the real lawbreakers in the case. The representatives of the people had drawn up legislation that was fair to all concerned, and it was passed by a comfortable margin, but these men in black had gone over the heads of the population to have the king annul a very fine piece of legislation, thus destroying the very moral principles of democracy. When the jury came back, they had reached their verdict—only one penny should be given for "damages."

In 1784, Patrick Henry was on the other side of the religious question. He and some others felt that there should be a general assessment for the support of religion in their new state. George Mason had written him, "Justice and virtue are the vital principles of republican government, but among us a depravity of manners and morals prevails, to the destruction of all confidence between man and man." Richard Henry Lee added, "Refiners may wave reason into as fine a web as they please, but the experience of all times shows religion to be the guardian of morals; and he must be a very inattentive observer in our country who does not see that avarice is accomplishing the destruction of religion for want of legal obligation to contribute something to its support."

The general mood of the population was pro-Church, but they were mostly opposed to the principles behind assessment. Again we find the Anglicans pitted against the other dissenting denominations. The Presbyterians and Baptists had worked hard to create an atmosphere where evangelical thought would thrive, and they were fearful of going back to a pre-Revolutionary setting. They also felt that this might be the first stepping-stone for the reestablishment of the Church of England in America.

The Baptist General Association met in September, 1785, and adopted the following seven-point program to fight assessment:

1. The civil power had no right to establish a religious tax.
2. The fear that religion would die without state money is "founded neither in Scripture, on Reason, or on Sound Policy."
3. The Assembly would be judging as to whom would receive the funds; thus it would determine religious principles.
4. If the Assembly had the power to establish all denominations, it had the power to reestablish one.
5. Incorporation of the Episcopal church (as she had requested) was inconsistent with human freedom.
6. Reserving ecclesiastical property would be a glaring distinction.
7. The indulgence granted the Quakers and Mennonites was an "open offense."

The Baptists and Presbyterians felt that their churches could and should stand on their own two feet, and that it would be an affront to God to suggest otherwise. A typical memorial read, "It is certain that the Blessed author of the Christian Religion, not only maintained and supported his gospel in the world for several Hundred Years, without the aid of Civil Power but against all the Powers of the Earth, the Excellent Purity of its Precepts and the unblamable behavior of its Ministers made its way thro all opposition. Nor was it the Better for the church when Constantine the great, first Established Christianity by human Laws. True there was rest from Persecution, but how soon was the Church Over run with Error and Immorality."

The bill brought up in the legislature went through two readings, but it was not read for the third time, which meant that it would not become law. This was considered to be a great victory for James Madison and those who stood for religious principles against the power of the state to dabble in theological questions. In the end it had been the weight of many petitions that settled the issue and stopped the secular processes that were moving it toward enactment. Virginia had taken another step closer to complete separation of church and state.

The Puritans had never asked for special favors of the king; all they wanted was for him to promise them religious freedom in the new land. The "evangelical churches" feared the Parliament's power to enact legislation to set bishops over the colonies. They completely supported the principles of freedom when it came to the question of mixing church and state. Penn may have been tempted to hoist his denomination into the driver's seat, especially when he was having troubles with the Assembly, but he resisted such a temptation and guarded freedom of religion in his province.

There were a good number of paradoxes in relation to the cold war before Lexington. Gen. Thomas Gage angered the clergy by refusing to allow a day of fasting and prayer even though he was sent there to try to pacify the colony. Rev. Patrick Henry of Virginia was a Church of England pastor, and he blasted the Presbyterians regularly; but when evangelist Whitefield came to the area, Henry opened his pulpit to him. Philadelphia had become such a morally depraved city that the Quakers almost blushed when they talked of it in low tones, but it was a town filled with churches of different denominations.

The Americans believed in Christianity and the good it

did in the community. But they were against compulsion when it had to do with faith or the practice of faith. They had already seen too much arm-twisting by the church establishment. Madison said, "That religion, or the duty we owe to our Creator, and the manner of discharging it, being under the direction of reason and conviction only, not of violence and compulsion, all men are equally entitled to the full and free exercise of it. . . ." Even the Episcopal church could not exercise enough power to place pastors in various pulpits—the churches individually did their own choosing.

It was the Great Awakening that helped to destroy the remaining ties of church and state. Even though preachers were willing at a minute's notice to preach to politicians, they did not want "men of Caesar" messing with their soul-winning endeavors. They wanted a strong church foundation, but not at the expense of the faith.

The age-old problem for men of the cloth is the question of how much they should dabble in affairs of state. Should a preacher express his political ideas from the pulpit? Should he back certain candidates? Tory Peter Oliver was infuriated that religious leaders ranted and raved about the king and his Parliament from the pulpit. They did this as they sensed that the establishment would take away from their liberties if they were not careful—and that would restrict their preaching of the Gospel, which was their main calling from Almighty God.

The Act of 1776 in Virginia exempted the different dissenting denominations from contributing to the support and maintenance of the church established by law. Even though this was on the books, it was not until 1779 that the church was disestablished, and it would be another seven years before Jefferson won the day with his Statute for Religious Freedom, which he called, "The severest contest in which I have ever engaged." Eventually the other states would gradually modernize themselves and put the power of religion back in the hands of the individual churches and their people.

VIII DARK SHADOWS OVER A RELIGIOUS REVOLUTION

They protested their innocency as in the presence of the God whom forthwith they were to appear before. They wished, and declared their wish, that their blood might be the last innocent blood shed upon that account. With great affection they entreated Mr. Cotton Mather to pray with them. They prayed that God would discover what witchcrafts were among us. They forgave their accusers. They spake without reflection on jury and judges bringing them in guilty and condemning them. They prayed earnestly for pardon for all other sins and for an interest in the precious blood of our dear Redeemer. . . .

CHADWICK HANSEN

A historian writes: "Contrary to popular opinion, New England's record in regard to witchcraft is surprisingly good, as Governor Thomas Hutchinson pointed out in 1750: 'more having been put to death in a single county in England, in a short space of time, than have suffered in all New England from the first settlement until the present time.' Through most of the seventeenth century the record is really astonishing. While Europe hanged and burned literally thousands, executions in New England were few and far between." In all the American colonies during the seventeenth century, there were fewer than fifty executions for witchcraft, and excluding Salem, there were fewer than thirty. "This is a genuinely exemplary record, considerably superior to Europe for intelligence and restraint."

It is surprising that about the only thing the secular world remembers about the Massachusetts Bay Colony are the witch trials. But how many of them have totally condemned Europe for a much worse record of bloodletting and destruction of human lives? Still, we who believe in Christ as our personal savior cannot allow this to warp our judgment of the value of one life in the sight of God. The much more horrendous record of the enlightened Europeans does not whitewash the activities that took place in the Bay Colony.

Of the twenty people who lost their lives, probably at least twelve people were innocent. No one can read their loving testimonies to the peace of God that reigned in their souls as they refused to lie and escape the noose by confession to something that was not true and not be deeply moved. They asked God to forgive the sins of the accusers and the court that brought in the verdict for their deaths. Nineteen of them were hanged and one gentleman was pressed for refusing to plead. In 1693, fifty-two persons were also indicted but only three were convicted, and each escaped the death penalty by confessing that they had made a league with the devil and were possessed of demons.

A number of historians and interested persons have come to the conclusion that what had happened in the Salem area was "image magic." But the question was much more serious for the clergymen of Massachusetts. They knew, what many moderns do not, that the idea of Satan having a forked tail and a hideous face was completely at variance with the Scriptures. According to the Bible, the Devil was an angel of light (II Cor. 11:14) and very powerful (Eph. 2:2,6:2), and he came to persons in many forms, some of them pleasing to the individual in question. Being the "Father of Lies," the evil one made an effort to possess the soul of any individual and used the best means available, whether it took gentle persuasion or violent action. "Most Protestant authorities agreed with Goodwife Osburn that, as Hamlet put it, 'the Devil hath power to assume a pleasing shape.'"

The questions raised in the hearts and minds of the clergy and laity in New England were very serious. One of these questions was whether or not the Devil could impersonate an innocent person. Also, they had to decide whether the Devil really did offer individuals whom he tried to possess things of value. One woman said that the Devil had come to her in a number of shapes but he told her "he was God" and that "she must believe in him." If she did this for six years he would give her many fine things. The most important question was whether or not God would allow the Devil to assume the shape of an innocent person and also possess believers.

We should not simply smile at the naïveté of these individuals of another age. Even Breuer and Freud reported a parallel case in their *Studies in Hysteria*: "A very distressed young girl, while anxiously watching at a sick bed, fell into a dreamy state, had terrifying hallucinations, and her right arm, which was at the time hanging over the back of the chair, became numb. This resulted in paralysis, contracture, and anesthesia of that arm. She wanted to pray, but could find no words [i.e., in her native language, German], but finally succeeded in uttering an English children's prayer."

"Pricking" was used as a test for witchcraft, and this seems absurd today. But psychologists Charcot and Janet used the same type of testing for hysteria two centuries later. Janet said, "In our clinics, we are somewhat like the medieval women who sought for witches. We blindfold the subject, we turn his head away, rub his skin with our nail, prick it suddenly with a hidden pin, watch his answers or starts of pain; the picture has not changed."

The New Englanders were not working off sexual frustrations as some historians have hinted at. The laws of every civilized nation at that time used the death penalty for witchcraft and the Puritans were simply following the Bible when they used capital punishment for this offense (Exod. 22:18: "Thou shalt not suffer a witch to live"). Rationalist historians have bent the record for their own purpose, which is to paint the Puritans in as dark a color as possible. But English law was even more exacting in its legal statutes against witchcraft. "One that shall use, practise, or exercise any invocation or conjuration of any evil or wicked spirit, or consult, covenant with, entertain or employ, feed or reward any evil or wicked spirit, to or for any intent or purpose ... or shall use, practise, or exercise any witchcraft . . . whereby any person shall be killed . . . or lamed in his or her body, or any part thereof: Such offenders duly and lawfully convicted and attainted, shall suffer death."

It is amazing that no other country or area was chastened for their crimes against humanity. But yet, the Puritans were not doing anything different than the other states of their day, and in fact, they were much less sadistic as we shall discover. One can only wonder at the total indifference authors of today have toward other areas or other groups such as the Roman Catholic church. All denominations should be judged alike.

Perry Miller states: "One point must be clearly understood at the start: witches were creatures whose existence was questioned by no one in his right senses, and even as late as the close of the seventeenth century hardly a scientist of repute in England but accepted certain phenomena as due to witch-craft." Still, not all the clergy were confused. Rev. Samuel Parris, a Puritan, did not believe the local doctor who said that two of the girls he had diagnosed were victims of witchcraft.

In Hartford, Connecticut, in 1662, Anne Cole, "a person esteemed pious," had violent fits a number of times during public worship and particularly at prayer meetings." Others also had fits during the court room sessions much to the surprise of those in attendance in Massachusetts. Even young people seemed to be dabbling in the occult. Problems with the evil one in Salem Village in 1692 could be traced back to the young people trying to find out various things by placing an egg in a glass and then praying to the devil. One such lass tried to find out her future husband's occupation and she was so struck by fear that she never married and lived a very unhappy life.

The common people had some strange ideas about the testing of people to see if they were witches. The most common test was the water-ordeal, which was based on nonsense. The victim was bound and then dragged through the water. If she floated, she was guilty because the water was rejecting her, as she had rejected baptism. If she sank, they'd try to rescue her because she had proven she was innocent. Another test was for her to repeat the Lord's Prayer and if she could not say it correctly she was a witch, as witches always said it backwards. Another idea that swept the community was that a female who could not weep was a witch, as she had lost her Christian charity and compassion for others.

A historian writes: "Many of the learned, including, Increase Mather and Deodat Lawson, rejected such tests outright as superstitions or as white magic or both." But there was one test that most of them accepted. It was a kind of laying-on-of-hands. The suspected person would touch the afflicted person, and if the touch cured the individual, it was assumed that the evil spirit had left. This was admitted as valid evidence by

Sir Matthew Hale, Chief Baron of the Exchequer, at a witch-craft trial in England.

They were not selective in who was accused. Rev. George Burroughs, who had been a minister of Salem Village, moved to Maine. He was suspected of casting spells. Others accused included Capt. John Alden; Hezekiah Usher, a prominent mer-chant in Boston; Judge Nathaniel Saltonstall; Phillip English (an ancestor of Nathaniel Hawthorne), who was a Salem merchant; and Andover Justice of the Peace Dudley Bradstreet.

Even the village attorneys believed in demon possession in Salem. But the accusers got out of hand. One of the con-fessions was read from the pulpit in that town. Anne Putnam said, "I desire to be humbled before God for that sad and humbling Providence that befell my father's family in the year about 1692; that I, then being in my childhood, should by such a Providence of God be made an instrument for the accusing of several persons of grievous crime, whereby their lives were taken from them, whom now I have just grounds and good reason to believe they were innocent persons; and that it was a great delusion of Satan that deceived me in that same time. . . ."

Cotton Mather was so upset by the accusations against many different people that he preached to his congregation against it. "Take heed that you do not wrongfully accuse any other person of this horrid and monstrous evil. . . . What more dirty reproach than that of witchcraft can there be?" The magistrates did not heed his warnings as they were anxious to convict those who came into the courts. The clergy told these judges that they should disbelieve all "things received only upon the Devil's authority." The people slowly began to see the light under the direction of their preachers. Thirty-nine neighbors of Rebecca Nurse signed a petition stating that according to their observations, "her life and conversation were according to her profession [as a Christian], and we never had any cause or grounds to suspect her of any such thing as she is now accused of."

The overall community was looking out for victims. But just any person who confessed to possession was not brought to trial, much less executed. Torture was never used on any of the accused, and they were free to state their own convictions about their guilt. Even Brattle, a sharp critic of the witchcraft proceedings, believes that the girls were "possessed." In Europe, those who admitted that they were possessed of the Devil would have been burned at the stake no matter how repentant they professed to be.

Rev. Cotton Mather had seen demon possession first hand. In the case of Goodwife Glover, she readily admitted that she had made a pact with Satan. She even called on him when asked who would stand by her. In her cell at night, the jailer could hear her berating Satan for abandoning her. She would torment the dolls she had in her keeping, and at the same time one of the Goodwin children would fall into sad fits.

Cotton Mather visited her in jail twice. He tried to convert her. When he told her that her prince was the Devil and that he had cheated her, she retorted, "If it be so, I am sorry for that!" He begged her to break her ties with Satan and "give herself to the Lord Jesus Christ by an everlasting covenant." He asked to pray for her but she said that unless her "spirits" would allow it she could not do so. Even then he dropped on his knees in prayer for her. But when he left she picked up a stone and put spittle on it and began praying.

The next time he asked her questions about her relationship with Satan. She told him that she would go to meetings where her "Prince," who was the Devil, was present with four other persons. She gave him the names but he never revealed to the public who they were, in fear that they might be accused themselves.

She said that even after her death, the Goodwin children would continue to be afflicted because there were others who were dabbling in spirit worship. This proved to be true and finally Mather took the oldest Goodwin girl into his own home. There he attempted to cure her through prayer and fasting. At first she could not read a religious book easily, as she could not read the words *God* or *Christ* outloud. She could not read the Bible and if others read it to her, she would have strange fits. Even a historian admits that she was cured —"not by her own [prayers], but that of Cotton Mather and other well-meaning members of the community who occasionally joined him."

We should not believe that all the pastors in the community took the same valid stand as most of the men we have mentioned. Even those cited would not be above criticism in today's world. But we must give them the benefit of the doubt because they genuinely were interested in the people involved, and Cotton Mather is credited with keeping some of the afflicted alive. Increase Mather was to follow with his manuscripts, *Cases of Conscience Concerning Evil Spirits Personating Men*, which roundly chastised the emotional atmosphere of the times and underscored the danger of false accusations. He was not alone as other clergymen began to act against the witch-hunters who were still popular with the people at large.

Once they realized what had happened, there was great chagrin among the leaders. During the early days of the witch scare, they called for a day of prayer and fasting, and now they humbled themselves "when Massachusetts proclaimed a day of fasting in repentance for the innocent blood shed at Salem." In 1709, Philip English and twenty-one others whose relatives had been executed petitioned the General Court to restore their reputations and make amends "as to what they have been damified in their estates thereby." Cotton Mather supported their position and took the lead as he preached a sermon about this before the Assembly.

One historian asked, "Finally, and most damagingly, proponents of the Puritan theory seem to be ignorant of the fact that the outbreaks of witchcraft occurred throughout Western civilization during the seventeenth century, and in every kind of religious community, Lutheran, Anglican, and Catholic as well as Puritan. If Puritanism was responsible for the hanging of nineteen people in Salem, what was responsible for the burning of nine hundred people in Bamberg?"

The nightmare was over. The Massachusetts Bay Colony showed genuine regret over what had gone on. Unlike the political conservatives who overlooked the repressive measures used by Spain's Franco, and the leftists who have said nothing about the bloodbath in Cambodia, which they virtually sanctioned by refusing men arms to defend their own liberty, these Puritans showed that they were not afraid to admit their mistakes and to pray that it would never happen again.

As late as 1736, England had the death penalty for witchcraft. A century later, Sir William Blackstone, the famous commentator on English law, declared "to deny the possibility, nay, actual existence of witchcraft and sorcery is at one to flatly deny the revealed word of God." But the Quakers were much more enlightened in their treatment of outbursts in Pennsylvania. It never got out of hand.

The handwriting was on the wall. With their position weakened, the British would be able to undermine the power of the Puritans in Massachusetts. Various laws and acts of the king and his Parliament would weaken the Congregational churches and strengthen the arm of the Anglicans in the years after the witch-hunts.

The Puritans did not think of themselves as a separatist group. In a booklet under the title *A Platform of Church Discipline* (later known as *The Cambridge Platform*), the

Puritans declared: "Our Churches here, as [by the grace of Christ] we believe & profess the same Doctrine of the truth of the Gospell, which generally is received in all the reformed Churches of Christ in Europe. . . ." Even back in the early days of the settlement, they detested the idea that they were "schismatic." An early Puritan writer thought endless wrangling over minor points was foolish and that the time should be spent in evangelism.

But we must remember that the Puritans came to America when every nation in Europe had a state church. Historians again show a double standard. They accuse the Pilgrims of narrowness, but never their persecutors. The Puritans stated that other denominations had freedom to stay away from their territory. As they lived very close to some other groups, there were bound to be problems when others wanted to enter their Puritan paradise.

The Bible was the key to understanding the controversy with Ann Hutchinson. She definitely had ideas that were not scriptural. So John Cotton asked her to leave as he followed Titus 3:10. As they wanted to maintain a pure doctrine in their colony, they asked her to leave. Even though we cannot praise narrowness today, political scientists don't get overly disturbed when members who differ with party policy are asked to leave; only when they deal with a religion that they know little about do political commentators condemn narrow-mindedness.

The Puritans were not looking for trouble, and they gradually came to accept a need for freedom of religion in America. But in the opening years, they were criticized for the very tactics that were being used all over Europe.

Much has been made over the contrast with the Keystone State. Every schoolboy knows of Penn's belief in the freedom of religion, but few realize that it was against the law for a Catholic to hold office in that province.

There is probably no other denomination in America that is freer from criticism. Everyone seems to have a good word for the quiet Quakers. It startles us to read the words of Thomas Jefferson as he describes them in his day: "A religious sect . . . acting with one mind, and that directed by the mother society in England. Dispersed, as the Jews, they still form, as those do, one nation, foreign to the land they live in. They are Protestant Jesuits, implicitly devoted to the will of their superior, and forgetting all duties to their country in the execution of the policy of their order." In the opposite vein, King George III was unhappy that the Quakers did not acknowledge their "submission to the mother country." Even though they were not still considered madmen in England, they could neither please the radicals nor Loyalists in the 1770s.

The Quakers knew, like the Puritans, what it was to live in a nation where they could be persecuted at the drop of a hat—even for not doffing their headgear. The Anglicans surely had not tried to live in harmony with other denominations, and the Quakers had seen 8,000 of their believers jailed in Old England.

Penn himself did not fight with his fists. He fought with his trusty pen. He was particularly miffed by Jonathan Clapham's *A Guide to True Religion*, which proclaimed that Baptists, Quakers, and other Dissenters were beyond redemption. He answered with biblical quotes and excerpts from patristic writings, along with any classical examples he could use. But he and his followers were accused of not believing in the Trinity and of being Jesuits in disguise. Next, Penn was tossed into a cell for writing *Sandy Foundations Shaken,* which was described as "an infamous and blasphemous pamphlet."

Like the Puritans, Penn would offer to debate those who differed with the Bible and his interpretations of it. The denominations of that time settled their disputes in debates instead of stuffing arguments under the rug.

The Quakers were accused of seeking martyrdom. It is said that some actually disrobed in Puritan meeting houses to stir up the Congregationalists. Whether this fervor for the Lord was edifying or not, they did seek to evangelize the colonies. Their main weakness was that they were dogmatic about the absence of dogma in their doctrinal position. In their narrowness, they began to lose power in America at just about the same time democratic concessions were being pushed on the province.

Penn came to realize that his practice of religious freedom was a plus in Pennsylvania. He believed in diversity that would strengthen the church. No doubt he was right because open competition with other creeds makes one continually search the Scriptures to find out if you are actually following the Bible or your own prejudices.

The Anglicans in America may have been a small denomination, but they had the power of the throne and British government behind them. This made them feel that others had no right to take unto themselves the power and prestige that had been their own back in the mother country. One such missionary boasted that he would "disperse the wretches." They particularly didn't like the Presbyterians and Baptists, who were zealous but rather uneducated. They even had harsh words for Roger Williams as well as the Reverend Mr. Cotton in Massachusetts.

The main difference between them and the Dissenters was their doctrinal positions and their church rites. The other dissenting sects believed that the Bible was the sole basis for doctrine, faith, and practice. The different denominations also criticized the Established church for rites that became dead formalism. They in turn felt that the other Protestant groups lacked intelligence and upper-class virtues.

The Toleration Acts were mainly to aid the Anglicans in getting a foothold in various spots where they had difficulty in making progress. They continually hoped to establish bishops in the colonies and to utilize the power from abroad to strengthen their position in church circles and in the missionary fields on the borders of the New World.

It is undeniable that the Catholics suffered more in America than in any other spot around the globe. But the colonists had tasted the use of force by Rome in the New World, and they all recalled the Reformation and persecution that followed. When John Winthrop came to America, he brought the Reverend Mr. Phillips, who believed that the Catholic church was as good as any Protestant denomination. John Winthrop later debated the Reverend Mr. Phillips in front of the latter's congregation. The result was that three other pastors admitted their errors in the faith.

In the House of Commons, there were debates over Catholic power in America and Canada. Even though there was much fear about Rome, the king and Parliament passed the Quebec Act which sent shivers up the spiritual spines of the Americans. Even though this was true, the colonies sent aid to the Catholics in Maryland. But it was not until John F. Kennedy broke the wall of prejudice in West Virginia, during a primary battle with Hubert Humphrey in 1960, that the Americans began to accept these people as equals in the political arena.

The forces of reactionism did not all stem from the pulpits of New England. There had been persecution in England because of Bible reading. The Anglicans, like the Puritans, had been very bitter against Baptist encroachment into their domain.

Roger Williams has often been an object for sympathy. His ousting from the Massachusetts colony and the openness of his province has brought him much well-earned praise. But he, too, took King George III apart with a bitter attack when he said that the English monarch had been a swearer from his youth and an oppressor and persecutor of good men. The attack caused the Anglicans to oppose him in his colony and to hope for his downfall.

We generally think of colleges of higher learning as being

free from bigotry. But Harvard College, as well as the Puritans, refused to open their doors to Evangelist Whitefield on one of his trips to America.

Even though each denomination felt that its own way was best, there were some signs of toleration in America. There would have been no problems, one theologian stated, if all the denominations were led by saints. Even John Winthrop continued to be a close friend of Rogers Williams after he had been banished from the Massachusetts Bay Colony. The one good thing about this competition, though, was the tendency to purify one's teachings when challenged by others.

There were both Calvinists and Arminians in New England. Both believed in the Word of God and in the salvation of man by faith. Much has been made of the Calvinistic tendencies of the Puritans. But even a secular writer acknowledged that they were not Calvinistic because they were in love with the image of John Calvin, but because they felt that the teachings of God were closer to the position of Calvin than to others. They were not hyper-Calvinists, as we can see when Cotton Mather tried to deliver a confirmed witch to the Lord Jesus. If, as some would contend, the Puritans believed so strictly in Calvin's teachings, then there would be no reason to preach to that type of person, as he would not be predestined to heaven anyway. But they knew that the Bible taught, "Whosoever will may come"—who would accept Christ was not up to man, but to God.

The spirit in America was changing. They were throwing off the yoke of a state-church mentality and becoming more open too. Cromwell had been very liberal and did not react against other groups until they forced his hand. Rhode Island had found that toleration paid off. When groups practiced persecution, their opponents grew. When no pressure was used, the denominations, such as the Quakers, did not make any headway. The more evangelical denominations had more of a spirit of democracy about them, and evangelistic work, such as Whitefield's, broke down denominational lines. This spirit continued as we see a pastor suggesting that both the Baptists and Methodists move into Kentucky to preach the Gospel.

During the revolutionary conflict, the Reverend Mr. Emerson visited an American army camp. As he looked out upon the different units, he could not help but see that some were in homespun and others in makeshift uniforms. As he stood there, he did not feel ashamed of the lads dressed in rags and tattered outfits that were beyond description. He smiled to himself and said that there was a beauty in the variety he saw before his very eyes. Perhaps he would have said the same today if he could see churches of evangelical persuasion in all the most important denominations. We are all brothers who have accepted Christ as our savior no matter what small differences there may be, and even these differences may be of God's making as he reaches out to all kinds of people who need his salvation. He has built a place for each one of them, and in that spot they can grow up in his love and shine for him.

IX *A TRUE*
PEOPLE'S DEMOCRACY

The Congregational Church in New England happened to be organized on a democratic basis, not because Puritans were in love with democracy but because leaders such as John Cotton and Thomas Hooker insisted that the First Church in Boston and the First Church of Hartford copy the exact organization of the First Church of Corinth and the First Church of Philippi, about which they knew very little, since the apostles and evangelists did not say much about them.

SAMUEL ELIOT MORISON

We would all admit that a mixture of state and religion is not good. First, if the religion is mixed up in state affairs it gradually supports ideas that may be directly opposed to the Word of God and public morals. Second, if the state supports one denomination, it is bound to overstep its bounds at times and suppress theological discussion simply because it feels a responsibility to back the denomination that provides it with votes at election time.

Governments are generally made up of groups that have their own special interests. Democrats in Michigan can expect the support of organized labor, and Nebraska farmers generally back the Republican candidate for political office. This is contrary to the teachings of the Word of God, because our Heavenly Father is not class conscious—all men are equal in his eyes.

At the time of the American Revolution, almost every class supported the ideals of Jefferson, Franklin, and Adams. There were no political parties, thus no complications in making decisions along emotional lines. The choices in elections were made on an individual basis, not because of party labels. In other words, they used the same criteria as God, who did not look on outward appearance but on the heart.

There was a very close philosophical brotherhood between political thoughts and religious thinking. A historian tells us, "The Fathers did not divorce politics and religion, but they denounced the separation as ungodly."[1] To divorce politics from religion would be setting aside the moral values they held dear. Each candidate would be judged on his inner being and his outward actions. Puritans were to be pure of heart and humanitarian in dealing with others. This was the ideal the voters had in mind when they went to the polls. De Tocqueville understood this very well when he wrote: "The Americans combine the notions of Christianity and of liberty intimately in their minds, that it is impossible to make them conceive the one without the other; and with them, this conviction does not spring from that barren traditionary faith which seems to vegetate in the soul rather than to live."

They built a government not because they prized an upper structure that would dictate to others, but because it was necessary for the administration of their daily lives. But this state should never supplant religion in making theological and moral decisions. President Stiles of Yale University said, "It was not so much their design to establish religion for the benefit of the state, as civil government for the benefit of religion, and as subservient, and even necessary, towards the peaceable enjoyment and unmolested exercises of religion—of that religion for which they fled to these ends of the earth."

Why subservient? Because they had lived in lands where religion was subservient to the government and it did not bring true freedom. The body of Caesar always deals with secular questions, whereas Christ's church deals with the spiritual. But this did not mean that they wanted one religion to dominate government either. They both were there to work for the good of the community, but along different avenues of approach. This was pointed out in the work of Rev. John Wise, under the title *Democracy Is Christ's Government in Church and State*, which was used in discussions of political philosophy at the time of the Revolution, although it was first published in 1687.

Were these principles really followed in political practice? Chadwick Hansen tells us that they were. "The clergyman was called to his position by the members of the church; the magistrate was elected by his constituency." There was a perfect unity in procedure, although one dealt in the political realm and the other in a spiritual sphere. This caused an English critic, a lawyer who had lived for three years in Massachusetts, to declare that "the government of the New England church was too democratical."

What was the total result of this practice? A new community, voluntarily gathered in New England, primarily for religious practice before Almighty God, organized into many independent churches, each a petty democracy, electing its officers and ministers without any control from any self-appointed bishops or priests, making its own laws, and regulating its own affairs, as far as possible, by the system of polity indicated in the Bible.

This religious faith was not built upon the ruins of civil government nor a civil government built on the ruins of religion. There was no church body to dictate to the legislature. But the church itself did have an interest in the legal apparatus that directed the secular affairs of the province. The very first code, under the charter of 1629, was drawn up by a minister. There was a yearly election, generally falling in the spring, and at this time there was a sermon preached for the edification of the listeners. It was often printed up so that each member of the Massachusetts Assembly would have a copy. But the preacher did not tell the people how to vote or whom they should choose for office. In fact, Rev. Timothy Edwards, Jonathan's father, preached a sermon entitled *All the Living Must Surely Die, and Go to Judgment,* when he had the honor of addressing the Connecticut General Assembly in 1732.

The early settlers realized the need for politics in their lives. Even before they left England on their pilgrimage to America, John Robinson wrote a letter about what the Puritans should do when they became "a body politic." He said that it was quite possible that no individual would stand out among them, but they were to chose leaders who were known for their love and interest in the common good of others. Just before the Revolution, at the time of the Continental Congress in 1774 at Philadelphia, the clergymen were reminded of their responsibility to inform their people of "the dreadful slavery with which we are now threatened," so that they might act wisely politically as well as spiritually in their private lives. This interest in the moral values of the political establishment continued into the nineteenth century. Theodore White writes, "And so a system of old moralists, led by the Protestant churches of the North, threw up new institutional leaders who founded the Republican Party, which mastered the slavery crisis by a war, changed the country's culture, but retained its form of state."[2] Kevin Phillips, a political scientist, believes the same stress on morality continued after Abe Lincoln of Illinois. He said, "In some measure, current presidential politics pivot on much the same set of factors that launched the Civil War and its attendant party system: an interrelated trinity of morality, money, and race."[3]

In Penn's woods, the colonists were very careful to point out that God was giving them the benefits of democracy. The draft to the inhabitants of the province read: "Divine Providence is about to grant you a favor, which few people have ever enjoyed before, the privilege of choosing deputies to form a government under which you are to live." This had echoed Penn's very own feelings when he founded the province. He had told his people, "God hath given me an understanding of my duty and an honest desire to do it uprightly." He also said that they should not put their trust in man in this "Holy Experiment," as men might fail. Even the government they were choosing could collapse if they forgot God. When the Constitutional Convention met later in Philadelphia, Rev. William White, an Anglican, led a religious meeting before the opening day, so that the delegates "may jointly offer up our prayers to Almighty God, to afford us his divine grace and assistance in the important and arduous task committed to us . . . in behalf of these injured, oppressed and insulated [people in the] United States."

In New England, voting was limited to those who were over twenty-one and "believers in Jesus Christ as the Son of God and the Saviour of the World." There were similar restrictions for voters in most colonies. In other words, "for its time it was democratic." But in many ways they had a deep interest in political problems. The New England states had their town meetings, and in Pennsylvania, Penn's first governor suggested that the people use a referendum in lieu of an elected assembly when he first took power.

Friends generally did not take an active part in prac-

tical politics. But they never shrank from promoting the basic
principles of liberty and justice based on the Bible. Penn
himself wrote a booklet called *England's Great Interest in the
Choice of a New Parliament,* which a secular scholar said
was one of earliest drafts of a party platform! When Penn
moved to the United States of the future, he continued his
interest in politics. In his Assembly, they even debated theological questions. For example, they debated whether it was
the will of God to refer to the days of the week and the
months of the year by the names derived from pagan myth-
ology. It was decided that they should continue to use them
because the original meanings had been lost.

Penn, like many of the Puritans, believed that he would
have little problem in running his province, as all were of
one mind and he could control the Friends (Puritan constituency). But this simply did not come true. As the citizens
did not mix politics with religion, they did not feel that
church affiliation had anything to do with how they voted.
By a second Frame, in April of 1683, his power was reduced
as he was not permitted to perform any public act without
the advice and consent of the Provincial Council. He assumed
that the Quakers would have a comfortable margin to control
Pennsylvania's first popularly elected Provincial Council and
Assembly organized one month earlier; but the Friends only
retained a one-vote margin over their opponents from up-
country, and that was because two rural members failed to
arrive on time to ballot for the speaker. Even before this he
should have felt the drift of sentiment, because when he first
tried to open the Assembly, only half of the elected delegates
were on hand and they were in a "belligerent mood." They
were not angry at him personally. They were upset because
they had been told that the Assembly was only to rubber
stamp LAWS AGREED UPON IN ENGLAND, and they
were not to have any discussion! But they had an ace up
their sleeve—they controlled the purse strings and could refuse

to pay the governor's salary if they wished, which they did on at least one occasion.

Moving south to Virginia, we see a movement away from the best traditions of democracy. Early in the state's history, every free white man could vote for the members of the House of Burgesses and there was no property qualification. But by 1670, they were back in the rut of Old England as they established property qualifications for voting. A man could qualify to vote if he had twenty-five acres with a house or one hundred acres of unsettled land in his name. But this did not mean that many of the lower crust rose to the surface. For the next hundred years, nine names provided almost thirty percent of all those who sat on the Governor's Council, as the aristocrats ruled the Old Dominion.

The first step to be taken in case of elections to fill seats in the House of Burgesses was for the governor to issue a writ that would order such a vote. Next, the parish pastor and readers in the various churches were then required to read the writ at the close of the worship service each Sunday.

On the day of the election, the sheriff checked to see if all was in readiness, and then he opened the election by reading the writ before all the voters who had assembled to cast their ballot. The general procedure was for a ruled paper to be used with the names of the candidates written at the top, so that at any time during the balloting you could tell at a glance who was ahead. Voters were not registered to vote and no poll watchers were on duty to see that everything was on the up-and-up. But when the individuals presented themselves to vote, the sheriff could refuse to take up their vote if he knew they were ineligible, and each candidate could challenge any voter whom he felt was casting his ballot illegally, either because he could not fulfill the land requirements or he wasn't of age. However, they seldom challenged voters, perhaps because they didn't want to anger an individual who might qualify for the next election.

The sheriff then asked each freeholder how he would cast his vote, and after hearing his choice the clerk would write down both the voter's name and for whom he cast his ballot. Very often the candidate would stand and thank the voter for his kindness. As the race swung back and forth, they might bring people to the polling area to influence the vote, as John Marshall (future chief justice of the U.S.) tried to do in one election. He had his friends entice the local Anglican clergyman and Presbyterian pastor to show their faces in the waning moments of the battle. But the men of the cloth were upset by this scheme, so they split their vote deliberately, so as to favor no special individual.

Indians, Blacks, and women were not allowed to vote. Also each voter was to be a believer in Jesus Christ, but probably nobody was asked about his faith. Even though the Anglicans were strong in Virginia, the politicians often courted the nonconformists too, as they were growing day by day and often felt more of an interest in the voting as they represented minority groups. Even though property qualifications were on the books, they were not very strict in disqualifying men on that basis. A Thomas Payne qualified to vote as he had a house that measured "4 and Half Feet Pitch, 4 or 5 Feet long, and 2 or 3 and a Half Feet wide" with a plank floor.

Tempers flared and even the first president of the United States was in a scrap when he was 23. He had supported George Fairfax, who came in second in a three-man race, where only twelve votes separated the trio. Mr. Washington must have used nasty language in the spat about the merit of the candidates, as William Payne knocked him down with a big stick even though the man from Mount Vernon towered over him. There was some talk of a duel, but George nixed the idea and they became fast friends. Most of the leading politicians were busy making friends instead of enemies by giving their friends plenty of liquid sunshine. Washington's agent supplied 160 gallons of liquor to 391 voters and "unnumbered hangers-on" when he was running for office himself in 1758.

There was a law that required eligible voters to cast a ballot or face a fine of "200 pounds of tobacco to be collected with costs by any informant." A lesser known fact is the Watergate-type of scandal in Old Virginny. John Robinson, Speaker of the House of Burgesses and Treasurer, up and died one day, and in checking through the files, they found that he had been helping out his friends on the side. He had withdrawn £100,761.7.5 from public funds and lent it out to many of his political acquaintances, including Patrick Henry, who had borrowed £11 in that way. Members of the Governor's Council owed him or the state £16,000, and in the House of Burgesses, it rose to a figure of £37,000. There was no proof that he had used any of the money for his own benefit. Thus, his friends chalked it off as a product "of his too benevolent heart," as Governor Faquier described it. The political establishment was willing to overlook moral breakdowns as long as they were the recipients.

South Carolina was much more enlightened than her Southern brothers. She had much better suffrage provisions than Virginia and even had the secret ballot. Some authorities believe that this was because of the spirit of the dissenting denominations in the state. The Anglican churches favored the status quo, while the evangelical denominations supported democratic principles.

The political establishment was bound to fall. First, there was a political revolution taking place throughout the thirteen colonies. Second, "the great evangelical revival" caused people to reassess their own thoughts on religion and politics. Lafayette understood this very well. He heard Americans talk about the possible revolution in Ireland. He said this would be impossible under the Catholics. It would have to be started by the Presbyterians first and then perhaps the Papists would throw their weight behind the revolution. The dissenters were the key to revolution. As a historian points out, "They [the Baptists] were democratic in politics as well as in religion, and whole-hearted in their sympathy with the colonial cause against England."

This was no rebellion simply for rebellion's sake. The revolutionaries believed that England broke the moral standards she herself had setup. Originally, the Parliament did not feel that there was any power in their Constitution, which would be counter to the provision granted by King Charles to Lord Baltimore in the charter for Maryland in 1632, and which said that neither the king nor his successors would cause any duties or other taxes to be imposed in the colony; and the king commanded his ministers never "to attempt any Thing to the contrary." The Parliament was consistent in this until 1764 and was in harmony with their Constitution. As Bernhard Knollenberg says, "If there were any principles which Parliament was obliged, morally at least to observe, 'no taxation without representation' was surely one of them." This went back to Article 12 of the Magna Carta, which declared, "No scutage nor aid shall be imposed in our kingdom, unless by the common council of our kingdom, excepting to redeem our person, to make our eldest son a knight, and once to marry our eldest daughter, and not for these, unless a reasonable aid shall be demanded."

How democratic was the England of that day? Few Britishers were upset that over half of the Parliament was elected by less than six thousand voters out of some five million people who proudly called themselves Englishmen. Even one of their liberal historians pointed out that a foreigner would surely be puzzled that "our commons [is] elected by so small a number of people."

The colonists began to ask themselves some pointed questions. Had England broken her own promises to the colonies? Did England set a good example for the provinces to follow?

The first question would be answered positively, because they were now expecting the American people to accept direct taxation without representation. The second query would be answered in the negative. A number of colonies were even more democratic than the mother country!

The relationship then was not based on morality or reason —the English wanted blind obedience. Friederich Gent put it this way, "The stamp act, in the first session of the year 1766, was repealed; but to preserve the honour of parliament from sinking altogether, with this repeal was connected a declaratory act, intituled, 'An Act for securing the Dependence of the Colonies'; in which the right of Great-Britain to legislate for the colonies in all cases whatsoever was solemnly maintained." Prime Minister North made it even plainer, saying that complete repeal could not take place until America would bow at the feet of Great Britain.

The colonies were not trying to break off their relationship with England. For decades they had been sending their legislation to Great Britain to get the stamp of approval from the mother country. They now felt that England herself was not being true to its own heritage. A joint committee of the Massachusetts Legislature, which included Thomas Hutchinson, emphasized the point that they traced their rights back to the Magna Carta and no reason "can be given why a man should be abridg'd in his Liberty, by removing from Europe to America, any more than by his removing from London to Dover. . . . Frenchmen, Portugals, and Spaniards are no greater Slaves abroad than at home, and by Analogy Britains should be as free on one side of the Atlantic as on the other."

The British began to use strong-arm tactics instead of persuasion. In South Carolina, the governor refused to administer an oath to Christopher Gadsden, who had been elected to fill a vacancy for Saint Paul's parish by an overwhelming margin, and then the Englishman dissolved the

House. Most of the members were immediately reelected and they denounced Governor Boone for high-handed actions. In New York and New Jersey, the English used another tactic. They secured more influence over the judges of the Supreme Court by reducing their existing "during-good-behavior" tenure by having this decision rest with the king. The Board of Trade said that rigid enforcement of the instruction (the granting of good behavior tenure to colonial judges) would be "Subversive of all true Policy, destructive to the Interests of your Majesty's Subjects and tending to Lessen that just dependence which the Colonies ought to have upon the Government of the Mother Country." No matter where the colonists looked, the British were banging their heavy brogans on calloused colonial toes.

America had a friend in England. When the Americans demanded that they be treated the same as other Englishmen, William Pitt spoke up for them in the House of Commons, saying, "I rejoice that America hath resisted." This was too much for Tory Peter Oliver. He said that this pronouncement had been construed as the voice of God. Or "as sacred as the Law delivered from Mount Sinai."

The patriots were upset by the double standard applied to them and to other areas under English rule. In 1737, the people of Edinburgh rioted. It was suppressed by armed might. The crown used this for an excuse to restore order in Boston, but the proceedings against the American town were very different. The proceedings lasted for about four months against Edinburgh; they lasted seventeen days in the case of Boston. The provost and magistrates plus the judges of Scotland examined many witnesses at the bar; in Boston the people were examined by the privy council and their evidence was suppressed. In Edinburgh, counsel and evidence were heard at the bar in front of the city magistrate; in Boston the agent refused a hearing at the bar. There were two members for Edinburgh and, overall, forty-five for Scotland in the lower House, and sixteen in the upper House; in the case of Boston there was not one member represented in Parliament nor for all or any part of America. The charge against Edinburgh was an open act of rebellion and atrocious murder, which was proved after a full hearing and by competent evidence; the charge against Boston was riot and trespass— no evidence was given and no hearing allowed. In Edinburgh there were frequent conferences held between the two houses to compare the evidence, etc., but in Boston there was no conference held at all. The punishment against Edinburgh was a £2,000 fine, whereas in Boston they lost their port and the lowest and most favorable estimate was £500,000 for the restoration of it; also, they were to be left at the king's mercy.

Not all the people in the colony felt that they had been trampled on. A number of them believed that the punishment was too light. Others complained about the American assemblies using their power to cut off the salaries against royal governors. These men were far from powerless. Governor Bernard of Massachusetts vetoed the choice of six of the newly elected twenty-eight members of the council. As a British historian put it, "Governor Bernard complains heavily and repeatedly, that the election of the Council at Boston in New England gives the people too much power. What idea can be formed of too much power in the hands of the people?"

The Loyalists continued to check for treason in their colonies. Governor Hutchinson of Massachusetts felt that they were only using the British ideas about rights of men to resist obedience to the power in London, and not because they were deeply concerned about liberty itself. His predecessor, Governor Bernard, was probably closer to the truth. All the Parliament needed to do was to have given the Americans limited representation in the home government in London. But Gov-

ernor Bernard personally felt that even the radicals would not
be happy if this sop was tossed their way.

Liberal political scientists of that age felt that "all lawful
authority, legislative, and executive, originates with the people."
They emphasized the point that the power in the people
was "like light in the sun, native, original, inherent and unlimited." The men of the cloth were shouting amen! Puritan
Hooker said in a sermon, "That the choice of public magistrates belongs unto the people by God's own allowance." Roger
Williams agreed by saying, "The sovereign, original, and foundation of civil power lies in the people." The Reverend Mr.
Wise of Massachusetts wrote, "A democracy, This is a form
of government, which the light of nature does highly value,
and often directs to, as most agreeable to the just and natural
prerogative of human beings." Samuel Stoddard gave his view
in an election sermon in 1703 and asserted that, "The abuses
that are offered unto a People by their Rulers, and the abuses
that are offered unto the Rulers by the People are deeply
resented by God." Mayhew's sermon was even more to the
point when he spoke on the birthday of Charles I. The parishioners must have winced as they heard him say, "There is
nothing in Scripture which supports this scheme [of unlimited
submission] of political principles. Neither God nor nature has
given any man a right of dominion over any society inde-
pendently of that society's approbation and consent to be
governed by him. . . . Disobedience is not only lawful but
glorious!" The net result of the thinking of the America clergy
would have to be direct election of the officials by the people.

The reason that the American Revolution broke out was
because the doctrine of the sovereignty of the people, which
had been nurtured in the towns, took possession of the whole
state. This is why the people were up in arms when the
Massachusetts Government Act limited the power of town
meetings and substituted an appointed council instead of

one elected by the freeholders. As de Tocqueville admitted—
the Americans wanted freedom, not simply independence.

One might have thought that the Americans only distrusted
government when it was enforced from afar. This has never
been the case. Winthrop, like many people today, believed in
limited government. Even though they would not be contented
with a moderate "share of Civil liberty," like some Tories,
they knew that mankind is likely to abuse the use of power.
A Puritan said, "Let all the world learn to give mortall men
no greater power than they are content they shall use, for
use it they will: and unlesse they be taught of God, they will
use it ever and anon. . . ."

A worthy Pilgrim, Edward Winslown, worried about the
ambition of leaders although he recognized the need for governors, etc. "Ambition in their governors and commanders,
seeking only to make themselves great, and slaves of all that
are under them, to maintain a transitory base honor in themselves, which God oft punisheth with contempt." Politicians
often overlook their own shortcomings but rant and rave about
the sins of others. Of the thirty-eight men of the Peter Rodino
committee to impeach the president, at least sixteen had accepted election contributions from the same milk producers
whose contributions to Richard Nixon's campaign they considered suspect. Politicians are not the only ones who seem
to think they are without sin; intellectuals have been thinking
only of their own special interests too according to Hofstadter.

De Tocqueville shook his head when he noted that America
continued to prosper even with imperfections in its political
system. The only thing that they could be happy about was
the freedom they did possess. Rev. Amos Adams gloried in
American liberty. He said, "Here we dwell in a land of light,
a region of liberty . . . religious liberty is one of the most
precious jewels on earth . . . a daring privilege. . . ." The
question is: What will we each do with this daring privilege?

NOTES

1. John Wingate Thornton, *The Pulpit of the American Revolution* (New York: Da Capo Press, 1970), p. 1.
2. Theodore H. White, *Breach of Faith* (New York: Atheneum Publishers, 1975), p. 223.
3. Kevin Phillips, *Mediacracy* (New York: Doubleday & Company, 1975), p. 85.

X BROTHER AGAINST BROTHER

So the Tories entered a bitter fight with pen, sword and the Bible.

NORTH CALLAHAN

The English continually had difficulty in gauging the Loyalist sentiments in the colonies. At the beginning they felt that a regiment could trot across the colonies and the people would rise in support of their king as wiser minds would prevail. The Tories understood from personal experience that this hope was a pipe dream.

Timothy Ruggles was one of these Loyalists who knew the score. He immediately began to organize a Tory group to defeat their foe—the Continental Association. Ruggles's group pledged to defend with their lives and fortunes their liberty

149

and their right of "eating, drinking, selling, communing and acting consistent with the laws of God and the King."

Others left for foreign shores. Rev. Jonathan Beecher tells of his emotions when he beached at Shelburne, Nova Scotia. "As soon as we had set up a kind of tent, we knelt down, my wife and I and my two boys, and kissed the dear ground and thanked God that the flag of England floated there, and resolved that we would work with the rest to become again prosperous and happy." Loyalists who landed in England felt the same elation as Louisa Wells, the daughter of a loyal South Carolina printer, as she wrote, "Oh! how shall I describe what I felt, when I first set my foot on British ground? I could have kissed the gravel on the salt Beach! It was my home: the Country which I had so long and so earnestly wished to see. The Isle of Liberty and Peace."

Many were still wavering in their decision in America. There had been no rush to push through the Declaration of Independence. Edward Rutledge was typical of those who later signed the precious document. He was tossed and torn and noted "the sensible part of the house opposed the motion" the first time it was offered. It finally carried by only one vote and even after that it was tabled again by the moderates who were still hoping not to be rushed into such a grave decision.

John Dickinson, who had written many brilliant articles opposing legislation prepared in London, could say sincerely, "As to GREAT BRITAIN, I glory in my relation to her. Every drop of blood in my heart is BRITISH; and that heart is animated with as warm wishes for her prosperity, as her truest sons can form." John Adams, one of the first to set his mind on independence, was warned by a Philadelphia gentleman that feelings were touchy to say the least. His friend told him, "Now you must not utter the word independence, nor give the least hint or insinuation of the idea, either in Congress or any private conversation; if you do, you are undone, for the idea of independence is as unpopular in Pennsylvania and in all the Middle and Southern States as the Stamp Act itself. No man dares speak of it."

Even after Lexington and Concord, the population seemed rather neutral. When Washington moved through New York City, on his way to take command of the forces in New England, he was given a rousing reception. Later the same day, the crowds turned out to see the new royal governor who had landed in the Fun City and they cheered lustily. The Loyalists even started a rumor that Martha was going to leave her George as she wanted to be loyal to the crown. Washington's own pastor, who had even taught the general's own stepson, remained loyal to the king and kept two trusty pistols beside him on the pulpit when he preached his sermons. Later, Rev. Jonathan Boucher left for England and wrote a book of sermons about the American Revolution—dedicating it to his old friend George Washington.

The war split families right down the middle. Virginia Tory John Randolph was the sire of Edmond, but the son remained true to the new nation while his dad hoped for an English victory. In South Carolina, Lieutenant Governor Bull remained faithful to his king but saw three of his nephews take their stand against the forces of the crown. Thomas Heyward signed the Declaration of Independence, thus becoming a traitor in the eyes of his own dear father who lived in South Carolina. Pennsylvania's Gouverneur Morris stood in the ranks of the ragged rebels while his own mother remained loyal to the British cause. Three sons of the Livingston family in New York supported the flag of Great Britain while one brave brother signed the Declaration penned by Jefferson.

In 1775, Samuel Quincy, whose brother was a rebel diehard, decided to depart from the unfriendly shores of New England. His sister pleaded with him not to go. She begged, "Let it not be told in America and let it not be published in Great Britain that a brother fled from his country—the wife of his youth—the children of his affection—and his aged sire, already

bowed down with the loss of two sons." He refused to listen
to this plea and stated that God would sustain both him and
his integrity and left for London town. He had expected a
quick victory to change his fortunes, but when news of Bunker
Hill arrived, he became very melancholy and wrote to his wife
asking her to join him in his political asylum. She never was
able to make the journey in the time of war and she passed
away in 1782, so he was unable to look on her face once again.

Samuel Curwen joyfully left his nagging wife in America
and fled to England. When questioned about his separation,
he confided in a friend that he had no desire to see her
again, and he was fearful of the possibility that she would be
buried by his side and would be the very first person he
would meet on the Resurrection morn, and he hated the
thought of that. Finding so many Americans in London made
his time move rather quickly, but he still had time to take
in a revival meeting under John Wesley, who had "the heavens
as his canopy."

General Ruggles, a gentleman we've met before, once sym-
pathized with the cause of liberty, even being the president
of the Stamp Act Congress; but now he was out of sorts
over the actions of the rebels. The man who had once been
highly praised by John Adams left for Nova Scotia at the age
of seventy-two with three sons, but his four daughters remained behind in New England.

The word *Tory* was first used in Ireland when it was
applied to outlawed Papists in the reign of Charles II. But
the word was soon to stir up a hornet's nest in the colonies.
One patriot gave his own definition of the term. "A Tory is a
thing whose head is in England and its body in America, and
its neck ought to be stretched."

The Tory historians wanted to have their day in court.
They pictured the patriots as an unruly mob who were moved
by passion, not principles. James H. Stark has left us his
impression of one of the rebel chiefs—Samuel Adams. "He is

only in his early forties but already gray and bent with physical infirmity, which kept his head and hands shaking like those of a paralytic. He was a man of broken fortunes, a ne'er-do-well in his private business, a failure as a tax collector, the only public office he had thus far undertaken to discharge."

Men of the cloth were very friendly with Royal Governor Hutchinson of Massachusetts. Some of them took an active part in fighting the propaganda that poured from patriot presses. Two Anglican clerics in New York took it upon themselves to supply "the speediest answers" to any radical publications "as appeared to have a bad tendency." Rev. Charles Inglis worked hand-in-hand with Rev. Myles Cooper, President of King's College, to keep an eye on "all publications that were disrespectful to Government or parent State, or that tended a breach between Great Britain and her Colonies. . . ." Inglis, Anglican rector of New York's Trinity Church, began to pen essays that were shipped off to local newspapers but he simply signed them "A New York Farmer."

In South Carolina, Rev. John Bullman began to preach sermons that supported his His Majesty the King. He belittled the members of his congregation from the pulpit for believing that they could run the national governments, as they couldn't even discipline their own homes. The congregation met after church and voted to give him his running papers— all the way to England if need be.

Rev. Mather Byles, a Tory comic, was a descendant of the famous Cotton and Mather clans. He also was a close friend of Benjamin Franklin, but this did not stop the local residents from calling for his hide. He was denounced at a town meeting in Boston, put on trial, and convicted. He refused to leave for England, so they put him under house arrest. He saw the humor of the whole thing and called the soldier, sent to guard him, an "observe-a-Tory." One day when the sentinel had to go on an errand, the spunky Dr. Byles took his place before his own door and marched up and down until the rebel returned, all the while carrying the sentinel's musket on his rounded shoulder.

Washington smiled when he saw the ships of Howe leaving Boston with their cargo of humans on board. Howe was leaving for Nova Scotia, and among his party were eighteen men of the cloth. General Washington had no sympathy for such sorts as he said, "There never existed a more miserable set of beings than these wretched creatures . . . no electric shock, no sudden explosion of thunder, in a word, not the last trump could have struck them with greater consternation" than Howe being whipped and leaving Boston at the mercy of the Virginian.

The defeats of the British at Lexington, Ticonderoga, Bunker Hill, and the evacuation of Boston bothered the Tories no end. Not all of the sympathizers were God-fearing. A spy captured in New York faced the gallows under orders by Washington, but the Tory refused to have a rebel chaplain, even though tears were running down his cheeks and he bellowed out, "They are all cut throats." Speaking of cutthroats, Rev. Eli Caruthers praised the adventures of Col. David Fanning, who had run amuck among the rebel population, leaving death and destruction in his path. Even though Cornwallis and Clinton had issued strict orders not to plunder, redcoats destroyed Bibles in Presbyterian churches because they assumed anyone using them "had the same political views as the Puritans of New England." Perhaps this is why Cornwallis made a Tory rector his chaplain during his retreat to Yorktown, or maybe he figured his forces were in need of prayer if they were to escape encirclement.

The rebel population was not indifferent to wealthy clergymen. In Connecticut, a missionary lived at the town of Hebron and preached at the local Church of England assembly. Rev. Samuel Peters had 7 houses on his property as well as 4 barns, 4,000 apple trees, and 6 Negroes who worked his 1,000 acres. Besides this he owned over 60,000 acres in the wilderness of New Hampshire. The local mob was angry because he "aped the style of an English nobleman," so they attacked his home and destroyed his belongings. He had to flee to save his very life.

A Sharon, Connecticut, pastor told his congregation that, "The New York Tories are rich, the Lord permitted his people to despoil the Egyptians and that it was lawful and right, because they were all Tories and to do it was no robbery." Rev. Nathaniel Whitaker thundered from his Massachusetts pulpit, "Liberty is the cause of God, laxity in taking up arms against an enemy is sin." James Madison was disturbed about Tory scorn and he wrote, "How different is the spirit of Virginia from that of New York. A fellow was lately tarred and feathered for treating one of our county committees with disrespect; in New York, they insult the whole Colony and Continent with impunity."

Not all of the Tory pastors were rich. Rev. Jacob Bailey was so poor that his breeches "just concealed the shame of his nakedness," but he was forced to leave his pulpit at Dressen, Maine, because he supported the king's cause. He had to leave for Nova Scotia with a young infant and two small girls, having almost no personal belongings. In Virginia, an Anglican cleric had to face "officers and armed parties" that "frequently entered his Churches with Drums, Gun, and Bayonets and with wanton outcrys and profanity disturbed the Sacred Service of Religion." When they could not silence him they nailed up the doors and windows of his houses of worship and posted a guard outside the buildings on Sunday.

In many communities, it was open season on Loyalists. Sarah Simpson claimed that the American army stole 27 fine shirts, 4 cloth coats, 2 dozen fine drill breeches, 1 dozen beaver hats, 2,000 weight of cheese, 4 barrels of pork, 60 pounds of tea, 128 gallons of brandy, 110 gallons of rum, and 26 barrels of cider. But not all of them got away with crime. In Connecticut, a rebel soldier killed a Tory family and burned the home to cover up his evil deed. He was caught wearing the dead man's clothing, tried, convicted, and executed.

In Pennsylvania, they drew up a "Blacklist" of Tories whom they considered to be guilty of high treason, but only 2 were hung out of 490 names. The New York Committee to Detect Conspiracies tried some 1,000 Loyalist "traitors," but 600 were almost immediately released with only a handful actually suffering for any imagined crime.

The king now decided that it was time to put these Tories in the field. Howe, in the summer of 1776, ordered Oliver De Lancy to raise the New York Loyalists, Cortlandt Skinner to form up the New Jersey Loyalists, and for Robert Rogers to gather men for the Queen's Rangers. These were to augment the New York Volunteers and the King's Royal Regiment, which had already been commissioned under Sir John Johnson. General Gage had hoped to do the same thing in 1775, as he listened intently to the view of John Connoly, British governor at Pittsburgh, when the latter drew up elaborate plans to strike fear into the hearts of the patriots by linking up the Loyalists of the border areas with savages and attacking in force. This fell through when Connoly was captured, but later in New York State, the Tories were to link up with their red-skinned friends as the lobsterbacks marched through the Mohawk Valley.

The first battle to be fought by the Tories was in North Carolina, under the leadership of General MacDonald, who had been a hero at Bunker Hill and had to slip through rebel lines to form up his British band. His force of a little over 1,500 troops was composed of 700 Highlanders, 700 Loyalists, and the rest regulars. They marched under a flag sewed together by a local tailor, but when they reached Rockfish Creek, they were met by a force under Col. James Moore, who quickly asked them to join him in the cause of liberty.

MacDonald refused the offer but did not stop to fight, as

he had heard fresh reserves would fill rebel ranks in a few hours. He slipped the noose and Moore sent Colonel Caswell chasing after him across the meadows and through the woods. MacDonald's luck remained good as he caught an American patrol and learned of his danger; he left a handful of men to bang away while he slipped away through the brush with his main body.

At Moore's Creek Bridge, the Tory crowd moved in to surround Caswell. But the crafty colonel had taken a page from McDonald's book, as he lit fires and moved away in the dead of night. McDonald was now out for blood. He chased after the shifty servicemen who now linked up with Lillington under the command of Col. James Moore. To get to the rebels, they would have to cross the bridge that the Southerners had stripped of planks and applied liberal amounts of soft home-made soap and tallow. The king's forces shouted, "King George and broadswords!" as they advanced. The fight was over within three minutes as the gallant soldiers slipped off the logs into the river below. Those who did not drown or die from the well-aimed shots of the sharpshooters were taken prisoner. Moore allowed these 850 prisoners to go home, and his generosity helped shift the sentiment of many of the Highlanders, who now threw themselves on the side of Washington.

This knocked the spirit out of the Loyalists. Only when British regulars were in command of an area would they feel confident to expose their true sentiments. As the typical American Loyalist was conservative, cautious, and an abhorrer of violence, he would need to feel secure if he was to continue to stand up tall for the king's name. In 1779, the British struck the port towns of Portsmouth and Norfolk in Virginia, and many of the Tories crossed through the lines to cheer the sight of an English banner; but they were to be disappointed because the presence was not to be permanent. A year later Cornwallis attacked the Carolinas and once again men came to join up with him, but the Tories under Ferguson gave them such a bad name that the rebels rose up to revolt, and the only place the regular could call secure was the ground under his very feet. Back in New York, Clinton outnumbered Washington three to one but was fearful of moving out of the friendly confines of that northern port city, because he had little confidence in the Tory troops that made up a part of his force.

At the beginning of the war, the English leaders tried a different tactic. They had offered pardons to a large part of the rebel supporters if they would lay down their arms and be peaceful. This was very helpful to the American troops, because when they were captured they could pretend to repent and would receive a full pardon. This infuriated the Tories who loved the king and had suffered for him. When they got under arms, they became even more brutal than the hated Hessians. They plundered, murdered, and reaped revenge on rebel radicals and their offspring. The Loyalists were suspect in relation to a plan for germ warfare, where they would leave sick Negroes, ill from smallpox, beside the road to infect the enemy. Even the leaders helped fill American ranks because of their bitter bombings of civilian towns. Lord Dunmore in Virginia issued a proclamation requiring every individual of military age "to resort to His Majesty's standard or be looked upon as traitors, subject to forfeiture of life, confiscation of lands, etc." Next, he ordered the destruction of Norfolk, which was called a "crowning piece of stupidity." It was "the one place in Virginia where the King had supporters and where the royal governor had been given a warm reception; and when he turned his guns against it, he insured the ruin of his own friends."

The last major battle for the Tory troopers was to be fought at King's Mountain. Cornwallis drubbed Gates, sending the general flying off the battlefield on a fast horse that took him sixty miles to Charlotte and safety. He confidently decided to make a three-pronged advance into North Carolina in a full-scale invasion of that province. The left flank would be under Major Ferguson and his hated Tories. The brilliant field officer took up a strong defensive position on the summit of the mountain and "defied God Almighty and all the rebels out of Hell to overcome him."

At the same time, Rev. Samuel Doak, a Presbyterian noted for his sermons that lasted a half day, was leading the "over mountain men" in prayer before these inexperienced men faced the task of attacking a strongly entrenched enemy on grounds that would favor the Tory band made up of men from New York, New Jersey, and the Carolinas, plus one hundred regulars. At the end of his prayer, the Reverend Mr. Doak shouted, "The sword of the Lord and Gideon!"

The American strategy was to hit the front and left flank at the same time, and then five minutes later the right wing was to go into action. The attack was brilliantly executed, and Ferguson was one of the first to fall under a hail of bullets. With their leader gone and facing the determined mountain men, the Tories laid down their weapons. The story of Loyalists under arms came to an end as far as major battles were concerned. Four hundred men lost their lives to the American's eighty-eight casualties, and the rest marched off as prisoners.

It is said that over 100,000 Loyalists left America during the Revolution and shortly afterwards. They had been piling up in New York for years; there were only 5,000 people to greet Howe when he forced the door open to New York, but by 1783, the population had grown to 33,000, with an additional 10,000 troops cramped for room.

Canada was a popular spot for the Tory evacuees. The population of Nova Scotia more than doubled, and the Tories became a strong political force in the province as they were now about half the population. The people who took up residence in the Maritime province of New Brunswick liked to boast of their close ties with Harvard and the upper crust of pre-revolutionary America, but one historian believes that this was just Loyalist propaganda. Quebec gobbled up 7,000 supporters of the king and the Americans couldn't have been happier. Most of the supporters of Congress felt that the Tories should love America or leave it, and they were not unhappy when their neighbors voted with their feet.

Longfellow's *Evangeline* underscored the problems of forced immigration. But few Canadians were sympathetic with the newcomers. Perhaps it was because of the liberal land grants to many of the loyal followers of King George III that induced them to sail northward to the cold and rocky shores of "New Scotland." Field officers received 5,000 acres each, captains got 3,000, lieutenants 2,000, and enlisted men 300 acres. Even noncombatants got at least 200 acres of free turf to launch their new life. It is estimated that by the year 1787, 3,200,000 acres had been given to the king's people in upper Canada alone.

The most prominent family to move to Shelburne, Nova Scotia, was a direct descendant of one of the Mayflower Pilgrims. We meet up again with Rev. Charles Inglis, who was to start a new church in this budding community. All the men of the cloth did not receive a warm welcome. The Methodist preacher, Rev. William Black, was stoned by the nonbelievers of the new port town.

In nearby New Brunswick, the grandson of the first president of Princeton University was filling the position as secretary of the province. Perhaps he felt right at home when Benedict Arnold moved into the province, as he had aided the traitor when he was a pastor back in the colonies and had also done other spy work for the crown. They had lots of time to compare notes and talk about their old acquaintances in America.

Even with the land handed out to most of the newcomers, things did not go very smoothly. Places were so hard to find that they even used a church building for shelter. At the Citadel in Halifax, thousands were under canvas and "every shed, outhouse, store and shelter" was crowded with people. At Shelburne, bursting at the seams and bucking to become the greatest port in North America, things were going from bad to worse. The provincial government raised the duties on imported goods, cutting sharply into the profits of the businessmen of the port on the southern tip of the peninsula. When the free issue of British government foodstuffs ended three years after the signing of the peace, the people began to leave in a mass exodus. They had never gotten used to the unfriendly climate and the need to suffer as pioneers once again. In three decades, the population dropped from 10,000 folks to a measley 300. Crime might have been one factor—a Black was executed in Halifax for stealing a bag of potatoes.

There were 1,440 families who left America for their mother country. Of these, 263 were from families from Massachusetts, 234 from South Carolina, and 204 from New York topping the list. Connecticut was the settlement that lost the fewest citizens; only 35 decided to return to England. In 1776, there were 139 families who shipped off for London, but the number dropped each year until after Yorktown, when 400 families left America for good for Great Britain.

Peter Oliver was sure that heaven punished rebels. Jonathan Sewall told all his American friends that they should tremble in fear of the fighting forces of England, so most of the individuals who left the colonies had done so expecting to return. They would just wait until the British flag was raised over the state capitols and then return as friends of the victors.

When Sewall set foot on British soil, he, and all the Americans, expected a warm welcome. It was very frustrating for them to face the cultural shock in their beloved London. He was astonished at the loose morality in the English center of culture, and it was nothing like the Puritan atmosphere of old New England. Like others, he detested the narrow views of the British citizens. The Tories also expected to be useful to the British government in explaining how America could be defeated or brought to the conference table. They were bewildered when nobody listened to them.

The ex-Americans would go to almost any extreme to find others from the old colonies. But passing the time was difficult. Some went to famous museums and others spent their time at theaters. Samuel Curwen was sickened by the plays he saw and thought they were very foolish. One of the high points in a Loyalist's diary was when he went to a public whipping of a female lawbreaker. Crowds of Tories also went to see the hangings in London.

One of the greatest problems was money. Some realized that they needed to rub elbows with important officials if they were to get anywhere, as it was almost impossible to succeed unless you had connections at the top. Francis Coffin was appointed as an army recruiter in 1786 in Birmingham, but he found it to be a terribly dull place. Otherwise, they were biding their time and hoping that the English government would smile on them with grants of money or pensions. This took a lot of paper work and often they became very discouraged.

One could safely assume that clergymen would have been in an excellent position, as there are always souls to save and good deeds to do. But it was almost impossible for Americans to find a church. Those who had been missionaries for the Society for the Propagation of the Gospel in Foreign Parts were kept on salary until it became apparent that the doors were closing in America. At that time, they were given assignments in other areas of the world.

Washington's old pastor looked and looked for a job. He finally found out that there was a vacancy—"the curacy of a parish in Paddington" could be had. When he got there, he found out that he would not become the head pastor, as it was already promised by the vicar to his nephew when he passed on to his reward. He had to be contented with his election as an assistant secretary for the missionary society until something better opened up. Rev. Samuel Peters, who had lived in luxury in Connecticut, was deeply disappointed in his reception and continually complained about the small sums given to him by the government and missionary society.

During the course of the war, some grandiose schemes were drawn up only to collapse. One was to take over the present area of Maine and fill it with Loyalists and rename it "New Ireland." When the British invaded the deep South, they were determined to set up loyal governments, so some of the Tories came back to America at that time; but the campaign was not completely successful, so the Tories had to leave the continent once again. Even after Yorktown, they kept pressuring the government to fight on to victory.

Benjamin Marston was typical of those exiles who longed for home. Even in 1792, he wished to be back in Massachusetts. His dream never came true as he died in West Africa, where he was working to establish a colony for the crown. The Hutchinson family, which had every reason to detest the rebels, liked to live on American type food and follow the customs of New England. Even though they, like others, were afraid of rebel "mobocracy," they wished to be back in America. Virginians settled in Glasgow, Scotland, but could hardly feel at home. Their feelings could be summed up by Sir William Pepperell, who said in 1778, "I earnestly wish to spend the remainder of my days in America, I love the Country, I love the People."

The Tories could not believe it when England gave up her fight to suppress the colonies after the fall of Yorktown. Some continued to kid themselves by dreaming that America, now that the fighting was over, would surely like to be back under the loving and protective wing of England. Those who wished to apply for permission to return could do so. Thomas Bradbury Chandler was delighted to return and was treated "with remarkable kindness and respect." But others, like the Hutchinson family, didn't wish to bow before American officials and request that the door be opened to them once again. Pennsylvania would not accept Galloway's request to return to the Quaker State. In the peace settlement, the American government did make requests to the several states to do something about the estates that were confiscated during the war, but this was mainly forgotten. The breach was never closed and the wounds never completely healed, and both lands gradually accepted the fate of those who had become outcasts from their chosen land.

XI NO KING BUT JESUS

And some began to cry out, NO KING BUT KING JESUS!

EDMUND S. MORGAN

"We must keep our eyes fixed on the supreme government of the Eternal King, as directing all events, setting up or pulling down the kings of the earth at his pleasure. . . ." These fiery words swept down upon the listeners in the pews below as Dr. Langdon gave his election sermon in May of 1775. Not many years before this, the population had followed the instruction of Saint Paul to "fear God and honor the King."

We should not venture to assume that the whole population in the colonies was about to arise and take hold of the reigns of power and bring in a political millennium before the world's very eyes. They were not about to allow anarchy to rule or watch the mobs directing traffic to send the local leaders to Philadelphia to form a new government. Another preacher wanted his pilgrims to reflect on a wise course under a new and wonderful ruler: "The great Creator, having designed the human race for society, has made us dependent on one another for happiness. . . . This proves that, in what is commonly called a state of nature, we are the subjects of the divine law and government; that the Diety is our supreme magistrate, who has written his law in our hearts, and will reward or punish us according as we obey his commands."

Jehovah never intended his creatures to have any other ruler than HIMSELF. The fact that they had demanded to have such a ruler proved how they craved to serve man instead of Almighty God. Even the political hacks of that day understood this truth. "The Israelitish government was of the free, or parliamentary kind. The people's demand of a change of the form of their government into monarchical was directly opposite to their constitution, and to the divine intention. Which, by the bye, shows the absurdity of the doctrine of regal government's being of divine origin."

That great evangelical, John Wesley, took these rioters to task for "despising His Majesty . . . with a perfect hatred." He found that even in England, the people seemed ill from a new type of political pollution. He said, "It is as much as ever I can do, and sometimes more than I can do, to keep this plague from infecting my own friends. And nineteen or twenty to whom I speak in defence of the King seem never to have heard a word spoken for him before. I marvel what wretches they are. . . ."

Back on the American side of the great drink, the king found strong supporters in Pennsylvania. Their first worthy leader, who had made it a colony of enlightenment, believed firmly that God had set the king on the throne to look after the needs of the people. He ruled that the political realm and the people were to obey, as the king had the "divine right" to govern, which was inherited from the people, and that he was their visible agent.

John Adams was angered because the Declaration of Independence made such sport of the king. He felt that George III was not a tyrant "in disposition and nature." John Dickinson, the "Penman of the Revolution," stated that the inhabitants of the colonies were unanimously devoted with the warmest sentiments of duty and affection to "your Majesty's sacred Person" and humbly begged leave to "approach the Throne" through a petition on behalf of the American people. Lafayette left for America under a cloud of royal disapproval, and even after he returned as a hero, he was reminded of the fact "that he had been disobedient to the King, and that he must consider himself under arrest until His Majesty's pleasure should be known." When he returned to Philadelphia to continue to give his all for a cause he so deeply believed in, he addressed the gentleman on the throne of France as "His Most Christian Majesty."

George III seemed to be a rallying point for the Loyalists to turn to. When Howe came to New York for a lengthy visit, almost 1,000 Tories declared that "we bear true allegiance to our rightful sovereign, George III, as well as warm affection to his righteous person, crown, and dignity." Rev. George Kribel, leader of the Bethlehem (Pennsylvania) congregation, chose to serve a jail term in an Easton jail rather than reject the man seated on the throne thousands of miles away. Rev. John Beach, an eighty-year-old clergyman, refused to budge when American soldiers entered his Anglican church in Hartford and said that he would continue to pray for the king "till the rebels cut out my tongue."

An Indian king believed that he was equal to the King of England, and his followers also felt that everyone should honor him. But the people of Great Britain acknowledged only their sovereign. "A loyal citizenry supported a just and loving

King in a joint and harmonious dedication to the well-being of the realm." Like their Tory brothers from afar, they could say, "The King . . . God Bless him! for we never had a better one, and no other nation ever had so good a one . . . who feels every calamity and misfortune of his people. . . ." He was also supported by intellectual scholars. Rev. John Vardill, professor at King's college, who was later to steal all of Silas Deane's diplomatic correspondence, remained loyal to his king. The chancellor, masters, and scholars of the University of Oxford and the University of Cambridge signed their names to a letter that acknowledged their support for His Majesty the king. The House of Commons, which in 1626 said, "Your faithful commons, who can have no private end, no object but your Majesty's service, and the good of our country," voted along with George by 270-78, 242-87, and 232-83 margins and even after the debacle at Yorktown sided 220 to 179 with their crowned leader.

By George, who was this man who caused such loyalty? His ancestors, who came from Germany, had a difficult time in mastering the language of the island empire that dominated the seas and half the world. Like his predecessors George I and George II, he was German to the core—hardly a drop of English blood could be found in his veins. Historians claim that he was brought up by a pious mother who was fearful about what worldly temptations might do to her sacred son.

A historian writes, "The Whig historians, though brilliant writers, were not very perceptive psychologists. With our knowledge of psychology, we can easily see that George III offers a clear psychotic case. He was a retarded youth, lethargic and rather stupid. . . ." The king continued to behave rather strangely. He often got excited and badgered his visitors in streams of strange, stupid sentences as, "What, what, what, what?" or "Why, why, why?" Later in his life, he got out of his carriage and bowed to a tree, as he assumed he was greeting some European ruler.

The end of life was much the same for kings and dignitaries as for the common fellow who labored long hours in a mill or plowed fields in lovely patterns. When Charles II suffered a stroke, they bled him and "plied his head with frying pans." But death could cause waves of concern among the people under his power, for when a new king took office, the old laws in the colonies could be subject to question.

George III was not about to hand in his scepter for a golden harp. He was to rule sixty long years. He was sure that God was going to aid him; and through the "blessings of Providence," he would gain the victory over his rebellious subjects in America. Although supported by most Anglican ministers, more than one clergyman in America believed that he was forcing his people in the colonies to make bricks without straw.

He needn't have worried if he fell flat on his royal face, because the English were always there to protect his reputation. Even though the people snickered about his strange eating habits and the rumors of his unbalanced mind, the cream of the crop were bowing to his every wish as though he were a god. Throughout English history, some person has always been available to take the blame from the shoulders of the blue bloods—just as if they were sinless personages.

William Penn's father was a victim of such prejudice. Sir William, Sr., won a victory over the Dutch fleet with the king's brother at his side. The critics were not appeased by the triumph; they thought he should have destroyed the enemy fleet completely. Seeing the duke was supposed to be the leader of the foray, criticism should have fallen on his royal head. But they did not want to make fun of one who might step on the throne of Great Britain some day.

Penn had heard these snide comments and decided that he should take the part of the duke. When some questioned the ability of the duke to ride the waves or direct battles, he quickly countered with the argument that the king's brother had written an excellent manual on naval operations. This only made things worse. Everyone knew, including Penn, that the future king had not really penned the paper; it was the work of the commander of the complete navy. So the critics leveled their guns at Penn, as he was a sitting duck, while the duke remained blissfully silent.

This event was to have a major impact on William Penn. When the duke became King James, he decided to give a silent but oblique word of thanks to the admiral. He gave the mariner a sizable chunk of real estate in America, which would be passed over to his son in later years.

This type of cover-up for the queens and kings has continued on down to this very day. Frank Hardie tells us: "The political role of the reigning Sovereign is, of all the processes of the British Constitution, that least known to contemporaries. This is true of our present Queen and has been true of the five preceding reigns. The innermost arcana of defence and foreign policy are not more closely guarded. The darkness in which the subject is enveloped is generally lightened only by death—by the posthumous publication, that is to say, of the biographies or memoirs of those concerned or the rawer material of their papers."[1]

How different this seems in light of the Profumo scandal in Great Britain—or the latest hot tips on how John F. Kennedy spent his off-duty hours. Throughout history, ordinary politicians have been open target on a field of black and white. But kings and queens have been pictured as pure or played up to be perfect, even though homosexuality existed in their putrid past. Men of brainy breeding have drawn a curtain over the lives of these individuals while they are alive, so that a public will revere their very being.

The rebels were only too happy to set the record straight. They took dead aim at His Majesty because he overlooked their petitions to him. Also, there were people in the Parliament who were very sympathetic to their claims and cries for help.

They could not indict the whole political family as the houses in Great Britain were divided over what measures should be used in treating the pleas of the colonists for more freedom and less taxation. But the king had set himself up against them and called for a bloody suppression of their wishes. In the Declaration of Independence, well over two dozen charges were brought against this sorry man who ruled over the vast kingdom.

When the British government decided to urge the savages to attack the settlers on the fringes of a white society, the men of America were very angry. When the English officers promised to free the slaves if they would take up arms against their former masters, the population was filled with fear. When the king himself requested foreign troops from a Russian queen, the Yankees foamed at the mouth. Every act by the throne only drove the moderates into the ranks of the radicals.

Then, too, the Americans didn't view His Majesty in the same shaded light as his followers in England. Having been schooled in Bible teaching, they would turn to I Sam. 16:7 for their enlightenment: "But the Lord said unto Samuel, Look not on his countenance, or on the height of his stature; because I have refused him: for the Lord seeth not as man seeth; for men looketh on the outward appearance, but the Lord looketh on the heart."

The Americans chuckled when a British cannon ball decapitated the portrait of King George II when the shell pierced the wall of the prayer hall at Princeton. In France, the Americans had a number of diplomats working for an alliance. One of them, John Laurens, spoke fluent French but "left the court with its collective mouth hanging open" because he had cornered King Louis XVI at a social function to win him over to the American view of the conflict. Even today, in a very different setting, the Japanese were shocked when Seiji Ozawa, the outstanding Japanese orchestra conductor, made a plea to His Majesty the emperor to save the Japan Philharmonic Symphony Orchestra from bankruptcy when he was invited to dine at a social gathering. The only thing that saved the situation was that Ozawa was dressed in black instead of his normal outfit of blue jeans and a flashy shirt.

Jefferson set the tone for the rebellion against royalty itself. He told a friend in 1810:

> I often amused myself with contemplating the characters of the then reigning sovereigns. Louis XVI was a fool. The King of Spain [Charles IV] was a fool, and of Naples [Ferdinand IV] the same. They passed their lives in hunting, and dispatched two couriers a week, one thousand miles, to let each other know what game they had killed the preceding days. . . . The Queen of Portugal [The Mad Maria], a Braganza, was an idiot by nature. And so was the King of Denmark [Christian VIII]. The King of Prussia [Frederick William II], successor to the great Frederick, was a mere hog in a body as well as in mind. Gustavus [III] of Sweden, and Joseph [II] of Austria were really crazy, and George [III] of England, you know, was a straight waistcoat. These animals had become without mind and powerless; and so will every hereditary monarch be after a few generations.

King George III wished to make himself archbishop. The kings and queens of England had a special moral standard all their very own. The Japanese could not look at the emperor when he passed by before the war. Today in Nippon, people are very fearful of marrying into a family that has some defect in its history. But the son of Meiji startled the Diet when he rolled up the speech he was to make and gazed out at them, like a child playing with a telescope, when he had come to read to them his words of wisdom.

King John, at the point of a sword, had to accept the great doctrine of the Magna Carta, even though he did not wish to do so. An English historian admitted that, "Our Kings and our Queens gave and took away the privilege of sending members [to Parliament], as pleased their fancy without regard to justice, or proportion." The American clergy taught that the king and Parliament had been robbing the people of their own inalienable rights. King George himself urged Bute to dismiss from office some of the members of Parliament who had voted against His Majesty in order to "frighten others" and bring them in line. No wonder pastors in New England were saying that the rulers of nations were above fear and were oppressive by nature.

The evangelical preachers were very liberal in their views and didn't want to bow to a master across the seas, even though the Anglicans generally supported King George III. But the people themselves had been attached to all the kings of English history, and they moved slowly toward independence. John Dickinson had invoked the idea of the king's parental love and emphasized the fact that Americans were "his Sons not Bastards" when he tried to influence the king to look favorably upon the complaints of his subjects. Others did not believe he would listen because there could be no reconciliation, as he had revoked the relationship between the two. The Declaration of Independence stated that he had waged a "cruel war against human nature itself, violating its most sacred rights of life and liberty." If he was not above enslaving the American people, then no one should have been shocked when he tried to bribe Joseph Reed.

Confusion reigned and Rhode Island was so overcome with confusion that she raised a rebel army in the name of the king! Scholars in England admitted that kings and lords had never been friendly to true liberty, but they still resisted changing a system so dear to their hearts. But here and there a voice was raised with not a tinge of uncertainty. A Presbyterian pastor stated clearly that George III was the same as the Pharaoh of of Moses' day and that Americans resembled the Jewish slaves. Thomas Paine could see no good in any monarch and turned to the Old Testament to prove that God himself frowned on the idea of creating earthly kings. A Loyalist claimed that the patriots had mocked heaven when they concluded a Thanksgiving proclamation with GOD SAVE THE PEOPLE instead of "God save the king." Yes, the emotions were mixed, but gradually calm would come out of chaos.

In Christianity, each individual is answerable to God. The crowd may rant, rave, and rebel, but every born-again believer must seek to know God's mind and will for his own life. A Lutheran preacher could not endorse the Revolution because of his oath to the king, but he allowed his sons to be active in the cause of the Founding Fathers. The Reverend Mr. Duche was the chaplain for the First and Second Continental Congress and even led in prayer those gathered to decide the fate of the colonies; but in the end he supported the king. Other Christians remained relatively neutral and, instead of taking verbal blasts at His Majesty the king, prayed that God might open his eyes.

And yet, the Christian who read the Bible faithfully could not get away from certain verses. "Let every soul be subject unto the higher powers. For there is no power but of God: the powers that be are ordained of God. Whosoever therefore resisteth the power, resisteth the ordinance of God: and they that resist shall receive to themselves damnation" (Rom. 13:1-2). These words stuck deep in the hearts of many a rebel. What could their answer be?

The ministers of New England did not believe in the divine right of kings, but they struggled with the idea about God placing in the hands of these rulers power to govern. Rev. E. Williams, in 1744, acknowledged that the Bible above "no doubt relates to Civil powers," but he believed that it was used arbitrarily to erect "a civil Tyranny over a free people." Cotton Mather argued that these men often used this power to create laws that were contrary to the laws of God found in the Bible. Rev. John Bulkley of Connecticut said, "It's not in the Power of Rulers to make what Laws they please, Suspend, Abrogate or Disanul them at pleasure. . . . As for Men's Civil Rights, as Life, Liberty, Estate, &c. God has not

Subjected these to the Will and Pleasure of Rulers. . . ." John Hancock's grandfather preached a sermon in 1722, long before any thoughts of revolt were harbored in the peaceful hearts of his hearers, and stated that the people were groaning under the burdens pressed upon them by the rulers, which invited "Divine Displeasure." He said, "An Oppression makes a wise man mad, so it makes a righteous God angry."

The Christian approach was not completely negative. Christians had a responsibility to follow leaders who were a "terror to good works." But these rulers had no authority from God to do any mischief, as they believed that "the prince upon the British throne" could have "no real interest distinct from his subjects." The clergymen liked to quote II Sam. 23:1-3 to their listeners: "Now these be the last words of David. . . . The Spirit of the Lord spake to me, and his word was in my tongue. The God of Israel said, the Rock of Israel spake to me, He that ruleth over men MUST BE JUST, RULING IN THE FEAR OF GOD."

Those who felt they needed a king based their reasons on goodness and an ability to govern. Others felt that the rulers should be developed as "no man is born a magistrate, or with the right to rule over his brethren." The Reverend Mr. Howard continues this theme when he asserts, "If a man, by the improvement of his reason and moral powers, becomes more wise and virtuous than his brethren, this renders him better qualified for authority than others; but still he is no magistrate or lawgiver till he be appointed such by the people." The seeds of democracy were sown in the hearts of the believers through reason and interpretation of the Word of God.

NOTES

1. Frank Hardie, *The Political Influence of the British Monarchy, 1868-1952* (New York: Harper & Row, Publishers, 1970), Introduction.

XII THE COMMON PEOPLE BECOME KINGS!

Printing opened the same resources to the minds of all classes; the post was organized so as to bring the same information to the door of the poor man's cottage, and to the gate of the palace; and Protestantism proclaimed that all men are alike able to find the road to heaven. . . .

JOHN STUART MILL

The tide may have been swinging in favor of the little men, but the Europeans hadn't received the good news as yet. While the upper crust nibbled away at the goodies prepared in the fields of the peasants, they prided themselves in seeing that government stayed in the hands of those who knew best how to rule—the aristocrats.

John Jay turned in desperation to the idea of having a King George enthroned in Washington after the victory, and he wasn't "pulling a Benedict Arnold" either. When he saw the riffraff in the streets, he was sure that the chaff was going to rise and rule, which was decidedly distasteful to him and most of the others who were in high political positions at that time. Pens may have scrawled republican ideals across parchment, but they were very skeptical of what would happen once the poor had rights equal to the fancier classes. Jay wondered outloud if Washington wouldn't be the first king of America.

The British, so class conscious themselves that they could not understand anyone really believing in unvarnished democracy, were still sure that high honors and fancy position were what men craved for. They were positive that every person had his price, perhaps because they did themselves.

Admiral Rodney wrote Lord George Germain a "private letter," in which he suggested that George Washington could be purchased if the government came up with the right amount of cash or the right deal. Seeing Arnold sell his soul for a package of British pounds convinced him that all the Americans were mainly fighting for political prestige or unprincipled wealth. He said, "Washington is certainly to be bought—honors will do it."

Sir John Dalrymple had the same thoughts when he wrote his ideas about the American Commissioners of England and their approach to winning back the colonies through negotiations. Basing his thoughts on history and applied psychology, he was sure that Washington could be talked into turning in his sword for special honors, such as a dukedom. He pointed out that General Monk had been won over by Charles II's personal application, and this proposal through Monk's friends made the king's position safe in England. Seeing Washington was of similar temperament—close lipped with plain understanding—Dalrymple thought the general would welcome such an approach. He was childless, wasn't he? He would never be able to see his son or daughter take the throne, even if America did win the war. This limited the ambition to Washington himself. Dalrymple suggested that the king himself write to the commanding general of the American army or have the ministers do so on His Majesty's command with the special offer of a dukedom, to be handed over to Washington by his old "bosom friend," who was now a Tory in London. This same individual, Mr. Lloyd Delany, was reliable because he had already secretly helped out in Dalrymple's scheme to undermine the worth of paper money in the colonies. Surely he would be just the man to contact the tall Virginian.

Perhaps the British elite were sure Washington would accept their proposal because of the very baseness of the American society. Samuel Johnson said, "Sir, they are a race of convicts, and ought to be thankful for anything we allow them short of hanging." Jean de Crèvecoeur's observation was that "the rich stay in Europe; it is only the middling and the poor that emigrate." As many as 40,000 convicts had been shipped to colonial shores (although most were convicted of petty crimes or religious beliefs—like the Quakers who refused to doff their bonnets in front of the privileged paragons of public virtue), and one in every fifty had a police record! In 1615, King James I proclaimed that convicted felons, except those guilty of "rape, murder, burglary or witchcraft," were to be shipped to Virginia. At that time, they also rounded up 100 homeless children from the streets of London and packed them off to the Old Dominion.

This image was strengthened by Rev. Jonathan Odell who was a Tory minister and a British spy from New Jersey. He put down his sentiments in a poetic vein:

> From the back woods, half savages come down
> And awkward troops paraded every town,
> Committees and conventions met by scores:

Justice was banished, Law turned out of doors;
Disorder seemed to overset the land;
Those who appeared to rule, the tumult fanned.

Rev. Samuel Auchmuty, a former pastor of Trinity Church in New York, who had been booted out of Harvard College because of unexcused absences but given a master's degree in 1745 by the same institution when he became a minister, heartily disliked the Presbyterians. He felt only members of the Church of England were loyal to the cause and he urged his followers to join the king's forces to fight the scum of the earth. His brother, a colonial judge in New England, remarked that he would never change his sentiments toward good old England and side with "the rude and unsettled states of America . . . a community which will ever be shunned by every true lover of liberty."

Even those Tories who tripped over to England during the bloody contest in the colonies continued to have a strong class consciousness among themselves. Former governor Thomas Hutchinson was the recognized leader of the New England Loyalists and the American Tories continually sought each other out in Great Britain, because of the kinship they felt for their brothers of the British faith. After Hutchinson died in 1780, Sir William Pepperell stepped into his staid shoes to keep the brethren together to fight for benefits from the government and to encourage the crown to keep up the good battle until victory was attained in America. When new arrivals paid Hutchinson a courtesy call, he would ask them to dine at his home. But unless the newcomers were of "high social status," the first invitation would be the last. The peons of society were encouraged to mix with their own.

Joseph Galloway believed that the radicals had incited the ignorant and vulgar to take up arms and by their muscle pull down the establishment with a bang that would send shivers through the upper strata of society around the world. The word *democracy* in that period had an entirely different meaning than now. It suggested civil disorder and mob rule. Even men like Rev. Andrew Eliot fretted about the "many inconveniences which would attend frequent popular elections!"

Boucher, Washington's old pastor, believed that ordinary folk were perpetually dissatisfied and "the Common People seldom, if ever, think or judge for themselves in Matters which concern the whole." He felt that the citizens had been made to feel they had a right to participate in government and their "early Prejudices were fostered by Education, and confirmed by Religion." He agreed with the ideas of de Tocqueville who wrote: "Aristocracies are infinitely more expert in the science of legislation than democracies ever can be. They are possessed of a self-control which protects them from the errors of temporary excitement; and they form lasting decisions which they mature with the assistance of favourable opportunities."

The station of birth meant a great deal to the British intellectuals then. Their works were almost certain to contain some mention of whether or not the individual was well born or his parents were on the lower rungs of the social ladder. Commenting on John Adams, the writer noted that he was born "of Parentage not very distinguishable." Even in British elections, Algernon Sidney, Penn's friend, who had leftist ideas, was attacked because he was not a resident of the spot where he was campaigning for a seat in government, even though all knew that in England there were no resident requirements for a candidate. When he persisted, they spread the word that he was not a freeman and thus ineligible to run, which was a blatant lie.

We should not assume that this prejudice against their poor country cousins in America was simply a product of the riotous mobs in Boston or bloodletting later. Charles Dickens stood solidly behind the Tory view of the uncouth Americans. In *American Notes* and *Martin Chuzzlewit*, he emphasized all the absurd national characteristics "like the seven deadly sins in a morality play." His pen wrote up weird descriptions of fictional characters who represented the various weaknesses of the Yankees, who were making their commerce "one huge lie and mighty theft." Hiding behind his work of art he enjoyed giving "the eagle a final poke under the fifth rib," as he put it.

The American politicians have always been careful not to make fun of the man in the sun. For generations, each candidate for president wanted to prove his humble origin by stating that he had been born in a log cabin. But before the Revolution, the elite, who were to write warm words about democracy, were themselves fearful of the masses. In Boston, they seemed to have it under control, and it became a lethal weapon in the hands of Sam Adams; but they were always worried that the workers would get out of hand and wallop the wealthy so sharply that the radicals would lose their power.

Rowdyism was not confined to North America. Bute, a close friend of the king, was attacked by a mob when he was on his way to Parliament. John Wilkes, who represented Aylesbury in the Parliament and was colonel of Bunkingham's County Militia, was the publisher of a scandal sheet that always took dead aim at some proud personage. He exploited the anti-Scotism spirit which was rampant in England. Wilkes suggested that Bute was the lover of the king's mother, which caused a few ripples in society; but his direct attack on His Majesty brought down the house around his insensitive ears. Halifax ordered a general warrant for the arrest of the legislator and his friends.

Wilkes of course could apply to the Court of Common Pleas for a writ of habeas corpus to plead for his release. This was granted because he was a member of the House of Commons and entitled to protection from arrest, and he was rewarded extremely heavy damages. He promptly wrote a friend, "The rod of oppression was lifted very high, but a few honest Englishmen have saved their country. . . . The joy of the people is almost universal . . . I hear from all hands that the King is enraged at my insolence, as he terms it: I regard not his frowns nor his smiles. . . . Hypocrisy, meanness, ignorance, and insolence, characterizes the King [George III] I obey. My independent spirit will never take a favour from such a man."[1]

Very often it was the poor who suffered injustice in Europe as well as in America. Men of the courts enjoyed the favors of many women and the society looked the other way. But the common man was expected to toe the mark. If rape was committed on "a woman of quality" of the same country, the guilty one was punished with death. But if the ravished one was of "inferior rank," the guilty man only had to marry her if both were single, "even though his rank be ever so much superior to hers."

The lower classes suffered all over the globe, and they always expected such treatment from their aristocratic brothers. But in America, where privileges of birth never existed and where riches did not confer special honors on the individual who possessed them, men were treated in a different manner.

A Frenchman was surprised that two Americans meeting in a foreign country immediately became friends. But he noted that such a situation was unheard of in cases where the two were Englishmen. Simply because they were citizens of the same nation did not guarantee that they would be friends—rank was more important. Unless they were on the same level socially, they might greet one another pleasantly enough, but in a few minutes they both would go their own separate ways.

The greatest share of the population of the colonies at the time of the rebellion was the farming class. We find that they were the ones who steadfastly served the cause of liberty while most of the Tories were city slickers. Jefferson would not have been surprised. He felt that those who tilled the soil were closer to the Creator. The Virginian said, "Those who labour in the earth are the chosen people of God, if ever he had a chosen people, whose breasts he has made his peculiar deposit for substantial and genuine virtue. . . . Corruption of morals in the mass of cultivators is a phaenomenon of which no age nor nation has furnished an example. It is a mark set on those, who not looking up to heaven, to their own soil and industry, as does the husbandmen, for their subsistence, depend for it on casualties and caprice of customers. . . ."

Even such an outstanding patriot of the Revolution as Robert Morris, who often came up with hard cash when Washington needed to stave off the wholesale desertion of the rabble under arms, was accused of profiteering. The reason men degrade themselves to such a level in the eyes of Tory Peter Oliver was because "we lower beings show an Ape." Just because a man was rich or intelligent did not alter his own inner wickedness.

Still, the royal governors in the colonies felt that America needed to be more like England. She needed an upper crust to lead and direct a band of baseless men who were unable to shift for themselves. Governor Bernard said, "A NOBILITY appointed by the KING for life, and made independent, would probably give strength and stability to the AMERICAN governments, as effectively as an hereditary NOBILITY does to that of GREAT BRITAIN."

The blueprint for the colony of Georgia was under the leadership of just such men. They would send people to populate the new colony and direct it completely with the intelligence of the upper class. They did not want deeply religious individuals because they distrusted "enthusiasts who take in their head that everything which comes uppermost is the immediate impulse of the spirit of God." The leaders of this project would grant the people a plot of land and supervise it like a welfare state. They were the employers and they would guarantee their workers the needs of life. The workers in turn would follow the specific directions from home and develop such industries as silk production to save England the expense of importing it from other foreign countries. They even put through a law that no one could be a representative in the Georgia Assembly unless he had at least one hundred mulberry trees planted and properly fenced in. Later, one could not be a deputy if one did not have at least one female in his family instructing in the art of reeling silk, or if one did not produce at least fifteen pounds of silk for every fifty acres owned. This type of paternal bounty from a just employer did not move the people to work hard; it made them completely dependent upon the leaders for their every need, and they did as little as possible in return. It failed because the immigrant prospered most when he had a stake in what he was doing and not when he was basically working for the riches of the upper classes, who watched over him from afar as absentee owners.

The Puritans had been taught that one should not look upon one's birth or the social position of others. What one did was more important than one's ancient ancestors or social breeding. Each man was a self-made individual answering only to God. So even the blacksmiths, forty-one of them, stood up for liberty when the Revolution approached—they would not work for any person who did not support patriotic principles. The swelling pride of the lower classes made one historian believe that laws in America were made by the poor themselves by their power in the ballot booth.

The American clergy was attacked by its opponents for encouraging mob violence. Even the elected assemblies were said to be housing "the mob inside." But the success of the American Revolution bringing in true democracy, when compared to France's revolution and the one in Russia under Mr. Lenin, was due to the fact that "the economic and social order was more, not less, democratic than the government."[2] Joseph Hawley wrote to Samuel Adams, who was a Boston delegate in Philadelphia, "The People are now ahead of you and the only way to prevent discord and dissension is to strike while

the iron is hot. The People's blood is too Hot to admit delays
—All will be in confusion if independence is not declared
immediately. . . ."

Graduation of ranks did not work in the United States
because the people were completely opposed to a territorial
aristocracy. In many states, there were many kinds of churches
and many different tongues spoken. It was natural that any
one group was not likely to find complete acceptance from
the rest. J. Hector St. John de Crèvecoeur, a Frenchman,
described this perfectly to his readers as he wrote about the
American farmer in these terms: "There, on a Sunday, he sees
a congregation of respectable farmers and their wives, all clad
in neat homespun, well mounted, or riding in their own humble
waggons. There is not among them an esquire, saving the
unlettered magistrate. There he sees a parson as simple as
his flock, a farmer who does not riot on the labour of others.
We have no princes for whom we toil, starve, and bleed; we
are the most perfect society now existing in the world."

Pitt struck out at the attitude of those in power in England.
He thundered, "The misfortune is, that gentlemen who are
in office seldom converse with any but such as are in office,
and such men, let them think what they will, always applaud
the conduct of their superiors; consequently, gentlemen who
are in the administration, or in any office under it, can rarely
know what is the voice of the people." This British politician
blamed such an attitude for producing the Stamp Act crisis.

Two hundred years have slipped by but this attitude may
prevail even in the high society circles of any capitalistic
nation. Rich American philanthropists invite Black radicals in
for tea while they jack up their white servants to act just
right for the occasion, or across town a billionaire conservative
hands over a check to his favorite foundation as flash bulbs
pop and he smiles demurely. Back in the days of Jefferson,
Henry, and Mason, the rich knew what it was to walk a

plowed field or help get in the harvest. Von Steuben gives us his impression of that period of time, "What a beautiful, what a happy country this is! Without kings, without prelates, without blood-sucking farmer-generals and without idle barons! Here everybody is prosperous. Poverty is an unknown evil."

When William Penn was rather young, he was accosted by a total stranger for not removing his hat. The drunken gentleman tried to attack him with his sword, but Penn disarmed him. A short time later he must have been less impressed with the styles of upper-class men when he carried some dispatches to the king. King Charles had been sleeping and came out to greet him in his bathrobe and slippers. He himself tried to stay away from special ego trips at the expense of others. Penn wanted his colony to be called Sylvania but was chagrined when the king made him add "Penn" to the province's title.

Franklin, who often opposed the pacifistic tendencies of the Quakers of Philadelphia, had a great interest in the underdogs of society. He wished to be a spokesman for all those apprentices who ran away from their masters, because he had done so in his youth. He wanted to represent the printers who dared to criticize their betters or challenge the government officials whom they believed were in the wrong. He wished to oppose all those Englishmen who "hoist themselves onto the throne of the King and talk of Our Colonies in America!" He was like President Martin Van Buren. He believed in the common folk. Van Buren said, "The sober, second thought of the people is never wrong, and always efficient."

We have not gotten over the special regard we have for the upper class. Many left-wing supporters of John F. Kennedy supported him simply because of "style." They detested the fact that "Texas" Lyndon came to sit on the throne and they continually made fun of him behind his back. No matter what we think of the two former presidents, we should all agree

that votes should not be decided by how one tips his tea cup
or holds his hankie, but by the soul he shows to the citizens.

The Pennsylvania government was controlled by the "haves"
in the early years of the province. But, after the Quakers
resigned because of their pacifist principles, the men from the
backwoods assumed leadership. These new men were determined to draw up a state constitution that would destroy the
power of the aristocratic and wealthy elements of the area.
This was symbolic of the feeling throughout the country. They
wanted to rest on one of the key verses of the Bible, "GOD
IS NO RESPECTOR OF PERSONS!" and build a society that
was based on ability not arrogance.

During the Watergate scandal, when President Nixon was
kept out of jail where lesser citizens would have been canned
for a considerable time, Peter Rodino reminded Americans
that King John had accepted the Magna Carta, but only "at
the point of the sword."[3] Two American political analysts,
Scammon and Wattenberg, warned the Democratic party officials that they were going to be swamped at the polls if they
labeled victims of crimes "bigots" simply because they complained about muggings on the streets of America.[4] The lower
classes heeded the haranguing of a George Wallace for a time,
because they knew of Senators and Congressmen who pushed
for forced busing while shipping their sons out of Washington
to special schools the average American could never afford.
A number of major journals admitted that they had misjudged
the pulse of the people in 1972, as the nation repudiated the
stand of the dovish politicians, the major portion of intellectuals, and left-wing columnists—proving that the common people
will do their own thinking and choosing whether the media
elite like it or not. This is true even though political scientist
Seymour Martin Lipset wrote: "I think of the United States
as a nation in which LEFTIST VALUES [author's capitals]
predominate."[5]

NOTES

1. Bernhard Knollenberg, *Origin of the American Revolution,* rev. ed. (New York and London: Collier-Macmillan Free Press, 1960), pp. 38-39.*

2. Dan Lacy, *The Meaning of the American Revolution* (New York: The New American Library, Mentor Books, 1964), p. 284.*

3. Theodore H. White, *Breach of Faith* (New York: Atheneum Publishers, 1975), p. 314.

4. Richard M. Scammon and Ben J. Wattenberg, *The Real Majority* (New York: Coward, McCann & Geoghegan, 1970), p. 168.

5. Seymour Martin Lipset, *The Political Man: The Social Bases of Politics* (New York: Doubleday & Company, Anchor Books, 1960), p. xxi.*

XIII   RACE RELATIONS AND THE REVOLUTION

Slavery deprives our republican example of its just influence in the world; enables the enemies of free institutions with plausibility to taunt us as hypocrites; causes the real friends of freedom to doubt our sincerity; and forces so many good men among ourselves into an open war with the very fundamental principles of civil liberty....

ABRAHAM LINCOLN

The first English slaver was Capt. John Hawkins. According to a historian, he was a devout Christian. The name of his slave ship was *JESUS!* Another captain who plied the trade from African shores was deeply interested in Christianity. Capt. John Newton wrote the hymn, "How Sweet the Name of Jesus Sounds," while waiting in his vessel off the Dark Continent for a fresh cargo of Black slaves.

191

It is difficult to understand the hearts of men of another century. Blacks were not the only ones who suffered enslavement. "The Most Christian King of France" thought nothing of having English prisoners spend the rest of their lives as rowers in his galleys. The Venetians, too, didn't care what the color of the skin was as long as they had strong bodies to do their work.

The slave trade by the English and Portuguese was almost infinitesimal when compared to the Arab business in Black flesh. Prince Henry's captains up to 1448 had taken only 927 slaves, "of whom . . . the greater part were turned into the path of salvation." This Catholic king had mixed motives in gathering men on the Dark Continent, but the obvious sin in enslaving souls was lost on many of the brightest minds of that period. David Livingstone leaves his testimony about the evil practice in Africa as he says:

> We had a long discussion about the slave-trade. The Arabs have told the chief that our object in capturing slaves is to get them into our own possession and make them of our own religion. The evils which we have seen, the skulls, the ruined villages, the numbers who perish on the way to the coast and on the sea, the wholesale murders committed by the Waiyau to build up Arab villages elsewhere—these things Mukate often tried to turn off with a laugh, but our remarks are safely lodged in many hearts. Next day, as we went along, our guides spontaneously delivered their substance to the different villages along our route. . . . It is but little we can do; but we lodge a protest in the heart against a vile system, and time may ripen it. Their great argument is: "What could we do without Arab cloth?" My answer is: "Do what you did before the Arabs came into the country." At the present rate of destruction of population, the whole country will soon be a desert. . . . The strangest disease I have seen in this country seems really to be broken-heartedness, and it attacks free men who have been captured and made slaves. . . . Some slavers expressed surprise to me that they should die, seeing they had plenty to eat and no work. . . . It seems to be really broken hearts of which they die.[1]

Back in the United States, critics of the abolitionists have tried to show that these zealots were no more than partisans of rural and conservative interests. They had toyed with the idea that those who opposed enslavement of any men were basically of Congregationalist-Presbyterian background, and they were working out their frustrations because they had been undermined by "social upstarts" and the industrialized class. But the appeal was three times as strong with the Methodists and Baptists than the other two denominations combined. The fight against slavery in the nineteenth century was located in the rural areas, as America was most rural at that time, but these were the areas where evangelicalism and Bible-preaching were the strongest and men without a predisposed view could not help notice the inconsistency of the practice when compared to Bible teaching.[2]

Was this spirit based upon humanitarian philosophy and completely divorced from Christianity? Historian Bertram Wyatt-Brown tells us: "The movement for 'immediate abolition' began as a direct extension of evangelical Christianity. In the columns of the *Liberator*, Garrison stated his goal as he developed it: the universal, immediate, and unqualified emancipation of all American slaves. Basic to his creed, just as to revivalism, was the conviction that sin was conscious, active disobedience to God. Being willful, it could be remedied only by conversion and penitence. . . ."[3] Professor Elizur Wright, Jr., echoed these sentiments in his call for immediate emancipation way back in 1833. Wright wrote: "Under the Government of God, as exhibited in this world, there is but one remedy for sin, and that is available only by a REPENTANCE, evidenced by reformation. There is no such thing as holding on to sin with safety. It is not only to be renounced, but the very occasions of it are to be avoided at whatever sacrifice. . . . This being the case, we might certainly expect that the entire agency which God has provided to reclaim the world should be adapted to produce IMMEDIATE REPENTANCE.

It certainly is so, if we take the testimony of the Bible. . . ."⁴

In Georgia, the trustees of that new colony were against the importation of Negroes. They felt that if the whites had slaves to aid them in the work, that the former would have very little reason to sweat in the fields themselves. They feared that the white would spend his time watching over his colored slave, and thus they would still be getting work from only one individual. But the southern colonies in not many more years would be importing these tragic victims of the sinfulness of men. Slavery was not confined to the South. By 1715, there were 2,000 Negroes in Boston with its population of 12,000. Twenty-five years later, one-quarter of the population of New York City was Black!

The British, who were prejudiced against the Scots, were not choosey when it came to putting fighting men in the field. Their government asked several nations to provide gun fodder for King George III, but they still came up short. Their next move was to urge the Blacks of the American South to turn against their masters and to take up arms for the king. Virginia Royal Governor Lord Dunmore not only invited them to join redcoat ranks, he had the breasts of their uniforms emblazoned with the slogan—LIBERTY TO SLAVES! The Loyalists in the Carolinas believed that it would be good to release the slaves, too, so that they could prevent mobilization by the white patriots. This touched the hearts of Southern men with terrible fear; they had always dreaded the thought of slave uprisings. They pushed the slaves into fighting for the rebel cause.

One does not have to read fiction like *Uncle Tom's Cabin* to realize the appalling situation of the Blacks in the South. But even Washington's pastor spread a yarn that was to become very popular as the nation moved toward the great Civil War a century later, when men would fight and die to free their dark-skinned brothers. Rev. Jonathan Boucher wrote:

Nothing is easier than to compassion by declamations against slavery. Yet I have seldom heard or read things of the sort which carried much conviction to my mind. The condition of the lower classes of mankind everywhere, when compared with that of those above them, may seem hard; yet on a fair investigation, it will probably be found that people in general in a low sphere are not less happy than those in a higher sphere. I am equally well persuaded in my own mind that the negroes in general in Virginia and Maryland in my time [1759-1775] were not upon the whole worse off nor less happy than the labouring poor in Great Britain. . . . Slavery is not one of the most intolerable evils incident to humanity, even to slaves; I have known thousands of slaves as well-informed, as well-clad, as well-fed, and in every respect as well-off as nine out of ten of the poor in every kingdom of Europe are. . . .[5]

These words of a Tory are just part of the reasoning used by those who supported an enlightened type of slavery, where it was the duty of the master to show paternal kindness to his Blacks. Rev. Thorton Stringfellow, a Virginia Baptist, wrote in the 1850s: "Job himself was a great slaveholder, and, like Abraham, Issac, and Jacob, won no small portion of his claims to character with God and men from the manner in which he discharged his duty to his slaves. Once more: the conduct of Joseph in Egypt, AS PHARAOH'S COUNSELLOR, under all the circumstances, prove him a friend to absolute slavery, as a form of government better adapted to the state of the world at that time, than the one which existed in Egypt. . . ."

Whether the arguments were old or up-to-date, these myths of men have come down to us today. In the original draft of the Declaration of Independence, there was a clause against slavery, but this was axed because of deep Southern opposition. The colonies south of the Mason-Dixon line gradually hardened their stand. In 1708, there were 1,400 Indian and 2,000 Negro slaves in South Carolina, but the Blacks were worth twice as much as the redskins on the selling block. In the early days of the Virginia colony, two white men were hanged for the murder of their slaves, but by 1753, this kind of murder was dropped to manslaughter, which carried no penalty at all! The Blacks even rated less consideration and charity than animals. A Virginian could be fined for beating his animal, but there was no levy for thrashing his slaves.

Lest one feel that only the rednecks were on the prowl, we would do well to check into the treatment Blacks received elsewhere in the world. When Carleton left New York for Nova Scotia, long after the guns of the Revolution had been silenced, he took a goodly number of colored folk with him, even though their old masters had asked for their return. As the Negroes were willing to work for lower wages than the veterans for the royal brigades, the whites rioted and burned down several colored homes. Later, the Afro-Canadians were executed simply for stealing food to sustain their lives. The lot of the dark race was not ideal anyplace in the world.

Now that the colored folk were being wooed to fight under the king's banner, the Americans began to wonder if they had missed a good thing in not asking these men, who were forced to be persecuted pilgrims in a land not of their choosing, to fight the British invaders. Lieut. Col. John Laurens of South Carolina was the first to wonder outloud whether or not it would be wise to put Blacks in the field to aid the cause of liberty.

The idea that a man from the Carolinas would offer to place himself at the head of a band of armed Blacks seems astonishing to us today. But he probably received his liberal views from his famous father who wrote his son on August 14, 1774: "I abhor slavery . . . I found the Christian religion and slavery growing under the same authority . . . I nevertheless disliked it. Not less than twenty thousand pounds sterling would all my Negroes produce if sold at public auction tomorrow. I am not the man who enslaved them; they are indebted to Englishmen for that favor; nevertheless, I am devising means for manumitting many of them. Great powers oppose me—the laws and customs of my country. What will my children say if I deprive them of so much estate?"

General Washington felt that the colored population was an untapped reserve that should be used in the fight for liberty, but he was not ready to move at that time. Laurens's close friend, Alexander Hamilton, had similar thoughts to those of the young South Carolinian. He gave Lauren a letter addressed to the President of the Congress, in which he supported the raising of three or four Black battalions to fight the king's men. When the commander-in-chief got wind of what was going on, he said he feared that the English would try to outdo the patriots in just such a policy, and there would be terrific bloodletting on both sides. Thus the idea died a slow death.

From the time of the Boston Massacre, whose first casualty was a Black, the Negro took part in the Revolution. A number of them detected British spies in Massachusetts and rejoiced that their brother was buried with the honored dead in Boston, where the colonies first felt the armed might of the British army. Another Negro was on hand when Benedict Arnold was trying to sell West Point and his soul to the English. Although he heard the discussions, he could not be very helpful, as Blacks could not testify in court against the whites. Not all the Black people were behind the scenes or washing pots and pans for their masters at rebel headquarters. The French were amazed at a Rhode Island regiment, which they described as the "best-uniformed and best trained," because it was three-quarters Negro. About 5,000 Blacks fought for liberty. In 1779, Congress proposed to pay the owners of Negro slaves in Georgia and South Carolina $1,000 a head for 3,000 Blacks to fight for the country, and after victory they each would receive $50 and their freedom. When these two states refused this offer, General Washington scolded them in no uncertain terms, as he believed that the Blacks would make excellent soldiers.

When the war ended, Washington was definitely against

accepting demands by former masters for the return of their slaves who had served in the ragtag Continental army. Washington had to think deeply about his own moral responsibility toward the slavery question. Some decisions could be made quickly. He immediately asked William Lee, his faithful slave who had been with him at the front throughout the war, whether he preferred his immediate freedom or his current status with an annuity of thirty dollars for the rest of his life.

This heart struggle continued after he had settled down, at war's end, to civilian life once again. Two years after Cornwallis handed over his sword at Yorktown, Lafayette got in touch with Washington. He suggested that they purchase a small estate where they could allow free Negroes to become tenants and learn a good trade, and the Frenchman also said that he would help personally in the project. Washington thought the idea was very promising but wanted to discuss it with the former general face-to face. In 1786, the Virginian answered another letter from Paris by stating that he was worried whether immediate freedom for the Blacks would be good for them, but saying that he definitely believed in gradual abolition of slavery, which he considered to be an excellent idea.

Throughout his presidency, Washington met with various religious groups. He moved slowly but surely toward the final decision of his life about slavery. He had so many slaves at this time that they were driving him into bankruptcy, but he definitely would not sell them off or hire them out to other neighbors. His main worry was about his wife and home. If he were to free them upon his own death, she might not be able to stay afloat financially; so he did the next best thing. He made a will that would free ALL his slaves upon the death of his dear wife, should he pass away before her.

Jefferson the great reformer had a less shining record when it came down to the practical application of his lofty principles. His first legislative effort in the House of Burgesses was a bill to emancipate the slaves. The leading light of the Democratic party preached to the king about his duties in regards to slave traffic across the ocean. He wrote: "The abolition of domestic slavery is the great object of desire in those colonies, where it was unhappily introduced in their infant state. But previous to the enfranchisement of the slaves we have, it is necessary to exclude all further importations from Africa. Yet our repeated attempts to effect this by prohibitions, and by imposing duties which might amount to a prohibition, have been hitherto defeated by his Majesty's negative; thus preferring the immediate advantages of a few British corsairs to the lasting interests of the American states, and to the rights of human nature, deeply wounded by this infamous practice."[6]

The author of the Declaration of Independence attacked His Majesty again in the draft of this world famous document. He continues, "This piratical warfare, the opprobium of INFIDEL powers, is the warfare of the CHRISTIAN king of Great Britain determined to keep open a market where MEN should be bought and sold; he has prostituted his negative for suppressing every legislative attempt to prohibit or to restrain this exerable commerce." This forceful fight for the freeing of slaves was thwarted by pressure from South Carolina and Georgia, much to the chagrin of the Northern radicals. But Jefferson did not find it in his heart to follow his liberal pronouncements when it came to his own Blacks. He only freed five upon his death, the rest being passed on to his family for use in building up their wealth and to add to their comforts in life.

James Madison, also to occupy the White House, was another Virginian. He saw the inconsistencies between what the Founding Fathers professed and what they practiced. When he moved to Washington, he addressed the Congress thusly: "Among the commercial abuses still under the American flag . . . it appears that American citizens are instrumental in carrying on a traffic in enslaved Africans, equally in violation of the laws of humanity, and in defiance of those of their own country. The same just and benevolent motives which produced interdiction in force against this criminal conduct, will doubtless be felt by Congress in devising further means of suppressing the evil." He also worked on his own plan, which was to send the Blacks back to Africa through the American Colonization Society, which was sustained by the gifts of churches and Christians, as well as other sources. After he left elective office, he even became president of this organization. The liberal advocates did succeed in shipping some Negroes to Liberia, but mostly it was a failure.

We now turn to the other racial group that came under the heel of the white settlers. The Indians were surprised when they saw the first foreign settlers land in their country. The new arrivals were also puzzled over the true identity of these red-skinned warriors. Some of them thought that they were related to the Jews of the Old Testament, perhaps the lost tribes, but their true background remained something of a mystery. The Christians wanted to have friendly relations with the occupiers of the land, and they often talked about the virtues of this brave race. But once they noticed that these lovers of nature were sacrificing their own children to appease the gods, the leaders wondered about how civilized they really were.

Rev. Joseph Doddridge observed the savage attacks on the settlers in Western Virginia in the latter part of the eighteenth century and leaves us with his observations. He says, "The Indian kills victims of his vengeances, because, if males, they may hereafter become warriors, or if females, they become mothers. Even the fetal state is criminal in his view. . . . He spares the lives of those who fall into his hands, for the purpose of feasting the feelings of ferocious vengeance of himself and his comrades, by the torture of his captive." These types of uprisings kept the white settlers on their toes and undermined any faith that might have remained.

Washington was said to have had a gift of oratory in the Indian language, but the British use of these so-called savages in battle angered the rebels. The Loyalists had urged the British to sign up these crafty fighters, and the two groups native to the American sod worked together in General Burgoyne's campaign. Sullivan struck into their country in reprisal, but he also signed up tribes to fight under the banner of the Continental Congress.

The Puritans had few reservations about these hardy hunters when they arrived at Plymouth Rock. Both of them exchanged kindnesses and worked in harmony during the first months of the colony. The Puritans noted that the red men were very faithful to the covenant they had made with the whites. To their shame, some of the whites did not deal rightly with the original inhabitants of North America and were caught stealing from these poor people. Even though they were punished, it was not a good witness for Christ and his religious teachings.

The Puritans were bothered also by other dealings with the Indians. In Puritan literature, we find a document that tries to answer a number of important questions. One of these queries was: "Did we any wrong to the INDIANS in buying their land at a small price?" One of the answers went this way: "Tho' we gave but a small Price for what we bought; we gave them their demands, we came to their Market, and gave them their price; and indeed, it was but little: And had it continued in their hands, it would have been of little value. It is our dwelling on it, and our Improvements, that have made it to be of Worth." Another question was about land that was not purchased. The authors wrote: "There was some part of the Land that was not purchased, neither was there need that it should; it was 'vauum domicilium'; and so might be possessed by virtue of God's grant to Mankind, Gen. 1:28. . . . The Indians made no use of it, but for Hunting. . . . When ABRAHAM came into the Land of CANAAN, he made use of

the vacant Land as he pleased: so did ISSAC and JACOB."
It is interesting to see that these Christians felt a need to
answer the questions dealing with other people, whereas most
of the leaders of that day on the political scene never were
bothered by their relations with the Indians.

The Quakers had a great deal of trust in the Indians. In
1748, the Quaker Assembly refused to vote any funds for the
defense of Philadelphia, but coughed up £500 for the Indians
and asked them to use it for the necessities of life. Eight years
later they formed the "Friendly Association for Beginning and
Preserving Peace with the Indians by Pacific Measures."

Even from the beginning, Penn desired good relations with
his strange neighbors, so he was willing to pay for the land
instead of simply taking it from them. He also offered any
help that they might need if they should wish to settle in
his cites. Penn's people were angered when the Paxton Boys
killed innocent Christian Indians, and they tried to force these
rascals to admit their failings and to see that they were punished, although some of the settlers sided with the riffraff. The
Quakers never lost their love and interest in the warriors of
the West, and Penn prohibited liquor sales to these tribes,
as they saw how it destroyed their lives and placed them under
the power of evil traders.

Their interest was even praised by a historian as he notes,
"Almost a century before Europeans were thinking of slaves
as human beings, the Quakers were concerned about their
souls." Puritan preachers also fought from the pulpit for personal freedom for minority races. It definitely was because of
their influence that men like Adams were to stand tall when
it was not so popular with the masses to preserve the rights
of all people, not simply themselves. Massachusetts was the
first to abolish slavery and New Hampshire followed. Pennsylvania and the other New England states supported "gradual
emancipation" of the Blacks.

Jesus Christ, an Asian, died on the cross for the sins of

all people. The great religions of the world have not come out of Europe but the Middle and Far East. It may be true that Arab slave traffic was much worse than that of the Europeans, but they were not as enlightened by the educational institutions of that century as the people of Europe were. In dealing with America, we must agree with the judgment of historian Dan Lacy, who wrote: "The most serious problem inherited from the Revolution was its failure to carry out its declaration of equality of all men."

It was the evangelicals who reached out to the Blacks in the 1700s:

> As Woodson, the Negro historian, has so aptly called it, "The Dawn of the New Day" in the religious development of Negroes occurred when the Methodists and Baptists began proselyting the blacks. The proselyting activities on the part of the Methodists and Baptists, as well as the less extensive missionary work of the Presbyterians, were a phase of the Great Awakening which began in New England and spread to the West and South. When the Methodists and Baptists began their revivals in the South, large numbers of Negroes were immediately attracted to this type of religious worship. However, it was not until after the American Revolution that large masses of the Negro population became converts and joined the Methodist and Baptist churches.[7]

NOTES

1. J. H. Worcester, Jr., *The Life of David Livingstone* (Chicago: Moody Press, undated), pp. 73-74.*
2. Louis Filler, *The Crusade Against Slavery, 1830-1860,* The University Library (New York: Harper & Row, Publishers, Harper Torchbooks, 1960), pp. 28-29.*
3. Bertram Wyatt-Brown, *Lewis Tappan and the Evangelical War Against Slavery* (Cleveland: The Press of Case Western Reserve University, 1969), p. 81.

4. John L. Thomas, ed., *Slavery Attacked: The Abolitionist Crusade* (Englewood Cliffs, N.J.: Prentice-Hall, Spectrum Books, 1965), p. 11.*

5. Jonathan Boucher, *Reminiscences of an American Loyalist* (Boston: Houghton Mifflin Company, 1925), pp. 97-98.

6. Paul Leicester Ford, *The Writings of Thomas Jefferson*, 10 vols. (New York: G. P. Putnam's Sons, 1892-99), 1:135.

7. E. Franklin Frazier, *The Negro Church in America* (New York: Schocken Books, 1964), pp. 7-8.*

XIV GOD'S MILITARY MIRACLE

If Historiographers should be hardy enough to fill the page of history with the advantages that have been gained with unequal numbers [on the part of America] in the course of this contest, and attempt to relate the distressing circumstances under which they have been obtained, it is more than probable that Posterity will bestow on their labors the epithet and marks of fiction; for eight years in this Country could be baffled in their plan of Subjugating it by numbers infinitely less, composed of Men sometimes half starved; always in Rags, without pay, and experiencing, at times, every species of distress which human nature is capable of undergoing.

GEORGE WASHINGTON

In 1776, Rev. Peter Thacher told his congregation, "The British nation is now become a great tame beast, instead of ravaging the American continent in a single campaign, with a single regiment, they have proceeded—one mile and a half in the conquest of it. . . . Formidable as was once the power of the British lion he hath now lost his teeth." Such bravado is often used in the opening moments of any war.

Where was the American army to fight the British regulars or the officers to lead them? Where was the American navy to defend thousands of miles of coastline against a seapower that ruled the waves? Rebels had only a handful of manufacturing plants in which to produce and supply the powder, guns, and equipment that every military force must have to stay in the field. The Americans had almost no source for the funds they would need to buy weapons from other countries, and it was debatable whether or not other nations would accept the credit from a band of bandits who were rising against the greatest government on the face of the globe. British cabinet minister Henry Ellis could write confidently to William Knox, "We know the real inability of the Americans to make any effectual resistance."

One half the officers in Massachusetts, the top brass, remained loyal to that other George—the one who sat on the throne of England. A Tory scoffed at the ragtag recruits playing with guns on nice greens and sneered, "Such is the army with which you are to oppose the most powerful nation upon the globe." Leonard, a Massachusetts lawyer, wondered out loud if anyone could be "so deluded as to believe that Great Britain, who so lately carried her arms with success to every part of the globe," would fail to conquer the weak and disunited American provinces? On the contrary, it was plainly apparent that, "with the British navy in the front, Canadians and savages in the rear, a regular army in the midst," America would be devastated. Old Judge Samuel Sewall of Boston skipped the country and from his safe hiding place warned an American friend: "Could you form a just idea of the immense wealth and power of the British nation, you would tremble at the foolish audacity of your pigmy states. Another summer will bring you all over to my opinion. I feel for the miseries hastening on my countrymen, but they must thank their own folly."

No wonder King George III chuckled to himself when he said he would just as soon have his boys kill Americans as Frenchmen. Part of this confidence rested on the poor showing of American recruits in the French and Indian War. General Wolfe, a hero to the Americans, called their rangers "the worst soldiers in the universe." The British brass thought the provincials were inefficient, poorly disciplined and riffraff. The colonists had been upset by the arrogant, overbearing, and condescending English officers. The English monarch told his prime minister that the rebels would give up meekly, and General Gage was sure he could end all the ruckus with one quick victory.

In February of 1775, General Grant rose from his seat in the House of Commons and told his listeners that 5,000 men under his command could easily march from one end of the American continent to the other and crush the rebellion. Unbeknown to him, Lord Stirling was listening, and when they met on opposite sides, at the battle of Long Island, Grant having 7,000 men and Stirling only 950 Delaware boys, the rebels attacked Grant six times and the Britisher had to call for reinforcements to turn the tide. Still, Major Pitcairn of the king's forces was sure that one sharp clash and the burning of two or three rebel towns would "set everything to rights."

Politician Dickinson of Pennsylvania was not opposed to throwing off oppression, but he believed that the radicals didn't have sense enough to realize that they would have to wait until they were much stronger before they challenged John Bull. The odds were completely against the patriots.

There was no question that the Americans could give a good account of themselves if all the country were unified in the effort to toss out the invaders, but they were divided themselves, without arms of quality and without a strong

Congress that could raise the funds necessary to equip an army. John Locke stated that more than a simple majority was needed to make any revolution a success. Galloway, an American Tory, told Parliament that "more than four-fifths of the Americans would prefer a union with Great Britain to independence." Maj. Gen. James Robertson testified that "the object of the war was to enable the loyal subjects of America to get free from the tyranny of the rebels, and to let the country follow its inclination, by returning the King's government." John Adams believed that one-third supported the revolution, one-third was Tory, and another third was neutral.

Was it a lack of willpower? King George was fully behind the war. Dartmouth also wrote to the secretary of war, Lord Barrington, in these words, "If you will resist and not yield, that Resistance should be effectual at the Beginning. If you think ten thousand men sufficient, send twenty, if one million is thought enough, give two; you will save both Blood and Treasure in the end. A large Force will terrify, and engage many to join you, a middling one will encourage Resistance and gain you no friends."

The Earl of Sandwich was sure that it would be a simple task. He angrily retorted to a hint that it would be difficult because of America's large population by saying, "Suppose the Colonies do abound in men, what does that signify? They are raw, undisciplined, cowardly men. I wish instead of forty or fifty thousand of these BRAVE fellows they would produce in the field at least two hundred thousand; the more the better, the easier would be the conquest; if they did not run away, they would starve themselves into compliance with our measures. . . . Are these the men to frighten us from the post of honour? Believe me, my Lords, the very sound of a cannon would carry them off . . . as fast as their feet could carry them. This is too trifling a part of the argument to detain your Lordships any longer."

By December, 1778, the British would have over 300,000

men under arms and still be asking for more as the new secretary of war requested 14,000 additional men. He admitted that this was "a military power considerably greater than had ever been kept in modern times." This prompted Horace Walpole to retort, "It was not so much to the honour of this country with such an army to have received nothing but disgraces, and it was ridiculous to hear more demanded of Parliament, as if 300,000 could not achieve all that 314,000 could." On the seas, the British navy consisted of 270 ships, with about half carrying 60 guns or more, against the Continental navy with 60 ships and not all of the latter were seaworthy at the same time.

Besides the homegrown variety of servicemen, the British had mercenaries from Germany. Then, too, there were 25,000 Tories about to sign up for the king. Galloway adds that at least 2,300 Americans deserted to Howe when he was in his winter resort in Philadelphia. How many more changed rebel rags for redcoat ribbons? Howe thought that he might leave the colonies if he didn't get more troops and believed that there would be a bloody civil war if that happened.

Not only did the Americans lack fighting men and arms, but they had to completely reorganize the army outside of Boston. "Search the vast volumes of history through," Washington wrote in January, 1776, "and I must question whether a case similar to ours is to be found; to wit, to maintain a post against the flower of the British troops for six months together . . . and at the end of them to have one army disbanded and another to raise within the same distance of a reinforced enemy."

After the British were forced to leave Boston because Continental artillery made them uneasy, they next decided to attack New York. The armada that moved in toward Long Island caused many a rebel to swallow deeply. On June 29, 45 ships sailed into the bay, and one day later, 82 more arrived. By August 12, an additional 67 boats had arrived off

New York, and with them were 32,000 seasoned veterans to face 20,000 Americans, many of whom had never fired a gun in anger in their life.

Before Trenton, the numbers of ill-clad soldiers under Washington had dipped to 3,000—and that was not the worst. If he did not win a battle to put starch in the backs of his young troopers, he would probably see most of them leaving him after the new year arrived, as their enlistments would be up. Throughout the war, the Americans had to hope that men would continue to fight under the stars and stripes without pay, without equipment, and without three square meals a day. Even when the French arrived to help put the squeeze on Cornwallis at Yorktown, they were perplexed, because they assumed that the rebel forces numbered about 10,000, when it was closer to 3,000. It was a great rarity for the Americans to have a numerical advantage on the field of battle, and until Yorktown, they never got their forces into position for a long seige.

Field Marshal Rommel, of Germany, told us that it is the quartermaster who decides battles. Whether or not this was just a case of humility on the part of the Desert Fox, we cannot be sure, but surely men cannot go into battle with their bare hands or amulets to ward off the enemy. The Americans did not have the means to make enough rifles, or even gunpowder, to support a single sustained campaign! Things became so bad that Franklin suggested that they use bows and arrows to fight the British and their cohorts. Often they were without food or clothing, and even their shoeless feet left bloody tracks in the snow. When the commander in chief learned there was a scarcity of gunpowder, he told them they would have to do with what they had as "the cause we are engaged in is so just and righteous, that we must try to rise superior to every obstacle in its support."

Money was another important item, so important that the British used a scheme to have it counterfeited to throw the

American economy into a spin. They may have been wasting their time, as things were in such bad shape, that freshly designed greenbacks would hardly be noticed. The Congress could not levy taxes, and it could only beg for troops. Paper money depreciated so much that the pay of a major general was about the same as that of an express rider in civilian life. Steuben was owed $220,000 by the Congress, but it was so worthless that he was forced to sell some of his silver spoons to feed one of his aides who was ill. It got so bad toward the end of the war that one bottle of rum cost $1,200! That must have cured the drinking habits of more than one man.

After all the problems about taxation without representation, the colonies had an uphill battle to convince their citizens that taxation was necessary. The British officers had to pay for their commissions on most occasions, but were rewarded handsomely once they were on the king's payroll. Washington, in contrast, received no salary at all and even dug into his own pocket to help pay for the needs of his army. But this was nothing compared to the soldiers in his army, because it must be remembered that the commander had a fine plantation. Men in Nathaniel Greene's army went without pay for two years!

Had it not been for the generosity of Robert Morris, America might have gone down the drain for want of hard cash. Washington often called on this patriot when things were dim. The British had carefully controlled the flow of money into the colonies and restricted their use of coins; therefore, the colonists used all sorts of money, as they could not mint their own. Late in 1776, George sent a fast messenger to Philadelphia to track down the busy merchant. Before noon on January 1, bulky bags of hard cash were arriving in Trenton, but what they contained was comical. There were "410 Spanish milled dollars, 2 English crowns, 72 French crowns, 1072 English shillings" plus the paper money that was losing value each passing minute. With inflation ruining the purchasing power of the troops, and having to rest upon the good will of other allies, one could easily agree with one patriot who wrote his friend as follows: "It is my opinion that America has much more to fear from the effects of the large quantities of paper money than from the operations of Howe and all British generals."

The first blood of the war was almost shed in Salem, where so many witches were given a hard time. In February of 1775, General Gage decided that it was time to send out an expedition to collect some hardware in the shape of several brass fieldpieces, which the Liberty Boys were hiding in that town. Brig. Gen. Alexander Leslie was chosen to lead the war party to Salem on February 2. News spread quickly, like it did when the British troops marched for Lexington, and the militia prepared for action. The people poured out of their churches earlier than usual to greet the lobsterbacks marching toward their town. They lifted the drawbridge, which meant that the redcoats could not enter the village at all. The British officer demanded that it be lowered, and in the scuffle a number of citizens were pricked by shining bayonets. One man shouted, "Soldiers, redjackets, lobstercoats, damnation to your government!"

The Reverend Mr. Barnard tried to calm the people down. He knew what the British had come for. During the morning service, Col. David Mason ran into the North Church and shouted at the top of his voice, "The regulars are coming after the guns and are now near Malloon's Mills!" A Quaker who lived near the church aided the men in hiding the weapons. Now Barnard faced General Leslie.

They then worked out a compromise that would satisfy the honor of the English officer. He would be allowed to cross the drawbridge and march his men thirty rods into the town, Barnard suggested, but if he did not find any arms, he would turn about and return to Boston. It was obvious that both would fight if necessary, but neither party wanted a scrap if it could be avoided.

Leslie's men marched across the bridge and turned about, retracing their steps as they played "The World's Turned Upside Down"—the same piece the British would play at York-town when they laid down their arms. As they passed a house on their return, a nurse named Sarah Tarrant vented her spleen from her open window. "Go home and tell your master he has sent you on a fool's errand and broken the peace of our Sabbath. What, do you think we were born in the woods, to be frightened by owls?" One of the soldiers pointed his musket at her, and she exclaimed, "Fire if you have the courage, but I doubt it."

If she had known what would happen in April of 1775, three months later, she might not have been so sassy. On April 19, Col. Francis Smith began an expedition to capture John Hancock and Samuel Adams, who were staying with Rev. Jonas Clark. Clark was a leader of his community and his wife was Hancock's cousin. The Britisher also was planning to seize arms and military provisions in Concord too.

Early in the morning the men of the area were roused from their slumber by warnings that the British were coming. Although the Americans officially had no army, they had been training in some areas of the colony. When Pitcairn's men in the British column reached the green, they told the rebels to lay down their arms, but the men began to disperse without following his command. The Reverend Mr. Clark, who was present that day, then saw the British fire the first shot of the war, and the first blood was shed. The forces of suppression moved on to Concord where they were met at the North Bridge, and after a sharp skirmish, the redcoats were sent fleeing toward Boston, and all along the route they were picked off from behind hedges, walls, and trees. In their hasty retreat, the British shot at innocent women and killed whole families when they burst into homes that they believed sheltered snipers. The British suffered 73 killed, 174 wounded, and 26 missing. The American casualties were 49 dead, 41 wounded, and 5 missing.

The next famous battle took place on Breed's Hill, next to Bunker Hill, which was initially occupied by the Americans. The rebels dug themselves into the hill, and when the British tried to take them by storm, their firing was withering. The English soldiers reeled back down the slope. On the third try, when most of the ammunition was used up and help was not forthcoming from other troops near by, the Americans were pushed from both Breed's and Bunker Hill; but 40 percent of the king's troops lay dead and wounded. Pitcairn, who recommended the burning of peaceful towns, was among those who lost their lives. "A dearly bought victory," Clinton wrote, "another such would have ruined us."

The Howe brothers, kings of land and sea, moved their forces into New York Bay. In an ensuing battle, the English outflanked Sullivan and won the day easily, though General Grant lost his life. Even though Washington managed a masterly withdrawal from the island to New York City proper, his forces had suffered 1,500 casualties, almost four times that of the British. Chaplains Fithian (New Jersey Militia) and Benjamin Turnball (First Connecticut Regiment) praised the fighting spirit of their comrades in arms, although the battle was lost.

The British routed more recruits at Kip's Bay, but Washington had a surprise for them at Harlem Heights. The general's plan to encircle them was barely foiled by hasty firing on the front, which sent the English troops running for cover just when the secret force under Colonel Knowlton and Major Leitch was turning the flank to get at the British rear. The king's officers were chagrined that their men had advanced backwards in rapid rout, with the ragged rebels hot on their heels. When Howe tried to turn the tables on the Continentals, they outwitted him by withdrawing to White Plains before he could outflank them.

When Howe attacked at White Plains he was met with a withering rain of bullets and shells from Hamilton's outfit, but the Hessians on the right hit General McDougall's exposed right flank; and the men in hunting shirts and brown hats moved away in the direction of New Castle. Once again Howe waited too long for reinforcements and lost out on an opportunity to win a meaningful victory.

If Washington was to sustain any morale among his tired troops, he had to win a victory. Although they had bloodied John Bull's nose and battered the British boys at Bunker Hill, Breed's Hill, and Harlem, they needed a brilliant victory to wipe out the effect of always moving on the defensive. This resulted in the attack on Trenton on Christmas Day, 1776, with only four Americans being wounded, among them future president James Monroe. The rebels took 918 prisoners and left 30 Hessians on the cold turf.

Charles Cornwallis began to chase Washington, and it looked like he had him boxed in in South Jersey. He was so confident that he boasted, "We'll bag him in the morning." But as the rebels left their fires burning, they slipped off in the night toward Princeton, where they would attack inferior forces and win another victory, while the main body of British men tried to catch up with them. George's men smashed the crack British Fourth Brigade, inflicting almost 600 casualties, while suffering 54 killed among their ranks. Once again the Americans moved to more friendly confines as the English licked their wounds.

London was upset and thought that they would recoup their losses with Burgoyne at Saratoga. But it wasn't to be. Gen. Horatio Gates made his name a household word with his victory over the British. With Maj. Gen. Benjamin Lincoln cutting off their chances to hoof it for Canadian soil, the English reeled in the wake of the first real jolt to their confidence, and France was making up its mind to commit men as well as money.

Gates's glory was to glow in contrast to Washington who had a bad day at Brandywine. It was basically a repeat performance of the battle of Long Island, and the same soldier, General Sullivan, was to be the goat once again. The position George had picked was splendid and his strategy brilliant, but he listened to Sullivan who said that recent intelligence reports showed there was no weakness in those British ranks Washington wished to attack. While they delayed, a farmer came on the field and told the tall Virginian that if he didn't watch out, Howe would have him surrounded. Because of the faulty position of Sullivan's men, they did not retreat in good order, and when the smoke cleared, the cause had suffered over one thousand casualties, including a light wound to Lafayette. Although he had not been outflanked or surrounded, Washington had a very poor day on the field of battle.

Germantown would be the next big battle, and Washington planned it after the classic victory of Scipio Africanus over Hannibal. The plan was to use four great pincers to crush the British. All went well for a short period of time, but perhaps the strategy was too complicated for the inexperienced Americans, because even though they pushed the British back and were moving toward victory, rumors spread that the enemy was behind the right wing and they ran from the field in panic.

Most Americans agreed with Wayne's judgment of the battle: "We ran from victory!" The ragtag army suffered heavier losses than the enemy once again, and they saw four hundred of their men become prisoners of war. Washington was criticized in Congress and the star of Gates was ascending in the heavens, causing many people to begin a conspiracy, called "Conway's Cabal," to have the Virginian replaced by the hero of Saratoga. The man from Mount Vernon could take some consolation in the fact that the battle also ruined the reputation of Howe, and he was soon to resign and return to England. A correspondent in England wrote, "Any other General in the world than General Howe would have beaten General Washington, and any other General in the world than General Washington would have beaten General Howe."

As the forces moved into winter quarters, it was the Continental forces that limped toward Valley Forge. About 2,500 men would never leave this famous spot, which was chosen because it was central and easy to defend. Nathanael Greene, an earnest Christian, was made quartermaster of the army and he tried to stem the discontent of men who were crying for meat. Even an enemy prisoner of war admitted that the force did not break up because "the spirit of liberty," and foreigners like Baron von Steuben, Louis Duportail, Thaddaeus Kosciusko, Johann de Kalb and young Lafayette shaped up the men into a fighting unit.

In the early months of 1778, the revolutionary troops brought pressure on the enemy and his lines of communication. This, along with the fear of the French navy sealing them in a trap, made the British evacuate Philadelphia without firing a shot.

When Washington heard the English were about to evacuate Monmouth Courthouse, he ordered Charles Lee, a veteran and hero of European wars, to attack, but the latter retreated instead. A deserter gave this precious news to the enemy, who then wheeled about and attacked the rebels, who fled from the field. General Washington intercepted the fleeing troops and called Lee down for such a shameful situation. The commander in chief immediately took over command and utilized the fighting spirit of Mad Anthony Wayne's Pennsylvanians to drive off the British, but they could not follow up on the victory, as the men were "beat out with the heat and fatigue." Lee was court-martialed for cowardice and cashiered from the army, so he spent his life taking care of his numerous hounds and hounding people about the terrible inefficiency in rebel ranks.

Tactics of the day differed from our modern use of concentrated fire power. Colonial muskets were not only heavy and cumbersome, but they were difficult to reload. The men from England liked to rely on the trusty bayonet as soon as the American had fired a volley, because the inexperienced Yanks often scurried from the field when they saw the glistening bayonets charging their way.

The "Paoli Massacre" made the Americans red with rage. On the night of September 21, 1777, the Tories told their political brothers that Wayne's men were sleeping peacefully near the town of Paoli. At midnight, the men serving King George III creeped into camp and went to work with their sharp bayonets, wounding several hundred unsuspecting Americans and taking a number of prisoners, while they lost only seven men. The forces of Anthony Wayne never forgot the fact that men had been stabbed to death even though they had tried to surrender.

Wayne two years later was to have sweet revenge at Stony Point, when his column of 1,350 men, all but one battalion attacking with unloaded muskets, struck in the dead of night, resulting in the enemy losing 63 killed, 70 wounded and 543 captured, whereas the Americans lost 15 dead and 80 injured. A couple of months later, "Light Horse" Harry Lee took a leaf out of Wayne's book of tactics and attacked Paulus Hook at four in the morning, where his men took the fort in a few minutes along with 158 prisoners. The men of America had learned their lessons well and the British units were paying for it.

All of the battles were not fought near Philadelphia, New York, or Boston. Washington decided to check the Indians and Tories, who had massacred settlers in the border areas of New York and Pennsylvania. He chose General Gates to head the band, but he turned down the offer to lead 4,000 men to strike into those two states. So Sullivan took these men and struck back at the hated foes, winning a key battle at Newtown, not far from Elmira, New York.

Henry Dearborn described one of these Indian villages: "The Army march'd at 8 o'clock. Proceeded thro the swamp & passed a learge body of clear land cover'd with grass, after leaving the clear land march'd one mile & came to a Small Lake call'd Konnondaguah. We . . . came to a pretty town call'd Kannadaguah [Canandaigua, Ontario County, New York] consisting of about 30 houses, much better built than any I have seen before. Near this town we discover'd very learge fields of corn, near which the Army incamp'd—several parties wear order'd out this afternoon to destroy the corn& c." These were typical tactics used against the Indians during the war.

Farther west, the Indians and British soldiers kept Kentucky and other areas on the defensive during the early years of the war. George Rogers Clark, only twenty-three, reversed the trend and captured Kaskaskia [below Louisville], Cahokia, and Vincennes. After he left for Virginia, "Hair Buyer" Hamilton swept down from Detroit and retook most of the same area. Clark drove them out of Vincennes but remained mostly on the defensive until late in the conflict. The Pennsylvanians made the Indians go on the warpath when they massacred Christian redskins at Gnaddenbutten. This caused Clark to make a counteroffensive into Ohio to protect the western flank of the colonies.

The British were now eyeing the South once again. First they struck at Boston, the head of the deadly serpent. Next, they hit the middle colonies. Now they were hoping to strike into the deep South and roll up the colonies one by one from the southern flank. Even though they had made a few attacks early in the war, this was their first big concentrated effort.

The British were trounced at Charleston in 1776, because of the courage of Rutledge and Moultrie who defied Charles

Lee and stuck to their guns, thus repulsing the British invasion. Four years later, the British forces transported ninety ships into the same area and broke the back of the resistance, and General Lincoln was humiliated in defeat as he lost the largest number of prisoners in the war and because the English exacted strict terms from him when he capitulated.

Savannah, Sunbury, and Augusta were to fall under the heel of Howe's forces in 1778. One year later, allied forces under General Lincoln and Admiral d'Estaing tried to recapture Savannah, but due to faulty strategy, they had to give up the attempt. Lincoln had done very well in other parts of Georgia, but the king's officers had not lost their relish for a new Southern strategy. With Frances Marion and Thomas Sumter rising from the swamps and using guerrilla tactics, it wasn't going to be pleasant for the invaders.

In 1780, Cornwallis's forces hoped to defeat the men of Dixie and then set up governments that would draw the people to the king once again. The battle of Cowpens was to throw a monkey wrench into these plans. It was the best-fought battle of the war from the American standpoint. Brig. Gen. Daniel Morgan, with a force of 1,000 men, lined up the raw militia in the front ranks, which had never been done before. In back of them were the veterans and hid from view was his cavalry. When a mixed force of 1,100 regulars and Tories spotted the Americans, they were looking for a swift victory. As planned, the militia fired their musket, but when the enemy charged, they ran. The regulars now stood up and hit the British with well-aimed shots, while Colonel William Washington moved around the right flank to trap the foe. In a matter of minutes, they crushed the entire force with a loss of only a dozen rebel dead. From this time on, the days of the English in America were numbered.

The revolutionary scene then shifted to Virginia, which had hitherto seen very little serious fighting. The British forces under the command of the hated Benedict Arnold moved into the Old Dominion with a large body of soldiers. They marched at will only to be parried now and then by a small force under Lafayette. Cornwallis, who had been badly beaten in the deep South, moved in from the Carolinas and linked up with the other English veterans.

Cornwallis was not worried as he moved into Yorktown. He was sure that his faithful troops, plus the strong right arm of the navy, would help keep him out of bad trouble. But this was just what Washington had been waiting for. He immediately got in touch with De Grasse, who then sailed north from the West Indies with the French fleet.

Washington made a few feints at New York and then hurried south. He passed his own church on the way, where he had joined in the fasting and praying in 1774 with other Virginians as they protested the closing of the port of Boston. Rochambeau with his fighting French forces accompanied his commander on the 450-mile race to seal Cornwallis in at Yorktown, which was not far from Jamestown where the first settlers had landed many years before.

De Grasse won a great naval victory off the American coast, which cut off the last exit for the British. The naval forces were pretty well balanced, but the French strategy had been much better than the British. After being whipped, the British fleet headed for New York to heal their wounds and to procrastinate and argue while their comrades in arms were being strangled to death in Virginia. This was particularly upsetting to Capt. William Cornwallis, the brother of the redcoat general.

The flag of capitulation was first sighted on the anniversary of the victory at Saratoga. As the guns fell silent, Johann Doehla expressed the feelings of many others as he said, "I had indeed just cause to thank my God who had so graciously preserved my life throughout the siege. Oh! how many thousand cannon balls I have escaped, with danger of my life hanging before my eyes!"

On the day of the surrender, the British and Germans were

to leave their posts at noon, but they were late. Cornwallis pleaded sickness, so the forces of King George III were led by General O'Hara as the bands played "The World Turned Upside Down." O'Hara held out his sword to Rochambeau, but the French general pointed to Washington in the opposite line. The British officer shuffled toward the tall Virginian, but the man from Mount Vernon did not accept the weapon. He pointed to General Lincoln, who had been humiliated at the surrender of Charleston. Lincoln accepted the sabre as the enemy winced. Their grief and rage was expressed by a German officer who said that they would never be able to understand how they could be surrendering to this pack of farmers and shopkeepers on October 19, 1781.

General Lincoln might have typified the average officer in rebel ranks. He was a deeply pious man who had a strong distaste for swearing, but he had little talent in the field. General Gates found Christ as his personal savior, and he quickly freed his slaves after the war and moved north from his native Virginia. Others, like General Schuyler, who had studied under a talented French Protestant minister, and Henry Knox, who had proclaimed that heaven was the guide of America's fortunes, would slide gracefully back into the footnotes of history. General Greene, acclaimed as the best officer the American army had, could go back to practicing his Quaker faith.

In Europe, it was said that "the church, the law, or the army were the only openings for sons of nobility" on the continent. On the British side, Gage, who opened the war in Massachusetts, was a Catholic. Carleton of Canada, who would bring the final terms to America and go back to England with the last troops who left New York, had a clergyman as his stepfather. Admiral Hood, who had wanted to fight on to rescue the forces at Yorktown when his superiors lacked the courage, was the son of a clergyman just like the great Nelson before him. Cornwallis, who had to write home about his mortifying loss to rebel rabble, was related to the Archbishop of Canterbury, as the Anglican leader was his wife's uncle.

When the guns went silent at Yorktown, nobody realized it would be the last major battle of the war. Back in England, they did not hear the news quickly. On Sunday, November 25, five weeks after the British lowered their flags in Virginia, official intelligence of the surrender reached Falmouth. Lord Germain was present when the message arrived, but without passing the news on to anyone else he hurried to see the prime minister. He got to Lord North's place between one and two in the afternoon and handed the message to the gentleman primarily responsible for waging the war against the colonies. In great agitation, Lord North could only repeat one phrase over and over again—"Oh, God! It is all over!"

On the other side of the ocean, the victory must have seemed like a miracle of God. The greatest country in the world could not subdue the spirit of a nation without arms, arsenals, or adequate finances. How could it have happened? Partially because Washington used the tactics that Mao was to make famous in China two centuries later. First of all, he avoided clashes when it was evident that he would be surrounded, outgunned, or outmanned so badly that he was bound to lose. The British played into his hands by using the same strategy as Chiang Kai-shek's Nationalists on the Chinese mainland. The English captured the key cities, but they were surrounded by a sea of humanity. The rebels used a scorched earth policy or kept the supplies from getting to the British, so the latter had to spend a lot of money bringing in goods from outside the areas of occupation. Catharine Macaulay, a British historian, predicted that a long, drawn out war would favor the Americans, and she was correct. Charles Carroll, the ony Catholic to sign the Declaration of Independence, knew one of key answers. When he received a letter from an Englishman who boasted that the king's men would easily march across America, he replied, "So they may, but they will be masters of the spot only on which they camp."

The American clergy stood behind their country in war as well as in peace. One man of the cloth called on people to enlist, but only after the service was over. Not believing that God was on the king's side, as some Tories claimed, a clergyman in Massachusetts called on Gage to repent and follow righteousness. Other clergymen took up arms and marched as privates in the cause of freedom. Still another used his power to talk the Indians into helping the forces of liberty. But chiefly the clergy carried out their calling by bringing the Gospel to the fighting men wherever they found them.

The end of the war was meaningful to those who trusted God. Not only were the forces of oppression broken, but the door swung open in favor of religious freedom. A historian wrote: "Religious bigotry had broken in upon the peace of various sects before the American war. This was kept up by partial establishments, and by a dread that the Church of England through the power of the mother country would be made to triumph over all other denominations. These apprehensions were done away with by the Revolution."[1]

NOTES

1. David Ramsay, *History of the American Revolution,* 2 vols. (London: John Stockdale, 1793), 2:315.

XV AMERICA AND ENTANGLING ALLIANCES

The nation which indulges towards another an habitual hatred, or an habitual fondness, is in some degree a slave.
GEORGE WASHINGTON

A leading historian said that the Quebec Act was the leading cause of the Revolution. The Americans had always been fearful of domination from Rome. Being avid readers of history and religious books, they had the dreadful feeling that history might repeat itself and the Catholic church might take over the colonies and stamp out their religious bodies, thus destroying perfect freedom in their midst.

The colonists most probably differed over whether or not the British had the right to tax them in an indirect manner. In fact, the people from New England to Georgia were quiet for decades about this issue. Others felt that the presence of royal troops would keep the Indians off the warpath. Many of them still loved the king, feeling that he was their friend and that he would listen to their sacred petitions. But as most of them were Protestants, they were united on one issue—the power of the Roman Catholic church must be checked to preserve freedom.

Adam Winthrop, the father of Puritan John Winthrop, who had led them to America, purchased a confiscated Catholic monastery for his home in England at Suffolk. Peter Oliver, arch Tory critic of the Puritan civilization, noted that the front of the *New England Primer* for small tots depicted the pope stuck with darts, which, as he noted, "creates and keeps up an aversion to Popery; & it had this Effect, until the honorable Congress wrote to the POPISH CANADIANS, that GOD & Nature had given them a Right to worship according to their Consciences." It was also a custom to parade effigies of Catholic popes through the streets of Boston. Rev. Ezra Sties reports, "This afternoon [November 5, 1774], three popes, etc. paraded through the streets, and in the evening they were consumed in a bonfire as usual—among others were Lord North, Governor Hutchinson and General Gage." But this anti-Rome sentiment did not stop the Catholics from joining rebel forces and some took an active part in the war. Rev. Pierre Dibault, delighted over the news of the American-French alliance, carried a proclamation from George Rogers Clark into southern Illinois to French settlements, assuring them that their property was safe and that the American forces would respect their religious freedom, so they heartily became "Virginians" in July, 1778.

They might allow these people religious freedom, and they also might glorify the relationship between Philadelphia and Paris, but the colonists were basically anti-Catholic. These gentlemen looked back to the Reformation for the birth of their churches. They differed with Rome over the infallibilty of the pope and whether or not the Bible should be the sole base for faith and practice. Most of them believed that the Catholic church had kept people in ignorance, so they could not bury themselves in the Word of God. Finally, they worried about the undemocratic tendencies in countries where the pope had great power.

Tom Paine lashed out at this new act that had established the Catholic church in Canada and had accepted French laws as basic. The radical wrote, "But popery and French laws in Canada are but part of that system of despotism which has been prepared for the colonies. The edicts of the British Parliament (for they want the sanction of British law) which relate to the province of Massachusetts Bay are big with destruction to the whole British Empire."

Both the Church and French had been foes of the American people. In the French and Indian War, the initial successes of these two forces sent fear into the hearts of the Americans, particularly those who lived in border areas. The Quebec Act extended the terms of the agreement to those French-speaking settlements in Ohio and Illinois.

Back in Quebec, the English were recognizing French civil law with slight modifications. A key part of the bill was the fact that the Roman Catholic church in Canada was sanctioned to collect tithes from all the inhabitants. Politically, there would be no direct election of officials by the people. The crown would appoint a legislative council of twenty-two persons who would be given the powers to make the laws for Quebec.

The priests in Canada, who held firm control over their parishioners, stepped in behind Carleton when he came to that area to organize a defense against the Americans. He was a benevolent despot, but the priests controlled the power behind his secular throne. But on May Day of 1775, when the act took effect, Carleton faced open opposition from the English-speaking mercantile minority because he secretly refused to follow the orders of the North's ministry, which had demanded that he preserve the right of habeas corpus and English law for civil suits, in which natural-born subjects were involved. He had to make hasty adjustments to please both sections of the population in the Canadian province.

Back in America, William Lee wrote his brother that "every tie of allegiance is broken by the Quebec Act, which is absolutely a dissolution of this Government, the compact between the King and the people is totally done away with." The Continental Congress itself was to endorse the Suffolk Resolves of Massachusetts, which also struck out at the bill. The tenth point of these resolves reads: "That the late act of parliament for establishing the Roman Catholic religion and the French laws in that extensive country, now called Canada, is dangerous in an extreme degree to the Protestant religion and to the civil rights and liberties of all America; and, therefore, as men and Protestant Christians we are indispensably obliged to take all proper measures for our security."

After Benedict Arnold defected to the British, he had to come up with a plausible excuse for his change of heart. He wrote that he was so shocked by the thought of an alliance with France, "the enemy of the Protestant faith," that he had decided he no longer could support the rebel cause. But this type of reasoning suddenly lost its power in America, and the people genuinely rejoiced at the new alliance.

A Roman Catholic believer was to take America by storm. This gentleman's name was Marquis de Lafayette. This young man had to face mounting opposition from his family, the threats of stiff penalties for disobeying the king, and had to separate from his young wife, pregnant with his child, to journey secretly to America.

He never saw his father, who had been killed in battle against the British. He was born on September 6, 1757, and baptized the following day in the little church in Chavaniac, France. He alone was the male representative of the family, as his dad's only brother had been killed in Italy and all other offspring were females.

Lafayette married a sweet young lass of a prominent family. The marriage was opposed by the girl's mother, but the father rejoiced in having such an ambitious young lad for his son-in-law. They were married on April 11, 1774, at a hotel in their native area.

Lafayette was supposed to enter into the service of one of the royal princes, but he did not care for this distinction; his refusal is said to have angered the king very much. Instead, he was attached to a regiment commanded by his cousin and stationed at Metz, where he accidentally met the brother of King George III, who was passing through the area. But his heart was in America when he heard about her cause. He wrote later, "Never had so noble a purpose offered itself to the judgment of men! This was the last struggle of liberty; its defeat then would have left it without a refuge and without hope."

France herself was not eager for personal involvement at that time; she looked down upon anyone who wanted to rush to the colonies to win his medals taking British lives. But he finally got Comte de Broglie to introduce him to various persons who would give him some aid in his determination to fight for the American cause.

At this time, his path crossed that of another adventurer, Baron de Kalb, who also wished to war for Washington. The German was about thirty years older than the Frenchman and had served through several campaigns with the French army during the Seven Years' War. Baron de Kalb could speak English, whereas Lafayette's knowledge of the tongue was limited.

They were not the only individuals seeking thrills in battle. Silas Deane wrote to Congress that the idea seemed to be the rage, and that he had received all kinds of proposals to enter the Continental army. The American diplomat stated that the French government had even forbade the discussion of the cause in French cafes. But Deane was impressed with de Kalb and thought that he would make an excellent officer if he could be transported back to the States in secrecy.

Matters moved slowly and de Kalb became very dejected. Finally, he suggested to Lafayette that they work together. To do this, it was suggested that Lafayette clandestinely purchase a boat and supplies with funds from his wealthy inheritance. Things were so touchy in Paris that Lafayette didn't dare contact Benjamin Franklin; he contacted the secretary of the American Commissioners instead.

During the waiting spell, he visited his uncle in London, who was the present French Ambassador to the Court of Saint James. During his three weeks in the British capital, he was shown around the "high spots" and was even presented to King George III himself! The nineteen-year-old could have taken this opportunity to spy out British shipping and other war preparations, but he felt that it would not be ethical at that time.

Back in France, he affixed his signature to the contract presented to him by Mr. Deane about his serving with the American army along with his personal aides. He was promised the rank of Major General and inked his contract exactly 165 years before the Japanese attack on Pearl Harbor.

The opposition from his family and friends had not abated, so he decided that he would have to leave his pregnant young wife and wee daughter without saying good-bye. The French officials would surely have arrested and placed him under orders of the king, as he was forbidden to set off on a wild-goose chase that could embarrass the nation and blacken his name.

The situation shifted momentarily to England, where it was learned that Comte de Banklay, marechal-de-camp in the army of the French king, had arrived in London and asked the British king to allow him to serve under General Howe with forces fighting the rabble in America. Even though this was rejected by Lord George Germain, it must have taken a little edge off the situation back in France for other adventurers.

Lafayette, having reached Bordeaux in the company of Baron de Kalb, discovered that the court knew where he was and the king might order his arrest. They slipped out of that city and headed for the Spanish coast, where they put into a little port on the Bay of Biscay, close to the French border. When Lafayette went ashore, he found out that two officers had been sent after him to demand his return, and they were carrying letters from his family and friends, which insisted that he give up his foolish journey. As time went by, the French government unofficially lessened their pressure on the expedition, and on Sunday, April 20, 1777, they embarked for America.

The trip took 54 days, and the force landed near Georgetown in South Carolina on June 13. He was delighted by the warm reception he received in the South and made his way toward Philadelphia with high expectations of how he would be accepted in the American capital.

He presented his papers to the Congress, but much to his surprise, they were not eager to recognize the agreement he had signed with Deane back in Paris. The Americans had seen many officers ship over and demand positions of honor with high wages for their gamble in the cause of the Americans. They figured that Lafayette was another glory-seeker on their doorsteps again, and so they were cool to the Frenchman, de Kalb, and the party of minor officers.

A member of Congress was appointed to meet them. He emphasized the point that they had asked Deane to send engineers to help in Washington's war, but they had not asked him to send boys to fight in a man's conflict. The Congressman said, "It seems that French officers have a great fancy to enter our service without being invited. It is true we were in need of officers last year, but now we have experienced men and plenty of them."

Lafayette retorted, "This is more like a dismissal than a welcome." After he calmed down he continued, "After the sacrifices that I have made in this cause, I have the right to ask two favors at your hands: the one is, to serve without pay, at my own expense; and the other, that I be allowed to serve at first as a volunteer." At this very time the Paris government handed the American Commissioners in Paris a letter insisting that Lafayette not be accepted into American service, but it arrived long after he had taken the field under Washington.

Lafayette's initial impression of the American army is an interesting one. The newcomer said:

> About eleven thousand men rather poorly armed, and worse clad, present a singular appearance. In the midst of a great variety of clothing, sometimes even of nakedness, the best garments were a sort of hunting-shirts, loose jackets made of gray linen, very common in Carolina. As for their tactics, it is enough to say that when in the line of battle it became necessary for a regiment to assume a position to the right without breaking ranks, instead of filing simply to the right, the left began a never-ending countermarch. They were always drawn up in two ranks, the small men in the front; but with this exception there were no distinctions made as to size. In spite of these disadvantages, however, they were fine soldiers and led by zealous officers. Bravery took the place with them of science, and every day improved their experience and their discipline.

Lafayette first served at Brandywine and Gloucester, impressing Washington with his energy and skill. Gradually, he rose to a place of prominence in the ranks and in the heart of the commander in chief, who almost looked upon him as a son. While other foreign officers made light of the American fighting forces and ridiculed their manners and customs, he stood up for his new friends. Near the end of the war, he was given his own command in Virginia and did remarkably well with his small body of men, who stayed out of the clutches of the enemy while proving to be a thorn in the flesh at the same time. The Frenchman was at the battle of Yorktown, and for many years he retained his love for the new country, often writing to the many acquaintances he had in the United States and making suggestions with a view of making it a broader haven for those seeking liberty.

The rebel forces had to turn away glory-seeking recruits, but the English were searching around for men to fill their ranks. The army that had once boasted it could crush the rebellion, by having only 5,000 trusty men march across the expanse of the colonies (while the riffraff ran for cover), was having troubles with 300,000 men in the field. It turned to foreign countries to fill the gap.

The British first turned to Catherine the Great of Russia. The king decided that he would ask her for 20,000 men to help crush the rebellion. The Earl of Suffolk said with glee, "I have been thinking about these 20,000 Russians. They will be charming visitors at New York and civilise that part of America wonderfully." She rudely turned down the English monarch, so George III had to look around for other warm bodies to beef up his forces.

This step was bound to arouse the population in the newly declared free nation. One author has even gone as far to say that this "foolhardy" policy of the English government sealed the case for independence in the colonies. Before that, many of the people were undecided as to whether they should throw their weight behind the radicals or seek reconciliation with London. Joseph Shippen said that "whatever Objections we & thousands of others may have to Independence, it appears to me, beyond a doubt, that a public Declaration of it will be made as soon as it is fully ascertained that a large Army of Foreigners has been taken into British pay to be employed against the Colonies."

The patriotic press had fun with the idea that the British were on the lookout for healthy specimens to bolster the army of the greatest and strongest fighting force in the world. In this spirit, a notice from London appeared in the *Freeman's Journal* in Portsmouth, New Hampshire, on March 22, 1777: "His Majesty intends to open this year's campaign with 90,000 Hessians, Tories, Negroes, Japanese, Moors, Eskimoes, Persian archers, Laplanders, Fiji Islanders and light horse. . . . He is resolved to terminate this unnatural war next summer . . . for heaven's sake ye poor deluded, misguided, bewildered, cajoled and bamboozled Whigs! ye dumb-founded, infatuated, back-bestridden, nose-led-about, priest-ridden, demagogue-be-shackled and Congress-becrafted independents, fly, fly oh fly for protection to the royal standard, or ye will be swept from the face of the earth with the besom of destruction, and cannonaded into nullities and nonentities, and no mortal can tell into what other kind of guiddities and quoddities."

A historian points out that the British never had mercenary armies in their distant past. As rumors spread in England, men started to speak out against the hiring of men of different nations. Captain Luttrell said that the hiring of the Hessians would cause five times the number to enlist in the army of Washington, and that the Germans would flee as soon as they set foot on American soil and turn against their officers. Chatham in the House of Lords attacked the use of "mercenary sons of rapine and plunder, devoting them and their possessions to the rapacity of hireling cruelty! If I were an American, as I am an Englishman, while there was a foreign troop in my country, I would never lay down my arms, never! never! never!" Even Frederick the Great said that any of these men who marched through his dominions to fight against the rebels would have to pay the usual cattle tax!

King George III was worried whether or not he would be successful, as he had written Lord North that "the laws of Germany are very strong against foreign recruiting." The instructions given to recruiter Colonel Faucitt were as follows: "Your point is to get as many as you can: I owe to you my own hopes are not very sanguine in the business you are going upon: therefore, the less you act ministerially (in dealing with the princes of Hesse Cassel and Brunswick) before you see a reasonable prospect of succeeding, the better. Get as many men as you can; it will be much to your credit to procure the most moderate terms, though expense is not so much the object in the present emergency as in ordinary cases. Great activity is necessary, as the King is extremely anxious; and you are to send one or two messengers from each place, Brunswick and Cassel, the moment you know whether troops can be procured or not, without waiting for the proposals of terms."

There was a good deal of jockeying over the terms, but the Germans had the king in a difficult position, as his heart was set on getting these mercenaries, no matter what the complete cost would be. He was asked to pay sixty German dollars for each man, but this fee was cut in half. Every soldier who was killed was to be paid for at a rate of levy-money, and three men wounded in action would count for one who lost his life for the British crown. The annual subsidy was figured at 64,500 German crown from the date the contract was signed, and double that price was to be paid for two years after the return of the troops to their own country.

The Earl of Shelburne commented, "Britain was able to raise an army of 300,00 men [in the Seven Years' War]; now she cannot find 50,000 soldiers." The British citizens didn't wish to fight their American brothers. King George III turned to his brother-in-law, Prince of Brunswick-Leneburg, who agreed to sell 4,300 men for £160,000. One other prince provided 20,000 mercenaries, almost 10 percent of the population of his province, for £3,000,000. The total amount of men shipped to America to fight totaled 30,000 Germans, which cost the British Government £3,000,000.

These poor Hessians faced many inconveniences. They were made fun of by the British, and occasionally clashed with their "employers" over petty differences. The English liked to blame them for any defeat and seldom gave them much praise at the time of victory. They were hated by the settlers because of their cruelty to prisoners and their desecration of churches; they even killed rebel pastors on occasion.

These men were excellent soldiers and struck fear into the hearts of rebel troops, as they rarely gave or asked for quarter. The first important victory for them was when they played the key part in the taking of Fort Washington. The fort's name was changed to Fort Knyphausen in honor of their leader. But in Trenton, they were beaten by Washington's gallant troops, who marched through a violent snowstorm to take the Hessians by surprise and defeat them. A Hessian court-martial convicted a dead man for this setback and the English criticized them instead of praising George generously. Washington's brilliant plan worked faultlessly, winning for him a stunning victory, just when many of his soldiers were about to leave the army as their enlistments had ended. Now they rejoiced in the cause of American liberty and stood firmly behind the man from Virginia.

After the Germans arrived in the New World, the Yankees decided to use a little bit of propaganda on them. Franklin instigated the plan to entice these homesick soldiers into deserting, and it was quickly translated into their mother tongue. Part of this booklet read, "Therefore that these states will receive all such foreigners who shall leave the armies of Britannic Majesty in America shall chuse to become members of any of these states; that they shall be protected in the free exercise of their respective religions, and be invested with the rights, privileges and immunities of natives, as established by the laws of these states; and, moreover, that this Congress will provide, for every such person, 50 acres of unappropriated lands in some of these states, to be held by him and his heirs in absolute property."

The Hessians were quite surprised by the religious atmosphere in the colonies. Even though they were housed in churches under the directions of the British, they noted that evangelical pastors often stood in the road with several of their believers and greeted them as they passed by. They were also surprised by the strength of the Baptists and the fact that this denomination did not baptize infants. But they were generally backwards. On a hot August day in New York City, early in the war, the Hessians and British tried to burn four rebel leaders in effigy. One was Rev. John Witherspoon, President of Princeton, and Generals Israel Putnam, Charles Lee, and George Washington. But when they were in the middle of their fun, a thunderstorm spoiled their gaiety, and they dashed for cover. They were badly shaken when they found that three of the figures burned completely, but Washington's remained intact, which served to "cause a great deal of fear among the Hessian troops, most of whom are very superstitious."

In their relationship with the people of America, the Hessians met a mixed reaction. Some colonists handed bread to Hessian prisoners of war, as they were marched through Pennsylvania after their defeat at Trenton. Others "screamed fearfully and wanted to choke us because we had come to America to deprive them of their liberty." Their band was detained in Philadelphia while the rest trudged off to camps for safekeeping. This musical unit delighted the citizens of the capital and even played rousing tunes for the first celebration of the Declaration of Independence on July 4, 1777, the first anniversary of that great document.

The Germans seemed to like the New World. Of the 30,000 men who shipped over to the States, 12,000 (or 40 percent) never returned to Germany! A goodly number settled in the rich farming country of the border areas and began a new life under liberty, instead of returning to Europe to suffer under some two-bit dictator.

The British not only had lads to do their dirty work, but they faced an old foe when the French began to think seriously of joining the Americans to break the shackles of London. At first, the French were skeptical of the ability of the rebels to make a success of their revolution. Even though they sent two private French citizens to work out an agreement to allow America to purchase munitions and powder, which was to be paid for by exports of farm produce, the king was far from convinced. Other diplomats sensed that the wave of the future in both North and South America would be a series of revolutions against European control, so Britain would lose the colonies eventually; but when should France commit herself?

The French wanted the Spanish to come in with them. They said that the English, when they lost the colonies, would probably eye French and Spanish possessions in the New World, wishing to recoup their losses. If Spain didn't form a block with France and the people under the American Congress, she would be the loser.

France moved slowly, as she did not want to be dragged into a conflict that would pull her down the drain. The Americans had been using her ports for sneak attacks on British vessels, but the French put a stop to that. They realized that there would probably be no reconciliation between the two parties, but open support was frowned upon. The budding nation in North America was not anxious for French troops, but they begged continually for more money, which bothered politicians in Paris. By the end of the war, the French endowment totaled $8,167,500, and Spain chipped in another $611,328 to grease the military wheels of Washington's forces.

The battle of Saratoga convinced various European nations that they should take the military power of the rabble seriously. The Franco-American forces, openly allied on July 23,

1777, put the British in a difficult position. The English envisioned a defensive conflict at that time.

Some have argued that the Americans might have won their independence more quickly if she hadn't made an alliance with the ancient foes of London, as this move played into the hands of the hawks in Great Britain. Gradually the King of England gained confidence that his forces would be masters of the situation. He even supposed that the French would have difficulties with the freezing temperatures of America; thus, they would be helpless before his royal troops. But French troops had already fought in Canada and other parts of the colonies during the French and Indian War without giving in to the elements. Anyway, the British quickly bottled up the French fleet in Brest, and so, for another three and a half years, it was of little help to America.

The man who was to lead the French ground forces into battle was affectionately known as "Papa" Rochambeau. He had studied for the Catholic priesthood, but turned to the army when he was young, fighting in most of the famous battles of his day. De Grasse, who was to bring the fleet north from the South Atlantic to take part in the seige of Yorktown, had been trained in a Jesuit seminary and a military school. where he learned how to fight the foe who lived across the English Channel.

When the French forces arrived in the colonies, they were not welcomed with open arms. In Boston, on September 17, 1778, there was a riot against the French and a number of them were killed and wounded in the uprising. There was skepticism about Europeans in general, and the French in particular. What if she should decide to try to take over the colonies by a coup of some sort? She was also likely to try to dominate the young nation once freedom was achieved.

Washington felt that the three kinds of foreigners in his service were the "mere adventurers, men of great ambition who would sacrifice everything to promote their own personal glory, or mere spies." It took him quite a while to change his views and this was done mainly through Lafayette who stood up for his new friends while French officers laughed at their clothing and their customs. Men like Von Steuben, Baron de Kalb, and Lafayette worked without thanks for a cause they believed was just.

Rochambeau acknowledged that his troops were not invincible when he said, "There are no troops so easily beaten when they have once lost confidence in their leaders." The first joint venture was at Newport, Rhode Island, when four thousand Frenchmen came ashore to link up with American boys. New England was supposed to add additional troops from their local militia, but they arrived too late. By that time, the British forces had put to sea with plans of bottling up the allies. D'estaing had to reembark with his French comrades and head out of port to meet the English sailing up from New York. A severe storm scattered both navies and the French admiral moved into Boston for repairs. Both Washington and the French government refused to send reinforcements, which the French commander had requested.

For over three years, the allies had been making wonderful plans on paper but none brought about a brilliant victory. According to the agreement between the two major powers, the officers were under the command of Washington, and Rochambeau did not try to assert himself in this situation. Washington was chiefly interested in utilizing the power of the French navy, but when he urged one officer to hurry into battle, the "frog" dragged his fleet. As the French had a healthy fear of the British navy, they often hinted that they might flee a scene of action.

Paris was perturbed by the inaction of the Americans. While American diplomats kept dipping their hands into the French treasury, the forces under Washington were so small that he could not use them in a big counteroffensive. It was not until Yorktown that the French could do much in the field themselves.

The Battle of Yorktown is considered in more detail in another portion of this book, showing that the part the French played in the final chapter of the war was very important. Some have even hinted that Rochambeau was the brains behind the brilliant moves that bottled up Cornwallis at Yorktown. The great naval victory off the coast under de Grasse and his willingness to take orders from Washington helped the allies to work in a unison that was hitherto absent. The future lover of Marie Antoinette admitted that the Americans had done even better than his own comrades in the skirmishes before the surrender. Washington and his aides saw to it that the British naval officers gave up their arms to the French, thus acknowledging the part these men had played in the final scene in Virginia. There were enough honors to go around, and both countries could each admire the courage of the other, and of the enemy as well.

XVI BROTHER EYES BROTHER

When Fieldmarshal Viscount Montgomery of El Alamein was asked who he called the greatest general of all times, he answered without hesitance: "Moses. He trained his soldiers for forty years in the desert. He trained his people, he trained his spies."

KURT SINGER

It was natural that the revolutionary men of the cloth turned to the life of Moses and the children of Israel as their examples for the future. Already, the Puritans quoted Old Testament verses to show that they were wanderers like the tribes of Jehovah, and they were looking over Jordan to their new home—America.

We find quite an unlikely name in the great hall of fame in Heb. 11:31. "By faith the harlot Rahab perished not with them that believed not, when she had received the spies with peace." The only reason it is considered unlikely is because present-day Christians would hardly be seen with the dregs of society unless they were to cross into the forbidden areas of the slums to smile at the drunks, junkies, and down-and-outers. They forget that Jesus Christ rubbed elbows with wine-bibbers and sinners to bring them salvation—"For all have sinned and come short of the glory of God." Salvation was only for those who would accept Christ as their own personal savior, and so the tax collector found salvation while the rich man went away sorrowing. Kurt Singer credits Rahab with being the first female spy in history.

Cromwell spent £70,000 pounds a year on espionage. Karl Schulmeister, Napoleon's daring spy, was the son of an unattached Lutheran minister. Delilah milked Samson of his secret power and betrayed him to his enemies. Theodore White tells us, "Sometimes the [LBJ] White House would have the advance text of a Goldwater speech, even in Spanish, before he could read it off the teleprompter himself." Even George Washington was accused of being a French spy during the French and Indian War.[1]

The Revolution was a unique war in the fact that anyone could be your friend one day and your enemy the next. Soldiers deserted their units or simply went home for the spring plowing or fall harvest. Many individuals felt no pangs of guilt, but a Quaker rejoiced that she could spy for the Americans and still not tell lies to her enemies.

The name of one spy is probably remembered by every schoolboy in America. His name is Nathan Hale. He may have been a hero and left a message for all at his passing, but he was a dismal failure.

Washington had just lost the Battle of Long Island, and he needed information about the enemy. He asked Lieut. Col. Thomas Knowlton to find a volunteer, because you can't very well order someone to risk his neck in a spying operation.

Knowlton looked up an old friend from the French and Indian War days but was turned down.

Knowlton's Rangers were then called together to see if one officer would volunteer to slip into British lines to be an agent. Every man in the room turned him down, but Capt. Nathan Hale said that he'd take the chance, even though he had been ill.

Hale was now a member of Webb's Connecticut Regiment, but a short time before that he was a teacher at Haddam in the same state. He shifted to Knowlton's Rangers after entering the service, but few would have chosen him for this difficult task.

The "James Bond" type of character is just the opposite of what a real spy would look like. A spy should blend in with the scenery and be so common that no one will think that he has the brains to do such important work. Hale was a strong, athletic type, but worst of all, his face had been scarred by exploding powder when he was young, and that feature alone would make his work very touchy. Then, too, he had a cousin who was a Loyalist and serving with the British at that very moment. Because he had volunteered before a group of men, it was likely that news would slip out about his new assignment. Hale was given no code, secret ink, nor any link with friendly forces.

Nathan posed as a teacher looking for a school. He carried his Yale diploma and set out abroad a schooner and was dropped at Huntington, Long Island. For a week he pushed on toward the British lines as Washington retreated. With the military situation getting worse, he would have a hard time getting back to friendly territory.

On the evening of September 21, he was caught. The captain of the British ship *Halifax* went ashore, and in the darkness, Nathan probably thought he was from a friendly vessel. Men from the ship helped seize the spy and he was taken before General Howe. There Hale readily admitted that he was an American officer and gave testimony to his belief in the cause of liberty. Instead of giving him a trial, he was hastily condemned to death and the time was set for his execution.

Nathan's brother Enoch was a clergyman. Nathan was also a very religious man. Even though Hale had no fear of death, he asked the British to send him a pastor that he could talk with before his end. This was denied. Next, he asked for a Bible to read during his last hours on earth. Again he received a negative reply.

In a few more minutes he was summoned to the gallows. Even though there were very few people present, a number of them have left a testimony to his courage in the face of death. His last dying words are memorized by many school children: "I only regret that I have but one life to lose for my country."

Farther to the north, a jack-of-all-trades may have been thinking about his first adventure as a spy, calling the Americans to resist the British, who were then on the march. His name is also well known—Paul Revere. Like churches at a later date, the houses of worship in Boston were used to help alert the patriots to the movements of the enemy.

Revere lived a couple of houses away from Maj. John Pitcairn, the British officer, who would be second in command on the march to Lexington. At the time, John Hancock and Samuel Adams were staying in the parsonage in the same town with Rev. Jonas Clark, whose wife was a cousin of Hancocks. If there was trouble and they were caught in the area, they'd not be handled gently. Revere's midnight ride historically outshines the ride of William Dawes; however, the mission of each was predicated on the possibility that the other might not make it through in time to warn the colonists, particularly Hancock and Adams.

Colonel Conant would be waiting for the signal from the Old North Church too. There were two lanterns stored at the church and the patriot rushed to find the sexton as soon as he heard the news that the lobsterbacks were planning an outing in the country the very next morning. He found Robert Newman and they headed to get the key from the vestryman, and then Robert climbed to the top of the belfry and lit the lanterns.

While Paul Revere hurried off with the news, the British officers moved in. They grilled Newman, who had slipped out the window after sleeping in the next room earlier in the evening. As they had seen him go to his room, they only could assume they were badgering an innocent man.

Revere borrowed a fast stallion and was off and winging across the open fields through towns and villages to alarm the land. They made it safely into Lexington, but when he left that famous hamlet for Concord with Dr. Samuel Prescott and Dawes, a surprise was waiting for them. They were stopped by British officers who grabbed Revere while the others got away. Not aware of Revere's purpose, the British simply took his horse, and he repaired to Lexington where he found Hancock still unaware of the presence of British soldiers. Revere helped hide Hancock's papers, and then they heard the ringing of the church bells that warned of the movement of the main body in the vicinity.

It is surprising that Revere and his companions weren't arrested long before this. One of the members of their spy ring was a Tory. This man was regarded as such a staunch rebel that they had even elected him to the Massachusetts Provincial Congress, which was making plans for a defensive war. This prominent person was Dr. Benjamin Church.

This noteworthy gentleman swore on the Bible that he would keep all the secrets of the rebel leaders to himself, and they had little reason to doubt him. In 1768, he implied that use of force by one party against another would break an existing contract and make it null and void. He wrote, "Breach of trust in a governor, or attempting to enlarge a limited power, effectually absolves subjects from every bond of covenant and peace; the crimes acted by a king against the people are the highest treason AGAINST THE HIGHEST

LAW AMONG MEN. . . . When rulers become tyrants, they cease to be kings." But this man sold his own soul to the same tyrant.

He rose to such prominence that he was appointed to the First Continental Congress and was also made the chief physician of the American army around Boston. For some vague reason, he began a questionable type of correspondence with General Gage, and he was discovered because a secret letter came into the hands of Henry Ward of Rhode Island.

The story of this twisting path to discovery reads like a work of fiction. A baker named Godfrey Wenwood brought the strange looking letter to General Greene, who handed it over to General Washington with a tale of how it had come into his possession.

It seems that Mr. Wenwood had been quite a man with the women in the Cambridge area, even though he settled on one likely female in his home town of Newport. His former girl friend turned up at his bakery with this very letter and a request. She asked her former beau to introduce her to Sir James Wallace, who was commanding the H.M.S. *Rose*, then stationed in Newport harbor.

He scratched his head in disbelief. Why had she suddenly turned up on his doorstep with a letter in her hand, desiring to get in touch with an enemy naval officer, whom he did not know personally? While he shuffled his feet, she said that if he didn't know the British captain, could he introduce her to Mr. Charles Dudley? He stared at her in disbelief. Mr. Dudley was the Royal Collector of Customs! Without batting an eye, she came up with a third name to liven up the conversation. How about Mr. George Rome? Surely he must know this prominent shipowner and merchant. He couldn't believe his ears—Mr. Rome was an arch Tory who helped support the British garrison bottled up in Boston.

She might not have been too bright, but he was using his brain. He suggested that she leave the letter with him. She probably thought that she had performed her duty and left.

The baker didn't open the letter addressed to a staff officer on General Gage's staff. He figured the best thing would be to contact a schoolmaster who would know what to do with the missile, and he knew this patriot could be trusted.

The friendly teacher, Mr. Adam Maxwell, did not wait one minute but broke open the seal to see what was inside. Neatly tucked in the envelope was a mysterious letter all in cipher. They decided it was best to hide the letter because they surely didn't want to aid the enemy.

Two months went by and then Wenwood received another letter from the same girl. She wanted to know why the letter had not reached its destination. How could she know? She also begged him to come to see her, as a third person wished to make his acquaintance.

Maxwell and Wenwood took the old letter out of its hiding place and went straight to Henry Ward, who was the secretary of the Rhode Island colony. Ward told them that they should deliver it to Gen. Nathanael Green, who was commanding that state's soldiers. Once Washington had seen Greene's interesting letter, he ordered the girl arrested and Gen. Israel Putnam brought her over for questioning.

They grilled her without results. It was evident that she had been carrying a time bomb all this time without any awareness that she was in danger. The only information she could give of any importance was the surprising news that Dr. Church had asked her to deliver the message to certain people in Newport. She surely could trust this staunch patriot.

General Washington quickly made his way to see the doctor. Dr. Church remained calm as he said that he was simply sending on a letter, which had been given to him by a friend. The general glared at him—after all, didn't Church know that he could send mail through the lines under a flag of truce like other American soldiers? The doctor wrung his hands, but would not admit to treason, although he did confess to being suspiciously discreet. As nothing was found among his papers to incriminate him, Washington could only put him under house arrest.

The letter was handed over to Rev. Samuel West and Col.

Elisha Porter, who would work along with Elbridge Gerry. The two different groups worked at deciphering the message and they both came up with identical papers. It was evident that Dr. Church had passed on information about the strength of American forces and their supplies. When confronted with the evidence, he said that it was true he had written it, but he had deliberately blown up the figures to deceive the enemy. The top brass didn't believe his story.

Church's luck still held good. The Continental Congress had forgotten to draw up a law against spies. He could not be executed, only fined and given thirty-nine lashes. The next month the Congress plugged the gap in their laws, but he had escaped the noose. However, an angry mob attacked his home, and if he had not jumped out a window, the patriots would have strung him up. He was quickly recaptured and protected from further threats.

In 1780, he was exiled by Congress to an island in the West Indies and threatened with death if he should ever return to American soil. He sailed on a small schooner but it was lost at sea, and he was never heard of again. The king pensioned his family so they lived in comfort the rest of their lives. Historians surmise that the doctor sold out his country for hard cash.

The greatest shock of the Revolution was the high treason of Benedict Arnold and the death of Maj. John Andre. If Arnold's traitorous scheme had succeeded, West Point would have fallen with 3,000 men and all its equipment; indeed, the cause itself might have been lost.

Arnold, who was impressed by high society, was delighted that he could trace his ancestry back to his great-great-grandfather, who had been closely associated with Roger Williams. But his ancestors had come on hard times and his grandfather lost most of the family fortune. This meant that his father was simply apprenticed to a copper, living in poverty until he married the widow of his employer and lived nicely on his inherited fortune. The very next Sunday, his dad strutted down the aisle to a front pew, while people tittered as they could see his poor brother Oliver seated far to the rear.

The first son was named after his dad but passed away within a few months, so when the future general made his entrance into a comfortable world, he was promptly given the same moniker. Things went fine at first, but soon his father over-expanded his business and then tried to cheat his creditors. They lost the fine reputation they had built up as well as the fortune. The relatives on his mother's side looked the other way when they saw him coming down the street, and even he was ashamed to sit in church with his family because it was obvious that people gossiped about the scandal, even those in the same pew.

Arnold studied during the winter season in Canterbury under the tutelage of his mother's relative, Rev. James Cogswell. By now, his mother had taken over the leadership in the home, because her hubby was usually grogging in the local tavern.

His mother was a very religious woman. She wrote that Norwich had been hit by yellow fever and the entire family came down with the dread disease. It was evident that two of his sisters were past help, and she urged him, too, to be ready to meet his Maker. "My dear, God seems to be saying to all, 'Children, be ye also ready!' . . . My dear, fly to Christ! If you don't know the way, tell Him. He is the way; He only is the door. Plead for the guidance of the Holy Spirit to guide you to that only shelter from death eternal, for death temporal we must all try sooner or later . . . God may mete you with this disease wherever you be, for it is His servant, but I would not have you come home for fear it should be presumption. My love to you—beg you will write us. I have sent you one pound of chocolate."

Like many a young woman of her time, she saw the darkness of life. Her message to her twelve-year-old son rang true, as she had lost her first husband and seven of her children. Only Hannah and Benedict remained. He heard the same message from the Reverend Mr. Cogswell in both the classroom and from the pulpit each Sunday.

In his eighteenth year, his mother went to her reward, although his father was still around to cast a shadow of shame over his only son. Soon afterwards, his dad was arrested for drunkenness and he then went completely down hill. Less than a year later, the homestead was sold to creditors and Arnold's dad stepped off into eternity.

Shortly afterwards, the town was struck by a terrible thunderstorm and many of the inhabitants fell on their knees in terror. But in Lathrops' shop, Arnold jumped up on the counter and cheered each thunderclap while he swore a blue streak and ridiculed the God his sweet mother had loved so dearly.

He continued to work hard at the apothecary shop and soon he was doing so well that the Lathrops gave him £500 to establish his own shop in New Haven. He then went to London on his first trip abroad to buy goods to stock his new enterprise.

Arnold swept New Haven off its feet when he returned, as he set up shop near the waterfront with a nice new sign telling the buying people who he was and what he had for sale. Living high off the hog, he soon had ten horses and a like number of servants to do his bidding. But within two years, he was sued by his creditors and imprisoned for six weeks. Only because an act for the relief of debtors was passed in May, 1763, which enabled one to settle his bills for a small amount of cash, was he set free.

In a few months, Arnold was on the rise again. He purchased back the old home his dad had lost and moved in with his younger sister to keep house. But ever restless, he was out to earn a fortune and the world's respect at the same time, so once again he sold the homestead and moved to Norwich with Hannah. He sold drugs, expensive books, "neat watches," necklaces and earrings.

With success he could move about at will. Soon, he left the store in charge of a partner and bought ships, which he sailed all over the Atlantic from Canada to the Indies, to London and back again.

Having other worlds to conquer, he captured the heart of a young beauty named Margaret Mansfield, who was high society, just to his liking. He not only received her hand in marriage, but formed a partnership with her father, who took over the work behind the counter while Benedict Arnold sailed the high seas once more.

In no time, he was back in trouble again with the authorities. It seems that two of his sailors had informed on him to the customs officials, and he almost lost his ship. Next, a New York merchant jumped him for a debt that Arnold was sure had been settled at least eight years before.

Rumors were spreading about his contracting a rather shameful disease while in Jamaica, and that he had been drunk continuously. Even at home, Roger Sherman considered him "an irreligious and profane character." In Honduras, he dueled with a British trader, who had called him "a damned American without breeding." All the extra rumors were not very comforting to his new wife, who finally had a chance to see him once again.

She should have felt better, because he was now back on home soil, sharpening his sword and ready to take on the redcoats by himself. After the battle of Lexington, he dressed up his troops in New Haven by using his own funds, and they were the snappiest attired men in all the colonies. His private orders made him a colonel, and he was to take Fort Ticonderoga and come home a hero.

Arnold would have to divide the laurels. Even though the Massachusetts Committee of Safety had directed him north to capture the British fort, Connecticut had authorized Ethan Allen and Captain Mott to do the same thing. Allen and Arnold finally agreed to work together, although their temperaments were very different; and with only 83 men they took the fort without a shot being fired. The British commander, without his trousers, asked by whose authority he was supposed to hand over the installation, to which Allen replied, "In the name of the Great Jehovah and the Continental Congress!"

Arnold was finally getting the applause he enjoyed. He looked around for new places to challenge. Even though he didn't get along well with Allen, they both decided that Canada would fall like a ripe plum if Congress would let them attack across the border. Allen joined up with General Schuyler, while Arnold talked Washington into letting him attack through Maine to take Quebec. Writing his friends in Quebec for information, he gave the letter to an Indian whom he trusted but who was actually a British spy. Saint Johns fell and Montreal was soon to follow, but then the forces joined before the ancient fortress that had been Arnold's goal. In a gallant attack, Gen. Richard Montgomery was killed and Arnold received a wound. Suddenly, the British decided to attack northern New York.

The gifted man from Connecticut was now given a new job—one that must have made him wince. He was to become Arnold the admiral, not on the high seas, but on Lake Champlain. His outnumbered fleet never had a chance, and some questioned his strategy of anchoring in a narrow channel between Valcour Island and the west bank of the lake, because it was twice as far from Ticonderoga as from the Canadian border; also, he had disobeyed the orders of Gates to stay at the American end. Mahan attacks these critics: "Never had any force, big or small, lived to better purpose, or died more gloriously. . . . That the Americans were strong enough to impose the capitulation of Saratoga was due to the invaluable year of delay secured to them by their little navy on Lake Champlain."

On the field of battle, America's hero could do no wrong. He was a fighting general and a daring admiral. But like many of his fellow officers, he was disturbed over his relationship with Congress. First, they were very slow in promoting him to the rank he and others felt he deserved. He based his wishes on seniority, but politics clouded his horizon. As long as the men sitting in Congress were deeply interested in their individual states, they were apt to show favor toward local flashes. Second, like many others, he felt cheated by the stingy government which was settled in Philadelphia. He had spent a sizable amount of cash in supplying his troops with necessities and he presented his bill to the colonial government. They carefully checked each item and quibbled about this and that. He felt his honor was being blackened by such action—they should accept his word by faith.

The British were now planning to make a three-pronged attack that would isolate New England and hopefully finish the rebellion. General Burgoyne was to have the main body, which would push down from the north, while a smaller force would hoof it through the Mohawk Valley to join up with other troops that would come from the south, all of them planning on meeting in Albany to celebrate. George III agreed that Howe must join Gentlemen Johnny to crush the American troops in eastern New York. St. Leger was defeated 110 miles from Albany at Fort Stanwix, and Howe declined to move up the Hudson. This meant that Arnold would be moving toward his old stomping grounds and his greatest glory—Saratoga.

Saratoga was a battle that changed the whole course of the war. It was Arnold's last grand entry on the stage of the glorious Revolution and from which everything would hence be on the downgrade. Gates and Arnold had a violent quarrel on the battlefield. Arnold insisted that Morgan's riflemen and Dearborn's light infantry be sent to check the movement by Burgoyne to turn the left flank. Arnold hit the center and split the forces of Burgoyne and Fraser, but Gates did not mention him in the battle report and withdrew him from the action.

After the battle of Freeman's Farm, Burgoyne was virtually surrounded. The climactic battle of Saratoga took place at Bemis Heights, when Gates's troops outnumbered the flashy Englishman's 11,000 to 5,000. Arnold was in disgrace and without command, but when the going got hot he charged across the battlefield and led some of General Paterson's and General Glover's men against the enemy and then when he saw that General Learned's men had appeared off to the left and were going to attack the British right, he dug in his spurs and took the lead of the latter's troops while they made a frontal attack on Lieutenant Colonel Breymann's position. At that point, his horse was shot from under him and he received a bullet in his leg, which was to finish his brilliant career as a fighting general under Washington. Burgoyne saw his star descending and surrendered his forces to the poorly clad rebels—sending shock waves around the world.

Injured in battle and on the sidelines, Arnold had a chance to think of a new mate as his first wife had passed away. Even though he had been engaged to Betsy De Blois, he had not seen her for over a year, and when he saw the charming Peggy Shippen, he broke off his engagement. Even though Peggy's dad was not very taken with the crippled rebel, his beautiful daughter was.

As commander of Philadelphia, he was having his troubles with the local politicians. This was in marked contrast to the offer from New York State, which wanted to show its gratitude to the hero—he was hoping that it would be a concrete proposal like "130,000 acres on the Mohawk." His enemies were striking out at him when he was down, and he could only find solace in the arms of the woman who would lead him into the enemy camp.

For a wedding gift, he purchased the most elegant place in that area and hoped to satisfy his Peggy with luxury, which would attract her attention. She loved the gaiety of Philadelphia when the British and Maj. John Andre occupied the city; and she had no desire to cramp her style under the stumble-bums. Rumors spread that Arnold had gone over to the enemy long before he gave it a thought, but Peggy was there now to keep after him, and he had time to think of turning Tory.

After all his troubles with Congress, local officials, and jealous generals, he said that he had become "ashamed of the human race." Once one can paint everyone else in the most evil colors, one can feel a little easier in the rationalization of one's own intentions.

Joseph Stansbury, a local crockery dealer, was the first person Arnold talked to about the feelings he had in his heart. When Stansbury reached New York, he was so nervous that he widened the plot by involving Rev. Jonathan Odell, who had been a British army officer before donning the garb of an Anglican minister; but now he worked for English intelligence.

Clinton was at first skeptical about Stansbury as he might be an American agent using Arnold's name to get information. Andre, under instructions from General Clinton, suggested that Arnold get an active command and allow his forces to be cut off from the main army, and he would be rewarded with a handsome amount of cash.

A year passed since Arnold and Peggy had decided to betray their country. In May of 1780, he began to plot in earnest, shifting all of his movable assets to London and rushing to Connecticut to sell his home. He urged the state to indemnify him and other soldiers for the depreciation of their salaries.

He continued his contact with Andre by using a code based on biblical names, and he raised his financial demands to £10,000 sterling. Clinton returned word that he would now like him to become commander of West Point, so that it might be taken for the king, but he said little about money.

Arnold in anger stated that he wanted to be guaranteed £10,000, no matter how the plot turned out, and an annual stipend of £500. If he helped turn over West Point, he would like £20,000, and he wanted an explicit answer. Clinton in return said that the latter figure would be alright if the stronghold was taken with 3,000 rebel prisoners and a large amount of equipment.

Now Arnold would have to work on Washington. When

he talked to the rebel leader, he was surprised when the general said that he thought Arnold could never be happy in such a quiet place as West Point. He suggested that the war hero be given a post of honor, such as leading the left wing of the Continental army. He was surprised when his guest looked depressed at the idea.

Washington must have felt pained when he saw his old friend limp away that day. Later, when he realized that Clinton had given up his expedition against Rhode Island, he decided to add a postscript to the general orders of August 3, 1780: "Major General Arnold will take command of the garrison at West Point."

Back in New York, General Clinton and his aide, Maj. John Andre, must have been delighted. After all of this, they must have felt a little uncertain about the rebel general. Now that he was going to command the great citadel on the Hudson, things were going well, and the young assistant must have dreamed about his part in striking the last blow of the long war.

John Andre was born on May 2, 1750, and was baptized in a French Protestant church in London two weeks later. His baptism was recorded in French, but he never gave the English any reason to fear he was not faithful to the cause of George III.

His schooling was entrusted to Rev. Thomas Newcomb. Since he was not rich enough to be a landed proprietor or pious enough to enter the ministry, the only decent thing left for him was to enter the army. Before his father died, he left orders that John would receive $100,000 in modern currency when he reached the age of twenty-one.

Andre was the exact opposite of Arnold when it came to philosophy. Benedict's blessed mother taught him that he needed to be saved and only the intervention of divine grace could redeem him. Andre's friends subscribed to optimistic humanitarianism, which held that men were naturally good. If men did not shine forth with a natural brightness, it was because they were taken up too much with the things of this world, but if they looked upon the good things of life, they would become outstanding individuals.

The poetic soldier with a taste for art was deeply disappointed after he purchased a first lieutenancy in the Seventh Foot for the Royal Fusiliers. Not only did he have no chance to glorify himself in battle, as peace prevailed, but his fellow officers were only interested in drinking, gambling, and wenching, whereas his own hobbies were music, art, and literature.

Andre's hopes for glory blossomed as unrest spread throughout the colonies. He was sent to America and then on to Canada, where he was captured when Saint John fell. During that time, it is said that he passed through Philadelphia, where he flirted with the future wife of Benedict Arnold.

When there was an exchange of prisoners, his heart leaped for joy. Now he proceeded to New York where he would take up his new post. Luckily for him, few of the limey officers could speak German fluently. He was just the right person to become General Howe's right hand man, and he was delighted at his advancement.

Many of his sympathizers painted the handsome young man as a gentle chap without any hatred in his heart for the forces under "Mr. or Major Washington," as he called him. But he took part in the Paoli Massacre and he was convinced that if a few more Yankees were stuck like pigs, they would surrender quickly.

The British government now recalled Sir William Howe to England, and along with him, General Grey, who had been Andre's immediate superior. The young social climber was worried about his new assignment, because he knew that Sir Henry Clinton despised Howe and any close relationship might work against him. But he soon became a favorite of his moody commander, and wrote the messages that were passed on to Arnold about the deal to sell America down the river—the Hudson river.

Soon, Major General Arnold was in full command at West Point. He waited anxiously for his beautiful wife to arrive.

The days were moving quickly and decisions had to be made. Arnold would have to arrange a rendezvous with Andre, so he asked a former Connecticut assemblyman, a Mr. Heron, to deliver a letter to the Reverend Mr. Odell when the gentleman from his home state visited New York to pay a debt. When he was out of sight, Heron opened the envelope and the contents seemed perfectly normal, involving speculation of some sort about money to be paid to a Mr. Stansbury; but he decided that it would be a patriotic gesture to turn it over to General Parsons, who might not like the commander dabbling in things like that.

Arnold did not know his message had not gotten through but guessed something was amiss when he received no reply. When Mary McCarthy, the wife of a captured Britisher, turned up with a pass from Governor Clinton, he asked her to deliver the letter for him in New York.

General Clinton did not like Arnold's suggestion that Andre sneak disguised into the American lines, because he did not want his beloved adjutant general to act like a spy, when his general line of duty was far removed from such wartime games. He was fearful that he would be caught and executed.

Arnold was living in a house confiscated from Col. Beverly Robinson, a Tory who was in New York. The plan now was for Robinson to come through the lines to negotiate about his home, which had been taken by the rebels. Arnold sent down the passes for the people who were to slip through the lines. As there was only one pass for one full-grown man to accompany Joshua Hett Smith, in whose home the treason was to be planned, and two servants who had come down to meet the British vessel, there was a discussion about whether Robinson or Andre should go.

As it was more important for Andre to meet Arnold, Clinton opted for his aide. Instead of meeting in no-man's-land, as Clinton suggested, John would go to the home of Mr. Smith, which was near the citadel, where he could talk comfortably with the turncoat. Smith's brother, William, was a Tory propagandist and a chief justice in New York City. Andre was to keep his uniform under a big coat.

When the two men met, they immediately got down to business. Arnold still had money on his mind and wanted the £10,000 indemnity, whether he was successful or not in turning over West Point to Clinton. Andre said that he could only offer £6,000, but gave in when he saw Benedict's emotions boil over. Next, Arnold handed him the plans of West Point, and they discussed details.

Andre hid in Smith's dwelling all day, expecting to be taken back down the river to meet the British ship that night as planned. But because of a brisk exchange between the vessel and a rebel battery, the other servants refused to row them down the Hudson again.

Smith said that Andre should change into civilian clothing armed with Arnold's pass, made out to a false name, and they would start toward the lines. A Black servant would accompany them. When they reached the area where the last rebel patrols were active, Smith said good-bye and headed back north.

As Andre neared Tarrytown, he was very relieved because he was far beyond the American checkpoints and nearing British lines. Just then he heard a shout and three ragged rebels barred his way. Even when he showed Arnold's pass for John Anderson, the name he was going under, they didn't look impressed. They demanded that he take off his clothing and be searched. He obliged and tried to remain lighthearted. Then one of them suggested that he take off his boots. They discovered some papers in the bottom of his stocking.

Only one of the soldiers could read, but what he saw made him start. "This," he cried, "is a spy!" The turned him around and marched north. All the time, he tried to impress upon them what trouble they would get into as he had the pass signed by Arnold.

The three captors delivered their prize spy to the American outpost at North Castle. Lieut. Col. John Jameson was the commander. After looking over the evidence placed before him, he made a decision. It was true, as the captive said, that Arnold had notified him that if a man named John Anderson appeared in his area from British lines, that he should be sent to West Point; but there was something strange about the valuable items in "Anderson's" possession.

Jameson decided to send the incriminating evidence on to General Washington, who was in the area; also, he sent a note to General Arnold that a man called Anderson had been taken prisoner and he seemed to have a legal pass from the commander—was it a fake one?

Back at the fort, they were making preparations for the arrival of Washington. If the papers in Arnold's handwriting caught up with the commander, then Arnold's doom was sealed. But if the other papers reached the traitor, he might escape.

On September 25, Washington and his party set out for an early breakfast with the Arnolds, but they stopped on the way to inspect some fortifications on the upper river. Meanwhile at the fort, Arnold sat at the breakfast table when two aides arrived to say that General Washington would be arriving in a short period of time, and that he would like to dine with Arnold and his lovely wife.

Just then, two more men burst in the door. They handed Arnold a dispatch from Jameson. He quickly opened it and gazed at the message intently. "I have sent Lieutenant Allen with a certain John Anderson taken going into New York. He had a passport signed in your name. He had a parcel of papers taken from under his stockings, which I think of a very dangerous tendency. The papers I have sent to General Washington."

Arnold turned on his heel and limped out the door. He commanded that his horse be saddled and ordered that his barge be ready to shove off. Those around him noticed that he seemed agitated.

Arnold quickly shuffled back to Peggy's bedroom. She was sitting up in bed smiling. He leaned over and whispered something in her ear—her smile faded. Arnold heard a knock on the door and listened as an aide's voice sounded through the door, "His Excellency is nigh at hand." Arnold moved toward the door and his wife fainted.

He almost knocked over the startled soldier. He yelled over his shoulder that he had to prepare the men to receive the commanding general and hopped on his horse and headed for his barge.

He ordered the barge to head for the *Vulture*. Once he was on deck, he announced dramatically that he was now a member of the British army, and that he was empowered to raise a Loyalist Brigade. He turned to the men who had brought him to safety and asked them to serve under him in the cause of the king.

None of the nine patriots moved to climb on board the British man-of-war. The coxswain exclaimed, "No, sir! One coat is enough for me to wear at a time." In a rage, Arnold now ordered each of them to be taken as prisoners of war.

Back at the house, Peggy was putting on the best act of her life. She screamed, moaned, and pulled at her hair. Hamilton and other officers tried to comfort her as they had no idea what had come over her.

It wasn't until mid-afternoon that the message caught up with George Washington. He casually opened the letters and his expression changed to surprise. Through ashen lips he blurted out, "Arnold has betrayed us! Whom can we trust now?"

Mrs. Arnold called for General Washington. When he appeared, she refused to believe that it was him. She screamed, "No, that is not General Washington! That is the man who is going to assist Colonel Varick in killing my child!"

John Andre had decided to stop pretending to be John Anderson. He picked up a piece of paper and wrote Washington a letter. He said that he had been forced to enter American lines by an unnamed military correspondent, against his very will, so he was thus a prisoner of war. He concluded that a prisoner of war had the right to attempt an escape wearing civilian clothing.

Five days later, John Andre walked into a little Dutch church that he had viewed from his cell window. Seated in front of him were the general officers of the American headquarters, all except Gen. George Washington. At this trial, he presented his reasons why he felt he should be considered a prisoner of war and not a spy. He did not realize that his testimony was contradicted by the letters of General Clinton to Arnold, which had been sent through the lines to Washington. The men listened closely to his every word, and then he walked slowly from the house of God while they pondered their decision.

When Andre was called back from his cell to face the board of generals, he was read the decision of the judges: "Major Andre, Adjutant General of the British Army, ought to be considered a spy from the enemy, and that, agreeable to the law and usage of nations, it is their opinion he ought to suffer death."

On the day after the trial, Gen. George Washington approved the sentence and ordered that "the execution of Major Andre take place tomorrow, at five o'clock, P.M."

He refused to be attended by a minister as he was a freethinker. He calmly allowed the noose to be placed around his neck, though he had asked to be shot like a gentleman. The executioner raised the whip and when it fell, the horses moved, pulling the wagon out from under the young man and "the world sprang out from beneath John Andre's feet."[2]

NOTES

1. Katherine and John Bakeless, *Spies of the Revolution* (New York and Philadelphia: J. B. Lippincott Company, 1962), p. 43.
2. James Thomas Flexner, *The Traitor and the Spy* (Boston and Toronto: Little, Brown and Company, 1953), p. 393.

XVII

THE ANTI-MILITARY ATTITUDES OF EARLY AMERICA

I would they were even cut off which trouble you. For, brethren, ye have been called unto liberty. . . .

These words formed the title of the sermon preached at the Boston West Church by Jonathan Mayhew on August 25, 1765. The Reverend Mr. Mayhew fortunately omitted the following clause, which read: "Only use not liberty for an occasion to the flesh, but by love serve one another."

It would be ten long years before the first guns would be fired in anger a few miles from this house of God, but the people were already up in arms about the Stamp Act, and news of the 117 sections of the statute had arrived in Boston almost three months before. On November 1, taxes up to £10 would have to be paid for prestamped paper, which would affect court documents, papers for clearing ships, newspapers, college diplomas, deeds for land and mortgages, as well as all bills of sale. It was evident that all of society was going to feel the firm hand of British rule, even as they went about their daily chores or sipped beverages in watering places that needed the stamp for their liquor licenses. A shadow hung over the city of less than 20,000, which would soon hear the marching feet of 3,000 soldiers sent to keep the peace and insure the free flow of money to the east.

Not long after the people heard this radical preacher and pamphleteer pronounce his bitterness in clear and concise terms, they took to the streets and attacked the houses of the Custom House officers, the register of the Admiralty, and the chief justice, who was their principal victim. Most of the mob consisted of individuals who made their living with their muscles, not their minds. Cordwainers, leather dressers, shipwrights, sailmakers, caulkers, ropemakers, a hatter and a housewright, as well as a distiller and even the local barber had fun in the streets. It was evident that the whole of society was very upset and willing to express their sentiments—and if necessary, press home the point—that they were not going to lose their liberty without a struggle of some sort.

The Reverend Mr. Mayhew rushed off an apologetic letter to Lieutenant Governor Hutchinson, but he shouldn't have worried so much about his role in the rioting. The mob had come to life on the evening of August 14, almost two weeks before Mayhew added fuel to the fire. In the 1740s, Boston saw three full-scale riots, so they were not the type of people to allow things to drift along without expressing themselves in deeds as well as words.

The repealing of the Stamp Act had very interesting consequences. The Boston Town Meeting on May 26, 1767, one year later, instructed its members to stand up for the total abolishment of slavery and to "move for a law, to prohibit the importation and purchasing of slaves for the future." Slaves began to take the issue to the courts and a spirit of freedom prevailed in Massachusetts, only to have the British government annul the act.

It was evident that the patriots controlled the situation. The mob was organized and turned off and on at will. The Sons of Liberty were not about to allow anarchy to reign and crowds only moved at their command. Governor Bernard was the typical politician who had to be friends with both sides to save his own shaky position. The commissioners who were to check ships for dutiable goods wanted the representative of the throne to apply for troops, but their plea fell on deaf ears.

They did the second best thing. They wrote to the homeland for aid and a frigate, two sloops, and two cutters were sent to help them control the situation. Commodore Samuel Hood arrived from Halifax with the H.M.S. *Romney*, its fifty guns prominently displayed for the patriots. Instead of staying out on Kings Road, it anchored uptown and moored very close to John Hancock's wharf. This was the first time England had brought military force to bear on the people of Boston.

For years, the British navy had been impressing seamen with her vessels, even though a sixty-year-old law forbade it in all the colonies. Three weeks after Hood's initial gunboat diplomacy, the town gathered to stop the impressment of Thomas Furlong, who was rescued as the crowd shouted insults and threatened to stone members who tried to take one of their citizens on board against his wishes. The commander ordered his crew to show their muscles by exercising the "great guns and small arms."

Poor Bernard was sitting on a powder keg and he knew it. He did not want to call for troops from England, because that would play into the hands of the radicals, as Sam Adams would call the Sons of Liberty to meet at "Liberty Hall," which was the area immediately under the Liberty Tree, and thousands would gather regardless of the weather conditions. From there they often marched the length of the town to show everyone that their group included some of the best men of the city. If the troops were needed to rescue the government, then that would prove the governor powerless and that the votes were "in the hands of the people of the Town."

During the Liberty riot, the crowd broke the windows of Inspector General Williams's home, so he left town for a nice, long vacation. But when he returned, the people threatened him once again, which might have provided Bernard with the excuse he needed; but when Williams faced the crowd of 1,500 people down from the balcony of the Town House, they simply allowed him to have his fun for a change and return home "in Peace & Quiet."

The commissioners sent Benjamin Hallowell to England with the news of the riot and how they had to move quickly to save their own lives. In less than two weeks Secretary of State (colonies) Hillsborough ordered the Sixty-fourth and Sixty-fifth Regiments in Ireland to immediately be transferred to Boston. Their instructions were explicit. They were to enforce "due Obedience to the Laws of this Kingdom . . ." and to see that the Bostonians were shaped up but fast.

The news spread about town quickly, though the Tories tried to keep a lid on it. The *Boston Gazette* carried a letter that expressed the sentiments of the townspeople. "Among a certain Set of People, Sir, I have observed that Mobs are represented as most hideous Things. I confess they ought not to be encouraged; but they have been sometimes useful. In a free Country I am afraid a standing Army rather occasions than prevents them."

The Quartering Act, which provided the royal governor with power to require the colonies to provide food, drink, quarters, fuel, and transportation for the king's men stationed in their towns or villages, had enough loopholes for the radicals to fight the governor every step of the way. The first thing they did was to call for a day of fasting and prayer.

Governor Bernard knew that he was in between the devil and the deep blue sea of humanity. As soon as the flotilla arrived off Boston, Bernard was boated out to Castle Island to tell Lieutenant Colonel Dalrymple that he was going to have problems with the council over quartering the troops. Penn had allowed quartering in his colony, but others believed that this would end true liberty of the masses. Dalrymple demanded that Bernard use his power to quarter them immediately.

General Gage soon arrived under the assumption that Bernard either had no power to get quarters or would not exercise the power he had because he wished to calm the feelings of his people. The civilians pointed out that Castle William was the place to quarter the troops, but the crown wanted the force settled in town to be a constant reminder of their power.

Private letters convinced Gage in New York that Boston was in danger of mob violence. Rumors spread by Samuel Adams hinted that 30,000 men would charge out of their villages and toss the king's men into the cold and salty sea. But when the troops marched through the city, all was completely calm. They were able to take 400 muskets that were on the floor of Faneuil Hall without a murmur from the patriots. The town was now disarmed except for personal weapons.

The war of nerves continued as Dalrymple demanded quarters for his troops in the very city itself. The act, made up by a civilian government, had been clear about one point—any officer who used "Menace of Compulsion" could be convicted before two justices of the peace and cashiered from service. He had to be very careful as the legal arm of the law might be under the control of the Adams boys. The officers rented quarters easily enough, but the troops had to live in tents until they moved to Faneuil Hall for temporary quarters.

The people of Boston immediately began to undermine the forces that came to show them who was boss. They urged the soldiers to desert, and within two weeks seventy soldiers had slipped out of Boston to the friendly countryside where farmers protected them from nosy Tory spies. Richard Ames, a private in the Fourteenth Regiment, was caught and executed before the rest of the redcoats, while the civilians watched in horror. If the army would kill one of their own, what would they do to the masses whose town they occupied?

Capt. John Wilson of the Fifty-ninth was in his cups when he met a group of Black slaves. He shouted, "Go home and cut your Masters Throats; I'll treat your masters, & come to me to the parade; & I will make you free; & if any person opposeth you, I will run my Sword throu' their Hearts." This kind of talk touched taut nerves, making the moderates question whether His Majesty's men came to stop violence or start it.

The same soldiers who would be turning churches into stables during the coming conflict were rubbing people the wrong way. The soldiers were lacking Bibles and proper books of devotion. On Sundays, they would play their band music outside church buildings, disturbing the services of God. Their antireligious nature disturbed Boston's God-fearing citizens.

Things were not only bubbling over in Boston, but also abroad. In London, the politicians were at play. They decided that something must be done to stop treason in the Massachusetts colony before it spread to other areas. On February 13, 1769, both Houses recommended to the king that a full investigation into sedition be made in Boston, and that those who were the worst offenders should be shipped back to jolly old England for trial under Henry VIII's treason act.

Bernard was hoping to leave for good and toss the time bomb in the lap of Mr. Hutchinson. But before he could leave the hostile climate of Boston, he was faced with another crisis not of his own making.

The navy was losing men through desertion. As they couldn't compete with the wages of merchant fleets, they had to find other means to fill their ranks. Commodore Hood ordered two of his ships to cruise between Cape Ann and Cape Cod to blockade the entrance of the bay and impress civilians in order to fill up the crews of his vessels.

The good ship *Rose* went about her business of trying to fill her normal complement of 120 officers and 24 marines. As she could only muster 89 naval persons and was lacking two marines, she set to work trying to get additional men. Exactly two months after the Parliament had suggested that George III get tough with rebel radicals, she set to sea under direct orders to blockade and impress civilian seamen for her use.

For one week she stopped ships to increase her numbers on board. The next day she sighted a ship and gave chase. To prove she meant business, she fired a shot over the bow of the civilian vessel, but as the ship did not acknowledge the warning, another shot was fired, and a twelve-pounder arched through the air to plop close enough to impress the captain with the message to cease resistance.

When she came within hailing distance, Caldwell shouted directions to the brig, which came under the lee of the *Rose's* starboard side. Quickly, a cutter carried Executive Officer Henry Panton, Midshipmen Stanhope, Porter Bowen, and seven seamen, including a Mr. Taynsford, who had recently been impressed himself. Captain Power of the brig allowed Panton to look over the ship's cargo, but the navy man seemed more interested in the list of men on board than what she carried below.

It was evident that Captain Power was not about to take directions from the intruder. As he would not order his men out, Panton turned to his men and shouted, "We must search for them." It was evident that the seamen were in hiding and Power was not going to offer any assistance to the Britishers.

Peering into the scuttle, they could see the rough outline of some men, but when they demanded that they come out of their hiding place, the Americans refused. As they gave every indication of resistance, he sent back the cutter to bring over more men to assist in taking the men captive against their will.

Panton tried to act calm as he asked the men to pass a candle around the scuttle so he could view what kind of place they were hiding in. One of the men moved the candle around the forespeak, but when he said that he wanted to climb down to have a closer look, a sailor named Pierce Fanning warned him that he had a musket and he would use it rather than be impressed into the royal navy.

Officer Panton ordered seaman James Sinclair to move in to take the men. The barrel of the musket poked out through the hole and Sinclair tried to pull it out of the forespeak. He pushed in a pistol loaded with powder only and pulled the trigger. The blast bloodied the lip of Michael Corbet, and he angrily screamed at Panton, "I'll kill the first man who tries to capture me!" Panton muttered, "If you kill anyone, you'll surely hang for it!" Panton then seated himself on a keg of salt near the opening.

Marine Private James Silley, who also tried to yank the rifle from the hands of the seaman, was standing by the side. Corbet grabbed a harpoon and thrust it out through the narrow opening. It struck the left side of Panton's throat who was sitting outside and the blood began to spurt from the jagged wound. Within a half hour the officer was dead.

Corbet and his two friends remained hidden. No sailor was anxious to try any heroics as the grisly scene proved that the American seamen meant business. The hours dragged on until Hugh Hill, a pal of the rebels, went down to talk them into surrendering. Corbet and the others blinked their eyes as they climbed out of their cramped quarters and were taken into custody.

Back in Boston, it was evident that things were getting sticky. The Whigs demanded a civilian trial, whereas the Tories wanted the guilty rebel hanged as high as Hamaan under the rules of the sea. Bernard's friends were members of a special court of the admiralty, which was set up to try offenders of "piracy, robbery, or felony on the sea."

"The statue of Henry," enacted during the eighth year of Henry VIII's reign (1536), stated that there should be a grand jury indictment and trial by jury just like an offense committed on land. At that time, England had no colonies, so in 1700, Parliament provided for a trial without jury of crimes on high seas. Commissioners sitting in the colony would pass judgment. Now it had to be decided which article should apply in this case.

The four Irish seamen were defended by John Adams and James Otis, the two top lawyers in Boston. It was evident that these radical lawyers would insist that the defendants were only defending themselves when they caused the death of the king's officer. The charge might be dropped to manslaughter, but this also was punishable by death. But the defendant, if he had a clean record, might plead "benefit of clergy" and thus escape capital punishment.

The authorities pushed for the immediate prosecution of Corbet. John Adams almost killed himself working night and day to prove that he should have a trial by jury. The Tories opposed a civilian jury, as it would be filled with farmers who would favor the rebels. Bernard was frightened by the tense atmosphere of Boston and decided to back Adams in his request for a normal trial. But Chief Justice Hutchinson juggled theories around to come to a decision that would please his Tory friends.

Hutchinson, who wore two hats, stepped in to twist the facts, as only a crafty chief justice can do, to fulfill the wishes of his own personal prejudices. He had to admit that if one read the 1717 statute literally, Otis and Adams were right; but the law also stated that the jury had to be filled with Englishmen or the criminals must be sent back to England for trial. Neither was possible in this case, Hutchinson decided.

The key to the case itself was whether or not the British boarded the vessel to check goods or to impress seamen. The confusing testimony on this point weakened the chances of the prosecution, no matter how prejudiced the Tory commissioners might be. Adams argued heatedly that impressment was illegal, thus his defendants should receive "an honorable Acquittal."

Suddenly the chief justice interrupted Adams's well-delivered plea and sent the judges out to deliberate the case. The judges returned with their verdict, "The Court have considered the evidence in support of the charge against you, and are unanimously of opinion that it amounts only to justifiable homicide; you are accordingly acquitted and discharged from your imprisonment."

Even in this tense atmosphere, Boston had been free of riots and sharp violence. Gage decided to send both the Sixty-fifth and the Sixty-fourth units to Halifax with one of the two remaining in the Castle and the other in Boston itself. The Sixty-fifth shipped out, but the day before four companies of the Sixty-fourth were to leave, Sam Adams pushed a unanimous vote through the House of Representatives which stated flatly that only those laws passed by the House would be binding on the people of Massachusetts. This sent General Mackay and Commodore Hood into a quick conference, and they decided to stay the order for the soldiers to leave Boston. Sam Adams, who had the representatives in the palm of his hand, suddenly decided that the recent legislation to resist British law might be altered after all. On July 4, the ships embarked, with four companies of men, for more friendly shores.

Three weeks later, two more vessels left the troubled port as Hood took the remaining companies of the Sixty-fourth and headed north toward Nova Scotia. This had reduced the forces by half and another sorry figure slipped on board the *Rippon*. Governor Bernard was leaving the colony for good, and the people cheered while flags flew and cannons saluted the victory of the radicals.

The soldiers who remained were not entirely happy. More deserted the king's forces and Gage worried about the loss. The general tried to keep the troops faithful by suggesting that the monarch would "Reward his Officers and Soldiers with the Estates of the Rebels." When Dalrymple sent out soldiers to recapture the deserters, the testy farmers refused to aid them in their search.

Those redcoats who remained in Hutchinson's haven had to be careful about what trouble they stepped into. In the warm days in the summer of 1769, a province statute that authorized triple damages for stolen goods was brought to bear on troops who took things from the citizen population. If they could not pay, they were to become indentured servants, which angered the Tories and troops a great deal. Other laws were passed to cramp the styles of the invading forces.

By February of 1770, it was clear even to the Loyalists that the soldiers had not brought real peace to the troubled town. The people were just as lawless as they had been before the unwelcome guests arrived. Even Gage knew that his men could not act on "Military Authority," and surely the civil authorities were not going to call for their aid. To send them home would seal the fate of Boston because complete control then would be in the hands of the liberty boys. To keep troops in Beantown would furnish all sorts of propaganda for the radicals.

On March 2, a soldier looking for off-duty-hours work came across a group of rope and cablemakers who were making ropewalks. The civilians asked the limey if he wanted to earn a fee. He nodded and the American sneered, "Then go and clean out my toilet!" Fists flew and the unarmed soldier had to flee the scene.

This was the first of many confrontations, which led to bloodshed. A rumor spread that a sergeant had been killed, which excited the lobsterbacks. On the evening of March 5, Thomas Preston was officer of the day, and Lieutenant Basset commanded the Main Guard. Private Hugh White was on guard at a small sentry box.

As the streets began to fill with hundreds of colonists, a church bell began to toll. Angry threats were shouted at White and snowballs arched through the air, forcing him to retreat to the Custom House where he loaded his gun and fixed his bayonet. A few blocks north, soldiers armed with bayonets, clubs and other weapons were seen by the citizens. It was evident that the Bostonians were not coming empty-handed either.

Preston was now faced with the decision of reinforcing White or trying to rescue the young lad and then take him off his beat until cooler heads prevailed. He finally called out six or seven men to assist the sentry. They fixed their bayonets, but their muskets remained unloaded. Henry Knox and some calmer sorts were trying to talk sense to both groups, but few were willing to listen.

Someone bellowed out, "Here comes Murray with the Riot Act." The reading of this act wasn't going to stop the mob now, as they pressed in close upon the soldiers. Some taunted the redcoats to open fire. By this time, their muskets were loaded, but the trembling troopers looked frightened as the townsmen moved closer. Some shouted at Preston, asking if the weapons were loaded and he replied in the positive.

A club was hurled through the air, and it struck a soldier, knocking him to earth. All along the line, bayonets flicked out at the mass of humanity. At the first shot, the crowd buckled and muskets banged away at will. Enranged Preston shouted at his troops to stop firing. He asked them why they had fired and they replied that they had heard him give the command.

In the street, men were covered with blood. A Black was the first to pass away, but four others were to fill the coffins that would be carried by a sad multitude to the cemetery for burial. They were buried in one large grave as the people from the immense procession wept. This was to become a memorial day that would be remembered for ages.

Men of all political persuasions rushed to the North End to inform Hutchinson of the massacre. When His Honor reached the scene, he stammered at Preston, "How came you to fire without orders from a civil magistrate?" The captain replied, "I was obliged to, to save my sentry."

Rumors were flying that men from the countryside were coming to town to revenge the deaths of their comrades, whose blood spotted the pure white snow. At a hastily arranged town meeting, the citizens demanded that Preston go on trial and that the British troops leave Boston proper. Hutchinson had to accept their requests or else bring on more angry confrontations. Tyler told the Loyalist, "The people of the best characters among us—men of estates and men of religion—have formed their plan to remove the troops out of the town and after that the commissioners."

Three hundred people, including John Adams, volunteered for nightly armed watches to keep the peace, and even the rebel lawyer could be seen walking up and down with a musket propped on his shoulder. The patriots suggested to Hutchinson that he activate the militia to keep order, but he could hardly explain to London why local troops should be used to watch over the activities of the king's loyal soldiers. The Sons of Liberty now controlled the situation and British officers could walk the street without fear. They even impressed a sailor for the *Rose* about two weeks after the massacre.

The next Lord's day after the killings, the Reverend Mr. Lathrop of Old North Church preached from Gen. 4:10: "The voice of thy brother's blood crieth unto me from the ground." Rev. Charles Chauncy tried to get one wounded man to sue Preston for damages but he refused. Attorney General Jonathan Sewall drew up the indictment: "Not having the Fear of God before their eyes, but being moved and seduced by the Instigation of the devil and their own wicked Hearts did with force and arms feloniously, willfully and of their malice aforethought assault one Crispus Attucks, then and there being in the peace of God and of the said Lord the King."

Hutchinson, who had been in such a hurry to bring Corbet to justice, now used his wiles to delay the starting of the trial. First, he refused to appoint temporary judges to fill the posts of Judges Cushing and Trowbridge, who were ill. Even at the end of May, Gage was hinting that "procrastination is our only course." Rev. Andrew Eliot expressed the thoughts of the moderates when he said, "People complain of the delay of justice. Perhaps it was best to delay the trial at first. The minds of men were too much inflamed to have given him [Preston] a common chance. But they are as calm now as they are like to be at all, and if judges have power to delay trials as long as they please, it certainly is in their power to say whether there shall be any trial at all."

Hutchinson's next move was to fix the court schedule to his liking. As only two judges attended the May 31 meeting, he could procrastinate some more. He refused to appoint a special judge until one of his own liking would be in charge of things. It would be the end of August at least before the men could be brought to trial.

It was rumored that the king was going to give the men a royal reprieve if there was a conviction. An alderman in London wrote to the radicals that this was both moral and religious and even good practical politics. Already the king had agreed to pay Preston's expenses himself, and in the end, he gave him an annual £200 pension for life!

In the middle of August, George Whitefield came to Boston to preach. Samuel Adams was so impressed that he said, "I hope to do by means of a political revolution what George Whitefield has done through a religious awakening." This was the evangelist's seventh trip to America, and he preached sixty hours a week, even though he had a very bad case of asthma. When people suggested he slow down he retorted, "I had rather wear out than rust out." He died on September 29, and many felt that because of his preaching, mob activity had dropped to a minimum.

Two weeks before this, the soldiers had finally been arraigned. When they replied, "not guilty," the clerk answered, "God send thee a good deliverance." Most of the Tories expected them to be defended by Loyalist lawyers, but radicals John Adams and Josiah Quincy stepped forward to aid the very men they had tried to keep from coming to Boston.

In choosing a jury, it seemed as though only the defense was allowed to challenge the selection of who would sit to hear the facts of the case. As they could not get enough men to fill the jury box, they had to collar spectators and "by means unknown" several men of Loyalist bias were seated. One of the men was heard to say that he "believed Captain Preston to be as innocent as the Child unborn and he would never convict him if he sat to all eternity." Seeing that Massachusetts required a unanimous verdict for convictions, we have to side with the ultraradical William Palfrey, who labeled it a packed jury.

The results then were a foregone conclusion. Preston and five others were acquitted, and two others pleaded clergy. Hutchinson had already given the judges orders to respite any conviction, but the two defendants who had pleaded clergy were burned on the hand for manslaughter—and they were then set free. These men smiled when they left confinement, but the feeling of the people of Boston was inflamed.

In annual orations for years afterwards, they would speak of the horrors of "THAT DREADFUL NIGHT" when Americans saw the "ground crimsoned with the gore of hundreds of fellow citizens." We have to agree with the historian who said, "Like no other incident before or since, the Boston Massacre permanently embedded the prejudice against standing armies into the American political tradition."

Whereas the colonists feared a standing army, they supported their militia. "The country towns, in general, have chosen their own officers and must exercise once a week at least—when the parson as well as the squire stands in the ranks with a firelock. In particular at Marblehead, they turn out three or four times a week, when Col. Lee as well as clergymen there are not ashamed to appear in the ranks, to be taught the manual exercises in particular."

Daniel Boorstin has said, "Since we are not a warlike people, we seem to have been afraid that studying wars would foster a bellicose spirit." But the ship that brought Puritan John Winthrop to America in 1630 had 28 guns on board. Even though they tried to get along peacefully with the Indians, they soon found out that they would have to arm themselves for defensive purposes. Then there was universal training in all of the colonies, except Pennsylvania, where the settlers lived in comfort, far from the threat of scalping parties, and felt no need to defend themselves. In most colonies, everyone over sixteen was expected to train themselves. There were fines for those who refused to muster or did not carry the proper arms.

Still, the colonists were not very interested in playing soldier. In 1632, the men of Virginia were expected to go through the motions of military drill every Sunday, but in ten years, they only soldiered once a month, and in 1674, it was mandatory only three times annually. New England retained some of its vitality, but the British were very unhappy because in North Carolina, where 15,000 names were on the books, the colonists had no desire to practice tactics and many of the names listed were dead or had moved away. In time of trouble, mothers would urge their children to fight, and farmers would leave their plows, but surely they were not interested in a standing army, and even Washington was unhappy with the militia that took the field.

In England, there was a long tradition of a standing army, and some historians in their homeland accused her of being more warlike than Old Rome. Even some Americans were anxious to take advantage of offers for commissions, because they would have a little military glory to boast about in the boondocks, and they would have half-pay for life after the campaign ended. In London, many military men also served in Parliament. William Howe, Charles Cornwallis, and flashy Johnny Burgoyne were among 64 army officers elected in 1761. Seven years later, Burgoyne got in a little trouble for going to the polling place with his own military guard and a loaded pistol in each hand, but after paying a fine of £1,000, he represented the same area until his death.

Rebel soldiers in England, who were on the wrong side of the king, were often put to death, jailed or sold into a type of slavery. Penn, who had been accused of treason himself, begged that he might have twenty of these men to take to Pennsylvania, where they could start a new life. The British civilians were fearful of the military because they had been used repeatedly to stop agitation, and two years before the Boston Massacre, soldiers had fired on a mob in Saint George's Fields, killing seven people. Where in America they were well armed to defend themselves, the hapless people of England were often unprepared. John Locke suggested that America needed no royal troops, but North and Clinton were fully confident that a military solution was just what the king ordered.

Back in America, the clergy was giving thanks from the pulpit for those who were risking their lives on the battlefields of liberty. But in times of peace, pastors such as Rev. Ezra Stiles, later president of Yale, were very worried about the morals of the soldiers and how it would disturb the populace.

America has a liking for military heroes—twelve generals have occupied the White House; but these men, when they became president, were very circumspect. It would have been easy for General George to feel himself above Congress, but he said, "Instead of thinking of myself freed from all civil obligations by this mark of confidence, I shall constantly bear in mind that as the sword was the last resort for the preservation of our liberties, so it ought to be laid aside when those liberties are firmly established." In 1783, Washington quickly blunted any chance for a military takeover by his old chums when they became restless about Congress's lethargy in acting on their promises to the servicemen who had served the country so well.

During World War II, Buddhist churches in Japan raised money to buy tanks for the Imperial Army. Stalin wooed the church so it would support him in his fight against Hitler. Two weeks after the invasion of Russia by Nazi Germany, Emelain Yaroslavaksy's famous "anti-God" weekly, *Bezbhzhnik,* was suddenly banned, and in 1942, the government put out a beautifully bound volume called *The Truth About Religion in Russia,* published through the efforts of the Central Committee. Even the intellectuals were carried away with their emotions, and they sided with Wilson in World War I.

We seldom complain when a new African nation is proud of their past and raises new flags over their office buildings. But we frown on nationalism when it comes to more advanced countries. Barbara Ward tells us that when people are blinded by national interest, they literally lose their grip on reality. "Unleased nationalism" removes all checks on a country and every action is considered okay. My Lai is an excellent example of what lengths patriots will go to when under the influence of military thinking. Even though Lieutenant Calley was from the lower class of society, where he was denied educational opportunities, that was no reason for making him a folk hero.

A preacher just before the Revolution put it this way: "Military aid has ever been deemed dangerous to the free, civil state, and often has been used as an effectual engine to subvert it. Those who, in the camp and in the field of battle, are our glory and defence, from the experience of other nations, will be thought, in time of peace, a very unproper safeguard to a constitution which has liberty, British liberty, for its basis." Perhaps that is the reason 83 percent of the college students during the Korean War reacted negatively when they were asked to fulfill military obligations.

Many countries throughout history have called for disarmament, even Germany under Hitler. But some left-wingers have hinted that the United States only supports this theory because it would open the world for economic domination. But Lenin may have cast a different shadow over this view when he said, "As long as capitalism and socialism exist, we cannot live in peace: in the end, one or the other will triumph —a funeral dirge will be sung either over the Soviet Republic or over the world of capitalism."

The act to draft American boys in 1940 passed by the big total of one vote. But some at that time believed that any defense was evil. "I [William L. Shirer] remember arguing that year [1939], whenever I was in London, with my Labour Party friends, particularly with men like Aneurin Bevan, whom I had known for years, that conscription was a necessary evil forced on them by Hitler and that it was not nearly so 'undemocratic' as they supposed. The experience of Switzerland and the Scandinavian democracies proved that. But they turned on me in scorn and fury. 'We have lost, and Hitler has won,' Bevan exclaimed when the conscription bill was finally passed. Arthur Greenwood called it 'criminal'."[1]

Everyone knows the Bible says that they turned their spears into pruning hooks (Isa. 2:4), but how many have read the verse in the book of Joel that says exactly the opposite thing— "Beat your plowshares into swords, and your pruning hooks into spears: let the weak say, I am strong." Perhaps the Bible is not as antimilitary as some would suppose.

The true Christian can be a very open individual. Whereas a politician must take sides, as his honor is at stake, the Christian does not need to do so. His home is in heaven, not on earth. He is simply a pilgrim passing through. Although he may love his homeland and admire its flag, he will quickly rebel against any ordinances that counter the teachings of the Word of God. He alone knows what it means to be completely free.

NOTES

1. William L. Shirer, *Midcentury Journey* (New York: Farrar, Straus & Young, 1952), p. 199.

XVIII SEEKING A PATH TO PEACE

Peace I leave with you, my peace I give unto you; not as the world giveth, give I unto you. Let not your heart be troubled, neither let it be afraid.

JESUS CHRIST

Plato says, "Only the dead have seen the end of war." In the same way, Jesus said, "And ye shall hear of wars and rumors of wars: see that ye be not troubled: for all these things must come to pass, but the end is not yet" (Matt. 24:6).

Nothing seems more foolish than war, but one might add that nothing seems as certain as war. After World War I, we heard the refrain that that was the war to end all wars, but within fifteen years the world was at it again. Man did not bring in the kingdom here on earth, although he may have believed he had the power to do so.

A famous historian, who has written many books about the Nazi plague and France's unpreparedness before World War II, believed that the United Nations would fill in the gaps left in the structure of the League of Nations and bring us a solid base for peace. William Shirer said, "The actual job of the conference, writing the Charter of a new League of Nations, has gone all right. We shall have our Charter before the middle of June [1945]. And it will have teeth in it whereas the League was pretty much of a toothless old woman. The core of the new league will be the Security Council, which will be mainly responsible for the maintenance of peace and security. It may make recommendations, but it is the Council that will make the decisions. . . . The old League never dared to apply armed force to restrain aggressors against the peace. The new League [U.N.] will specifically call for such application and will have a Military Staff committee to aid it."[1]

Where and when was the world's first peace society founded? It was founded in 1815 in the U.S., when the New York Peace Society came into being. Its founder was David Low Dodge, who was an elder in a Presbyterian church in Connecticut. He was "deeply imbued with the evangelical and philanthropic spirit of his time, and this spirit provided the main source from which his pacifism sprang." His book was entitled *War Inconsistent with the Religion of Jesus Christ* and was considered the best volume on the subject for decades to come.

Dodge was one of the first men in denominations other than the Quakers, Mennonites, or Dunkers, who believed that pacifism and peace were essential to mankind. He was disturbed that men of deeply religious principles were involved in the question of slavery but hadn't given much thought to the question of war and peace, even though this should have become everyone's chief concern. He based his book almost completely on the Word of God and his interpretation of key passages.

"I had been a pacifist in the First World War, and until after Munich I had hoped that a pacifist attitude would be possible in relation to the Nazis. I have never been a theoretical pacifist. I have always held that some wars have done more good than harm and that such wars are justifiable." These are the words of Bertrand Russell. Even though he had tried to follow the way of peace, he had found that the world simply did not allow him to fight evil and propound pacifism at the same time.

This was particularly true as America moved toward the Civil War. Those people who had grown interested in slavery gradually had to make a choice in their own hearts and souls. Which was worse—the institution of slavery or physical combat between individuals when nonviolence should be the strategy of the day? Closest to William Lloyd Garrison in his intense hatred of both war and slavery was Rev. Henry Clarke Wright, who was a Congregational minister. His pacifism "stemmed directly from his sternly Puritan and Bible-centered religion."[2] But even Garrison modified his position when he agreed that violence could be used for good, saying, "I believe that . . . culprits may be seized and condemned without a necessary violation of that principle of love; consequently, that civil and criminal jurisprudence ought to be supported by Christians, to a certain extent . . . I also believe that physical force may sometimes be used in the spirit of love, as in family government, and restraint of drunkards, lunatics, and criminals."

If the British pressed the point, there was only one decision that freedom loving Americans could make in the eyes of the patriots. But before that, they sent an Olive Branch Petition to George III and Jefferson told John Randolph that he was "looking with fondness towards a reconciliation with Great Britain." George refused to accept it and Lord Suffolk gave the world the sad news when he said, "The King and his Cabinet are determined to listen to nothing from the illegal congress, to treat with the colonies only one by one, and in no event to recognize them in any form of association."

There was a £500 reward out for the capture of the man

who first signed the Declaration of Independence. John Hancock scribbled his name in large letters and grinned: "There! His Majesty can now read my name without spectacles, and can now double his reward for my head. That is my defiance!" This president of the Continental Congress had been forced into a corner like all liberty loving Americans:

> We are reduced to the alternative of chusing an unconditional submission to the tyranny of irritated ministers, or resistance by force. The latter is our choice. We have counted the cost of this contest, and find nothing so dreadful as voluntary slavery. . . . With hearts fortified with these animating reflections, we most solemnly, before God and the world, declare that, exerting the utmost energy of those powers which our beneficent Creator hath graciously bestowed upon us, the arms we have been compelled by our enemies to assume, we will, in defiance of every hazard, with unabating firmness and perseverance, employ for the preservation of our liberties; being with one mind resolved to die freemen rather than to live as slaves.[3]

Major Pitcairn, who was to march on Lexington and Concord, but lose his life when shot from a house in Charlestown (the British burned the town after his death), felt that the rebels had bitten off more than they could chew. He wrote the Earl of Sandwich that General Gage had told the Whigs, "What fools you are to pretend to resist the power of Great Britain; she maintained the last war with three hundred thousand men, and will do the same now rather than suffer the ungrateful people of this country to continue in their rebellion."

Many Americans must have shaken in their boots when they thought of the great power they must face on the battlefield. England was the strongest nation in the world. The sun never set on her empire. In modern day terminology, was it better to be dead than red? Amusingly enough, they never ask whether it is better to be dead than to be under fascist rule, although Hitler was a piker when it came to killing people, as Stalin murdered over 20,000,000 and Hitler only put to death about 6,000,000. The colonists, who considered themselves just as English as the boy in Bristol, felt that they were oppressed because they had suffered "taxation without representation" in the Parliament. Would only the radicals support the theory that it was better to be dead than suppressed by redcoats?

"Why have not peace with people who, it is evident, desire peace with us?" cried Sir James Lowther after reading the Olive Branch Petition that the crown had refused. Pitt had come out against using "measures of Force . . . in the Settlement of our Colonies upon a proper Foot." Burke called out in debate in the House of Commons, "The proposition is peace. Not peace through the medium of war; not peace to arise out of universal discord, fomented from principle, in all parts of the empire; not peace to depend on the juridical determination of perplexing questions, or the precise marking of shadowy boundaries of a complex government. It is simple peace; sought in its natural course, and in its ordinary haunts. It is peace sought in the spirit of peace; and laid in principles purely pacific. . . ."

The American people were not a warlike population, although they did fight to protect themselves in battles against the Indians. Alexander Hamilton, who was the right arm of Washington during the war, proposed to create a Christian Constitutional Society in imitation of the Jefferson-controlled Democratic-Republican Societies. This group was to support the Christian religion and the Constitution. He lost his life because of his ideals, as he threw away his shot in his duel against Aaron Burr.

The people around Boston were angry but they did not resort to arms until Lexington, and then they believed that the English had fired the first shot. Before this, Pitcairn said, "I often march out with our battalion six or seven miles into the country. The people swear at us sometimes, but that does us no harm. I often wish to have orders to march to Cambridge and seize those impudent rascals that have the assurance to make such resolves. They sometimes do not know what to think of us; for we march into the town where they are all assembled, but we have no orders to do what I wish to do, and what I think may easily be done—I mean to seize them all and send them to England."

War veterans Sir Jeffrey Amherst and Lord Frederick Cavendish refused to accept active commands of posts in the colonies. General Henry Conway condemned the war policies of the king and Parliament. The Earl of Coventry termed the coercive measures "madness and absurdity." The Bishop of Peterborough believed that the colonists were contending for "an opinion of liberty," which he believed to have a deep resting place in the hearts of the Americans. Even the merchants were worried about their trade with the colonies. Nineteen lords protested against the war "because we cannot, as Englishmen, as Christians, or as men of common humanity, consent to the prosecution of a cruel civil war, so little supported by justice, and so very fatal in its necessary consequences, as that which is now waging against our brethren and fellow-subjects in America. . . . When we consider these things, we cannot look upon our fellow-subjects in America in any other light than of freemen driven to resistance by acts of oppression and violence."

Jefferson worried about America's image abroad. The humanitarian philosopher said, "The love of peace which we sincerely feel and profess has begun to produce an opinion in Europe that our government is entirely in Quaker principles and will turn the left cheek when the right has been smitten. This opinion must be corrected when just occasion arises, or we shall become the plunder of all nations." But this is the very image William Penn would have been proud of—he wanted his homeland to be a "haven of peace and truth."

The gentle followers of George Fox were opposed to both revolution and war. One would assume that their pacifistic tendencies would have kept them out of trouble, but such was far from the case. William Penn's own father was an admiral and could well have wished that his son follow in his footsteps. The British Quakers had to face persecution from a government that supported a state-church concept and a population that saw them as Jesuits in disguise. Many times in his life, William Penn was accused of masquerading as a lover of freedom when he really wanted to bring the Pope of Rome back to England and seat him upon the spiritual throne of the church.

Penn and his followers decided to test the rights of free speech, free assembly, and freedom of worship. Three of them, including a recent convert, decided to hold a Quaker religious service that was in violation of the Coventicle Act, which stated that any group other than the Anglicans needed official permission to hold meetings to worship the Lord. They were immediately arrested on a flimsy excuse, so they would have to have a jury trial. This also would bring the whole jury system of England into question too.

For some strange reason, they tried Penn and his new follower separately from the other Quaker. Immediately, they got into trouble over hats. When the two marched into the courtroom, a bailiff snatched their headgear from their polished pates and immediately he clapped them back on in front of the Lord Mayor and Sir Samuel Sterling, who was the presiding judge. This was ruled an act of contempt, and they were fined £5.

The so-called mild-mannered Quakers immediately decided to make an issue of their blessed bonnets. Penn pointed out that when he and his companion crossed the courtroom threshold, their heads were bare and that either the bailiff or the judge himself should be fined, because they were the ones who were responsible for placing the hats back on the hallowed heads of the two religious personages. The judge would not listen to this reasoning, as he knew full well that they would have replaced their hats if nobody else had done so.

When William was asked whether or not he was guilty,

he promptly questioned the legality of the law in question and not his own action. The prosecutor reminded him that he was being accused under the common law. To which Penn retorted, "If it is so hard to understand it is far from being very common."

During the trial, witnesses for the prosecution were paraded before the jury, but Penn was denied the right to cross-examine and, on top of that, the right to subpoena witnesses for the defense. Quickly, the judge asked the jury to make their verdict, but when Penn and the other prisoner were being taken away to prison, the quiet Quaker shouted, "Must I be taken away, because I plead for the fundamental rights of Englishmen?"

To everyone's surprise, the jury brought back a verdict of not guilty. Immediately, Judge Sterling lost his temper; he said that the verdict was against all the evidence that had been presented. He ordered the jury out to reason again about the guilt of the two defendants, which was a clear violation of the English legal system. This upset the members of the jury so much that even the four who had voted for conviction now stood with the rest in calling for acquittal. The stiff-necked judge then fined each one of them for breaking their oaths to return an honest verdict! These gallant persons remained in jail for two long months, despite hundreds of demands for their release!

One should not get the idea that William Penn was in favor of the actions of those who disturbed the peace or that he never became angry. One time in a Quaker meeting, two soldiers believed that they would have a little fun and interrupted the service. Penn immediately bolted from his seat with the intention of throwing the offenders into the street. If others had not intervened, he most surely would have done so.

When Penn set up shop in his colony, he figured that things would go very smoothly. As his province expanded to the west, an imbalance became very apparent to the politically alert persons who populated Penn's woods. Most of the Quakers were on the east coast, which was far away from the trouble spots. There they could practice their faith and nonviolence easily because there were no people to provoke them. But on the borders, the settlers lived in a very different situation. They had to plant their crops with one eye on the wooded regions, as Indians might be on the warpath at any moment.

Penn was having problems with London. In 1693, his government was taken away by the king and given to the governor of New York. The next year, it was restored, but it was quite evident that things were not going smoothly. The Parliament was touchy about the fact that the Quakers controlled the Assembly but there was not much they could do at that time.

Four years previously, the colonists were informed that England had declared war against France, a war which became known as King William's War. Governor Blackwell immediately pressed for a militia that could defend the territory. One replied, "I see no danger but from the Bears & Wolves." Another insisted, "If we should put ourselves into Armes, The Indians would rise against us, suspecting we intended to harm them." A third reminded the governor that the king was completely informed of the Quaker sentiments, when he gave the patent to William Penn so he should not be angry if things did not go his way when there was actually no danger anyway.

In 1701, Queen Anne's War broke out. The Pennsylvanians refused every appeal of the governor to enact a military law. Eight years later, London decided that she would like to conquer Canada and expected the people in Philadelphia to vote to provide 150 privates and officers. The Assembly was not about to ask for men to do battle, and when Governor Evans asked for £4,000 for defense, they declared that "were it not that the raising of money to hire men to fight or kill one another, is a matter of Conscience to us and against Our Religious Principles, we should not be wanting, according to our small abilities, to Contribute to those designs."

From this time onward, the Pennsylvanians realized that they would have to bend their principles a bit. They decided that they would give the queen £500, and she could use it anyway she wished. This was upped to £2,000 after some battling, and it was in lieu of the province's quota of men.

The next war that touched the peace-loving citizens with Quaker doctrines was the War of Jenkin's Ear. One year later, it expanded into a European conflict, when once again England was fighting the two Catholic states of France and Spain. The conflict now was given a new name—King George's War. The Assembly even refused to take any action against Spanish privateers on the Delaware.

Governor Thomas decided that he needed to change the Assembly if he was going to be successful in getting the population to support English conflicts. He decided that the Parliament might be able to remedy the situation by excluding Quakers from sitting in the statehouse.

The Quakers suddenly woke up to the fact that if they didn't get to the polls, they might be shoved aside. In 1741, they elected a large majority of their men to the Assembly and began making trouble. They decided that they wouldn't pay the governor his salary or enact any laws. Thomas now tried to wrest control out of the hands of his opponents, and in the next elections there was rioting by sailors in the City of Brotherly Love.

Four years later, they finally got things back on the track when the Assembly appropriated £4,000 for "Bread, Beef, Pork, Flour, Wheat or other Grain" for those who had recently captured Louisburg. Thomas broadened the interpretation and immediately substituted gunpowder in place of "other Grain."

When the peace came at Aix-la-Chapelle in 1748, after nine years of bloodshed, it was the northern colonies who had suffered the most; the people of Pennsylvania had made a killing in profitable industries while contributing very little. Benjamin Franklin, speaking for a new spirit in the colony, wrote a booklet entitled *Plain Truth,* in which he chastised the Quakers for their attitude toward the needs of defense for the bulk of the people who lived in the territory. It was not long before a plan was drawn up, mainly by him, to put 10,000 men in the field from Pennsylvania and the area that is now called Delaware.

The French and Indian War was to shake up the whole political situation in the land of the Penn family. It was obvious that the frontiersmen were going to face foes with little more than their faith if the local government didn't do something. Up until this time, the Quakers could count on the vote of the Germans, who sided with them over the principles of religious practices. Now, there was a switch, and they began to join with the Scotch and other groups on the borders in fighting the political influence of Penn's people.

If the Quaker-controlled Assembly sat on their hands, then the people would have to go over their heads directly to London. Immediately, a petition was prepared and sent to the provincial agent to be presented to the Privy Council. The message read that "Numbers of your Majtys. good Subjects, on the sed Frontiers have been recently barbarously murdered, by bloodthirsty Savages; & whole Townships broke up, & driven from their Habitations." A committee was appointed and it found that the construction of Penn's Charter did not exempt the colony from military service.

Even the Quakers began to understand that they stood for a principle which would leave the people unprotected, and even their area might come under the occupation of the French Catholics if something was not done. Immediately, some of these peace-loving people began to resign from the Assembly and the control shifted to those who did not accept the principles of nonresistance.

In the yearly meeting of the Quakers in Philadelphia in 1775, they said that they did not approve of what the British were doing, but they themselves "did not believe in war or revolution and would not be a party in overturning the beneficent charter of William Penn, nor aid in throwing off our ultimate allegiance to the Kings of Great Britain."

On October 27 of the same year, an address to the Assembly by a committee of Quakers on behalf of their society emphasized their religious scruples against bearing arms, and said that they were relieved from any responsibility by the contract that had been entered into by Penn and the crown. Four days later, the Committee of the City of Philadelphia, which numbered sixty-two persons, marched two-by-two to the Assembly and denounced the above because "it bears an aspect unfriendly to the liberties of America, and maintains principles destructive of all society and government. . . ." They were particularly upset because they knew that the Quakers themselves would be receiving all the benefits of the struggle without paying a single penny or shedding one drop of blood.

The Reverend Mr. West, in an election sermon preached in Boston in 1776, came down hard on the pacifists. He said:

> We find such persons are very inconsistent with themselves; for no men are more zealous to defend their property, and to secure their estates from the encroachments of others, while they refuse to defend their persons, their wives, their children, and their country, against the assaults of the enemy. We see too what unaccountable lengths men will run when once they leave the plain road of common sense, and violate the law which God has written in the heart. Thus some have thought they did God a service when they unmercifully butchered and destroyed lives of the servants of God; while others, upon the contrary extreme, believe that they please God while they sit still and quietly behold their friends and brethren killed by their unmerciful enemies, without endeavoring to defend or rescue them. The one is a sin of omission, and the other is a sin of commission, and it may perhaps be difficult to say, under certain circumstances, which is the most criminal in the sight of heaven.[4]

It is one thing to wish for peace and quite another to keep the peace. King George decided that the rebels must be told to shape up when he said:

> I have as yet not heard from Lord Weymouth concerning the debate in the House of Lords, and consequently am much pleased with your attention in sending me a copy of Lord Chatham's highly unseasoninable motion, which can have no other use but to convey some fresh fuel if attended by the rebels. Like most of the other productions of that extraordinary brain, it contains nothing but specious words and malevolence, for no one that reads it, if unacquainted with the conduct of the mother country and its colonies, [but] must suppose the Americans poor mild persons, who after unheard-of and repeated grievances had no choice but slavery or the sword; whilst the truth is, that the too great lenity of this country encreased their pride and encourage them to rebel.

The king decided that he must suppress the people of New England. He wrote Lord North, "I am sorry that the line of conduct seems now chalked out, which the enclosed dispatches thoroughly justify; the New England Governments are in a state of rebellion, blows must decide whether they are to be subject of this country or independent." His Majesty's navy turned their guns on Norfolk and bragged, "The detested town of Norfolk is no more." Bristol, Rhode Island, had to buy off a bombardment by the British fleet with two hundred sheep and thirty fat cows, after Rev. Parson Burt had been injured. Perhaps George III believed that he could frighten the natives into submitting to his rule. But even a patriot could write his friends with these words: "For God's sake let there be a full revolution, or all has been done in vain. Independence and a well planned continental government will save us. God bless you. Amen and amen."

Patrick Henry paraphrased the Scriptures when he intoned, "Gentlemen may cry peace, peace—but there is no peace. . . . Is life so dear or peace so sweet as to be purchased at the

price of slavery? Forbid it, Almighty God—I know not what
course others may take; but as for me, give me liberty or
give me death!" Whether these words are the exact ones that
tumbled from his lips or whether his biographer used a little
license, they essentially describe the mood of the times. These
men believed that peace with slavery was no peace at all,
because it robbed the heart of its essential blessings—the
freedom of worship, speech, and press.

A clergyman asked a special question of his congregation.
"That ever-memorable day, the nineteenth of April, is the date
of an unhappy war openly begun by the ministers of the king
of Great Britain against his good subjects in this colony, and
implicitly against all the other colonies. But for what?" Even
a British citizen realized that the Americans were only fighting
a defensive war. Dr. Price wrote, "The truth is, we expected
to find them a cowardly rabble who would lie quietly at our
feet, and they have disappointed us. They have risen in their
own defense and repelled force by force. They deny the
plentitude of our power over them and insist on being treated
as free communities. It is THIS that has provoked us; and
kindled our governors into rage."

Washington could find no other avenue of action. The king
and Parliament had denied "our Petitions and Remonstrances
and Prayers," so there was nothing else to do but to take up
arms in self-defense. The Earl of Shelburne underlined the
feelings of the Virginian when he wrote, "The noble Lord
laughs at all propositions of conciliation; repeats his imputation
of cowardice against the Americans; says the idea of rights is
to be driven out of their heads by blows; and ridicules the
objections to employing foreigners and papists. Is this a language, my Lords, becoming so great an officer of state?"
Because of this harsh attitude, many people called on God
himself to protect them and encouraged people to enlist, even
from the pulpits.

Throughout the war, there were overtures for peace. The

first offer of pardon came through General Gage, after the fighting had gone on for two months. He said that the king's troops had not been prepared for vengeance when they took the road to Lexington, but even after the bloodshed, he was willing to pardon everyone but Samuel Adams and John Hancock. Many men did not step forward, because there would have been no change in the relationship between the crown and the colonies—they still would have had to beg favors from the king's hand.

Richard Penn, the grandson of William, took the "Olive Branch Petition" to England after it had been signed by virtually all the members of Congress four days after the date we celebrate as Independence Day. This petition was written by the moderates of the Congress, but George III would not even accept it. It even led to a debate in the House of Lords as to whether or not they would even hear the gentleman who had traveled so far, because they were fearful that this would be some recognition of the Congress, and they did not want to give that impression to the members who had gathered illegally in Philadelphia to carry on the business of the thirteen states.

The Howe brothers were named by the king as peace commissioners under the authority of Parliament. They tried to negotiate with General Washington, but he refused to bargain. Five days later, after the rout of the American forces on Long Island, Howe put forth his offer for peace again through General Sullivan, who had been captured. Congress was not too happy to see Sullivan, and they debated whether or not Howe actually had power to negotiate a settlement on terms they would accept. The moderates decided to send John Adams and Benjamin Franklin to see if the offer was reasonable, but the two came to the conclusion that it was meaningless, as there was no offer of independence to the thirteen provinces.

The next thoughts of peace arose when the French-American

alliance was about to be formalized. The British watched in horror as their historic enemy sidled up to her children. The Carlisle Commission was drawn up with the purpose of breaking up this new duo that might make things pretty messy for His Majesty. The British agreed to keep no standing army in the colonies in time of peace, to make no change in colonial charters unless requested by the assemblies concerned, and to consider representation of the colonies directly in the Parliament. If these concessions were made in 1774, it is highly probable that they would have been accepted with glee; but now that Sir Henry Clinton was forced to evacuate Philadelphia, and the French alliance might assure victory, the love offerings fell on deaf ears.

Now we turn to the king's personal thoughts about peace negotiations:

1. "The present [August 12, 1778] from America seems to put a final stop to all negotiation. Farther concessions is a joke. . . ."
2. "The present [June 11, 1779] contest with America I cannot help seeing as the most serious in which any country was ever engaged: it contains such a train of consequences that they must be examined to feel its real weight. Whether the laying a tax was deserving all the evils that have arisen from it, I should suppose no man could alledge [sic] that without being thought more fit for Bedlam than a seat in the Senate; but step by step the demands of America have risen: independence is their object to a MOMENTARY and inglorious peace must concurr with me in thinking that this country can never submit to: should America succeed in that, the West Indies must follow them, not independence, but must for its own interest be dependent on North America. . . ."
3. "The fate of no question [debate on General Conway's motion for a bill for pacifying America] in this Session

more sincerely interested me than that of yesterday [May 6, 1780], and as such Ld. North will easily believe how much I am pleased at the majority. It was founded on fatal experience that every invitation to reconciliation only strengthens the demagogues in America in their arts to convince the deluded people that a little farther resistance must make the mother-country yield. . . ."

4. "It is difficult to express which appears more strongly, the manly fortitude to the great majority last night [June 9, 1781] in rejecting the hacknied question of a Committee for considering the American war, or the impudence of the minority in again bringing it forward; for whoever the most ardently wishes for peace must feel that every repetition of this question in Parliament only makes the rebels and the Bourbon family more desirous of continuing the war, from the hopes of tiring out this country. We have it not at this hour in our power to make peace; it is by steadiness and exertions that we are to get into a situation to effect it; and with the assistance of Divine Providence I am confident we shall soon find our enemies forced to look for that blessing."[5]

Winning the peace was almost as hard as winning the war on the battlefield. The king did not want to give up the colonies, because it was evident that the monarchy might fall too. The French, who were supposed to be mutual partners, tried to dictate the peace terms to America. Bonvouloir, a French agent, boasted that he could do what he wanted to do with Congress and probably this attitude infected all the top French politicians who dealt with the new nation. Yorktown toppled Lord North, like it gobbled up Cornwallis and his redcoats. The next regime worked for peace, but the two sides were far apart, because Franklin wanted Canada and the British wanted the debts owed the Tories to be paid. The key question was independence, and after the English gave in on that point, the smaller problems were worked out with the French still gazing over the shoulders of the Americans.

War has embittered men and it has ruined society. After such conflicts, people want to get back to the status quo and settle down. After the last war, Gabriel Kolko wrote, "Man became degraded and uprooted, and having lost his commitment to an interest in the conventional ways and wisdom, he sought to redeem himself and his society in order to save himself."

Man has always tried to save himself. The Briand-Kellogg Pact was a representative manifestation of those times when mankind was going to outlaw war and make nations bargain, not fight, over problems. The pact, which was signed in 1928, came into effect on June 24, 1929. It read:

ARTICLE 1. The high contracting parties solemnly declare in the names of their respective peoples that they condemn recourse to war for the solution of international controversies, and renounce it as an instrument of national policy in their relations with one another.

ART. 2. The high contracting parties agree that the settlement of solution of all disputes or conflicts, of whatever nature or of whatever origin they may be, which may arise among them, shall never be sought except by pacific means.

The key articles read well and they should have solved the age-old problem of armed conflicts. But shortly after the signing, Japan was on the march and the Spanish Civil War would make nations choose sides. But the pacifists were still sure that the people would vote for peace. In England, the pacifists called for a "Peace Ballot" to prove to the world that the citizens of Great Britain were solidly behind the pacifist movement. The intellectuals had already sworn that they would never go to war to protect their nation. Now it was time for the common folk to vote. Of the 11,000,000 who voted, 10,000,000 demanded economic sanctions against any aggressor, and by a 6,750,000 to 2,360,000 margin, they would also support war if need be.

Who promised to do the following?: "The_____govern-
ment is ready to agree to any limitation which leads to abolition
of the heaviest arms, especially suited for aggression, such [as]
the heaviest artillery and the heaviest tanks. _____declares
herself ready to agree to any limitation whatsoever of the
caliber of artillery, battleships, cruisers, and torpedo boats. In
like manner, the_____government is ready to agree to the
limitation of tonnage for submarines, or their complete abolition. . . ."

Another famous world leader said, "What is the alternative
to this bleak and barren policy of the inevitability of war? In
my view it is that we should seek by all means in our power
to avoid war, by analyzing possible causes, by trying to remove
them, by discussion in a spirit of collaboration and good will."

The two leading actors on the world stage that day were
Adolf Hitler and Neville Chamberlain. Their programs seemed
very reasonable—but they led to war; and the intellectuals
were proven wrong.

The same thing was true during the Vietnam War. Even
though the press pointed out that the American people believed
America had made a mistake in entering Vietnam in the first
place, Nixon won the next election by a comfortable margin.
In fact, it was his mining of the harbors of North Vietnam
that won him the election of 1972, according to a famous
political scientist.[6] As the elections came, the North Vietnamese
came to the conference table, because they realized that the
electorate backed Nixon's "peace-with-honor" theme on the war.

Stalin signed a pact with Hitler and then called for the
nations to settle their differences and have world peace. Japan
in her history has attacked three countries while she was nego-
tiating with them. The dangers of war are all around us.

There are two distinct dangers to peace. One is the mutual
hate countries have always had for one another. Egypt's Gamal
Nasser stated, "Israel's existence in itself is an aggression."
The other is when political philosophy leads a state or group

of states war. Lenin said, "The main argument is that the demand for disarmament is the clearest, most decisive, most consistent expression of the struggle against all militarism and against all war. But this main argument is precisely the principal error of the advocates of disarmament. Socialists cannot, without ceasing to be socialists, be opposed to all war. In the first place, socialists have never been, nor can they ever be, opposed to revolutionary war. . . . Secondly, civil wars are also wars. . . . Thirdly, the victory of socialism in one country does not at one stroke eliminate all war in general. . . ."

Mao Tse-tung told us, "Power comes out of the barrel of a gun." His nation has stated her determination to retake territory that was lost to China ages ago and has "expanded" into India's and Russia's border areas to show that she is not bluffing.[7] No wonder John F. Kennedy presented a program for peace that would seem very hawkish today.[8]

Even though the United Nations is a very valuable organization in many ways, it has not brought peace to this world. Still, the Americans feel that there is less danger of a world conflict today than in recent years. But is it possible to have a lasting peace?

The men of the revolutionary war period had actively sought peace. They did not rush into the conflict. It was pushed upon them. Man is simply too unstable without God to manage his own affairs. Without the Prince of Peace, the world will continue to have wars and rumors of wars until Christ returns.

NOTES

1. William L. Shirer, *End of a Berlin Diary* (New York: Alfred A. Knopf, 1947), p. 43.*
2. Peter Brock, *Radical Pacifists in Antebellum America* (Princeton, N. J.: Princeton University Press, 1968), p. 3.*
3. Gaillard Hunt, ed., *Journals of the Continental Congress,*

1774-1789 (Washington, D.C.: United States Government Printing Office, 1904-1937).

4. John Wingate Thornton, *The Pulpit of the American Revolution* (New York: Da Capo Press, 1970), p. 312.

5. W. Bodham Donne, ed., *The Correspondence of King George the Third with Lord North, 1768 to 1783*, 2 vols. (New York: Da Capo Press, 1971), 2:207, 252-55, 319.

6. Samuel Lubell, *The Future While It Happened* (New York: W. W. Norton & Company, 1973), p. 12.

7. Harrison E. Salisbury, *War Between Russia and China* (New York: W. W. Norton & Company, 1969), p. 106.*

8. John F. Kennedy, *The Strategy for Peace* (New York: Popular Library, 1960), pp. ix-xv.*

XIX HEROES OF THE REVOLUTION

The History of our Revolution will be one continued lye from one end to the other. The essence of the whole will be that Dr. Franklin's electric Rod, smote the Earth and out sprung General Washington. That Franklin electrified him with his rod—and thence forward these two conducted all the Policy, Negotiations, Legislatures and War.

JOHN ADAMS

The loud speakers on the vehicle of the local Buddhist temple blasted the early morning calm in Taipei, Nationalist China. The citizens listened to the message being announced to the public. The message was: "Lincoln was a Buddhist believer, why don't you become one, too? He found the meaning of life in the teachings of Buddha and you will also receive this same peace when you believe!"

Unbelievable? This is a true story. The Buddhists as well as the Christians wish to claim the great ones as their very own. This seems to provide them with more confidence in their own faith. Needless to say, "Honest Abe" must have turned over in his grave when he got the message.

The world often tries to deify human figures and place them on a pretty pedestal. Historian Thomas A. Bailey says, "The Lincoln cultists have one bond in common with the Washington cultists: they regard criticism as unholy. If the Father of his Country is godlike, the Great Emancipator is Christlike—'the mystic mingling of star and clod.'"

Author James Barron Hope called Washington America's "Messiah." John R. Thompson said that the capitol square would be "henceforth to all a consecrated place that holds a sacred shrine." Bernard May scribbled, "George Bancroft, for example, saw clearly the Hand of God in American history and Washington as divinely ordained." A Virginia poet has acclaimed our first president with these lines:

> And future ages, when thy fame they scan,
> Will deem thee Freedom's myth—thou more than man.[1]

As George Washington symbolized national independence, Thomas Jefferson was the epitome of personal liberty. The first was so lofty in character and personality that we have rare glimpses of his true being. Jefferson is move lovable, with the warmth of humanity wrapped about his very bones. The friend of the common man did not have a memorial built in his memory until the New Deal came along. For more than one hundred years, his home had been neglected and his tombstone mutilated. But today, more than 250,000 pilgrims make the trip to see Monticello annually. His works have become so popular that they are continually quoted—just like the Bible.

One author hints that Americans need stirring symbols to worship. When we see how our present-day politicians are treated in comparison to Mao, we would doubt if that is true. But Americans have applauded national heroes in every generation. Jefferson said that Franklin was "our Patriarch, whom Philosophy and Philanthropy announced the first of men, and whose name will be like a star of the first magnitude in the firmament of heaven when the memory of those who have surrounded and obscured him will be lost in the abyss of time." John Adams noted: "His reputation was more universal than that of Liebnitz or Newton, Frederick or Voltaire, and his character more beloved and esteemed than any or all of them."

Not all beings are judged exactly alike. Samuel Adams was a hero of the radicals, but he was described as a devil by the Tories. Dr. Benjamin Rush, who helped undermine Washington in favor of Gates, quoted John Adams as saying, "I have been distressed to see some members of this house [Congress in 1777] disposed to idolize an image which their own hands have molten. I speak here of the superstitious veneration that is sometimes paid to General Washington."*

Even intellectuals idolize certain liberals and applaud their every word and deed. Dean Acheson tells the story of individuals visiting the White House and of Miss Wilson pointing out her father's typewriter to the visitors who gazed at it in silence, and then "the door was reverently closed." Bailey tells us: "The Wilson cult is vigorous and vocal, though it boasts few visible tabernacles. The birthplace at Staunton, Virginia, though imposing for a Presbyterian manse, is not a palatial residence. . . . But the memory of Wilson is cherished, almost fanatically, by the thousands who recognized him as a martyr to a glorious cause. . . . Criticism of the fallen warrior seemed to be unsporting, even sacrilegious."[2]

Whether or not we should bow or bend our knees to these famous fellows is questionable. But surely men should be applauded for rising above circumstances that have floored fellow

---

*See p. 216.

citizens. We have to agree with Richard B. Morris—God surely granted America the grace of having a great group of talented gentlemen at this crucial point in her history.

Washington's life is bathed in myth. He was a tall individual with slightly rounded shoulders and a heavy lower torso. He did not have the flashing eyes of a Paine of the manly features of Patrick Henry. It is said that he seldom smiled, principally because of his false teeth, which some have said weighed several pounds and needed personal adjustment quite often. When one thinks of an athlete, one pictures a man with a broad chest and square shoulders. George didn't have this build, but he could ride a horse with ease and was very agile for a male of his size.

His mother was very possessive and tried to dominate his life. He continually had to show his own willpower or she would have tried to control many of his actions. She lived to be eighty-one years of age and was the first of ten mothers who saw their sons put in the office of the president of the United States. His father died when he was a boy of eleven, but his dad left most of the property to George's half brothers. He was badly shaken when his oldest half brother, Lawrence, died before he came of age.

Washington's great-grandfather had been an Anglican minister in England but was forced from his pulpit by the Puritans when they took over under Cromwell. His grandfather shipped off for America, married a rich woman, and settled down to the life of a farmer in Virginia. Augustine, his father, worked the plantation but did not encourage his young son to have an education on the college level, although Lawrence benefitted from such teaching.

His lack of education did not keep him from wielding his trusty pen, and we have enough letters and papers to fill thirty-seven volumes; but many of them do not give us much of a glimpse into the heart of this silent creature, as they deal with the monetary problems of running a plantation in that age. At first his writing, spelling, and use of grammar left much to be desired, but gradually he improved his ability and became the equal of most of his famous colleagues who were not self-made men.

He had an active interest in politics, often taking the stump for family friends or local politicians. He himself was later elected to office but generally did not win as many votes as other celebrities. He was a poor speaker and hesitated to warm the crowd with flights of fancy words. But he erected a personality in his soul, which made the public watch in awe as he went about his business as first president of the United States. Similar to the administration of another military hero named Ike, the press was hasty to pick on the president's right hand man—who in this case was Alexander Hamilton.

Although Washington received many newspapers, many free, he seldom took the time to read them. John Tebbel tells us, "Even when they were complimentary—and the Federalist press treated him like a deity—he did not trust the papers. As he became president, he observed gloomily that the day would soon come when 'the extravagant (and I may say undue) praises which they are heaping upon me at this moment' would be turned to 'equally extravagant (that I will fondly hope unmerited) censures.'"

His part in the top ranks of American officers in the French and Indian War must have been helpful at the polls, before he stepped up to a higher position at the direction of Congress at the beginning of the struggle. Even though he had seen weapons fired in anger, he frowned on duels to save one's honor. He married a rich widow who brought her brood to Mount Vernon. They remained childless but he took an active interest in his step-children's education and upbringing. Jackie Custis was a sickly youngster but he arrived at Yorktown to see the British humiliated, dying a few days later at home. Custis left two children to be reared and his granddaughter was to marry Robert E. Lee, famous general and outstanding Christian of the Old South.

Although Washington was the first of six presidents to

remain childless, he took many people into his heart. One of these was Lafayette, and he left a glowing description of his leader. The enemy made wild charges about his person, as often happens in the time of war, but they respected him, and the king was hopeful he would be taken from office, as surely a new commander would be easier to defeat than steady George.

He is often pictured as being a very distant gent and a man with little personal charm. Congress demanded that he be painted in the manner of Cincinnatus in an ancient toga. He felt this was silly and wished to be sketched in contemporary dress, but he was overruled. Few men shed tears when a stiff and formal personage says good-bye, but we read that every spectator was in tears when Washington resigned from the army in December of 1783, and many members of Congress were seen dabbing at their eyes too. He was simply exchanging his spear for a plowshare, but the people believed that they were losing a widely loved hero.

President Eisenhower described George Washington as "the greatest human the English-speaking race has produced." But some people simply cannot stand veneration of their fellowmen, particularly if they have Puritan ways and thoughts. Emerson said, "Every hero becomes a bore at last. . . . They cry up the virtues of George Washington—'Damn George Washington!' is the poor Jacobin's whole speech and confutation."

This latter-day attitude has led to the art of debunking. The modern critic loves to take to task this type of Hogan's hero and to liven up their literature with all types of odd stories to make a buck and a name for themselves. Fawn M. Brodie wrote a lively book about Thomas Jefferson, but it enraged Dumas Malone and other historians, as they claimed it was not a work of scholarship, but simply of sensual sensationalism based on guesswork.

But what do we do when we come to Pastor Weems? Honest historians have cracked this clergyman across the knuckles. They say that there is no truth in his fables about George and the cherry tree tale, etc.; that the Reverend Mr.

Weems wrote these from his vivid imagination. We cannot applaud this type of dishonesty of course, but part of the historians' criticism rests on their hatred of his moral precepts. He was labeled "a Victorian before the Victorian era!" They detested this do-gooder attitude and the obvious conclusion that they, too, should follow the straight and narrow path.

Weems had the last laugh. His version, written about 1800, went into forty editions! At the time of publication, there were numerous people still living who knew Washington intimately. Surely, they would have known if these tales were too tall to be stuffed down their throat. John A. Krout gives us his reasoning about the case. "The creation of the folk hero is but superficially the work of those who write. Weems's stories bore the mark of truth not because they were told with zest, but because they recorded what men and women were saying about Washington. Fantastic they might be, but they were widely believed."

The Founding Fathers took life seriously. Jefferson ran a very tight ship and lived a regulated life. He hardly ever dabbled in frivolous exercises. Franklin followed Puritan virtues when it came to work patterns. John Adams was a hard worker. And Washington himself said that he never recalled when he had ever broken his word in his life.

John Marshall, first supreme court justice of the United States, wrote a biography about the gentleman, whom he called "the father of his country." His work is basically the same as the volume written by the Anglican pastor penned four years before. Washington Irving decided to write five volumes about his namesake, and he used poetic license in drawing a nice picture of the man from Mount Vernon. Both Bancroft and John Fiske claimed that they were going to make a man of the revered saint but ended up making him the supreme leader of the revolutionary era, which probably did a grave injustice to others of that age.

In size, Washington's monument towers over Saint Peter's in Rome and the great pyramids of Egypt. The "debunkers" came along to rip down that mammoth tower. W. E. Woodward used "the shock-tactics of debunking." These critics hailed him as a champion of sorts—winner of the first prize as the top swearer on his general staff. They insist that he must have dabbled in forbidden flesh, simply because he had 277 slaves on his plantation when he left this earth. They drew up lively tales about his relationship with Sally Fairfax—his lovely neighbor. As wiser minds have stated, they were reversing all that Weems wrote.

General George swore very seldom and drew up orders that told his troopers to restrain themselves. The British spread wild rumors about his womanizing, but those who have searched the record say it is only an immoral myth. Another biographer, one who did not worship Washington, tells us that authors have read too much into his friendship with Ms. Fairfax, and that there was nothing amiss in their relationship. They echo the words of Britisher Marcus Cunliffe that "the man is the monument; the monument is America."

But was George Washington a religious man? Richard B. Morris writes, "He drew equally upon the revolutionary rhetoric to which he was exposed, upon a moral fervor which expressed his special religiosity, and used apt biblical metaphor to hammer home his message. The man who wished that 'the most atrocious' speculators be hung 'upon a gallows five times as high as the one prepared by Haman,' who looked forward to the day 'when every man could sit under his own vine and fig tree, and there shall be none to make him afraid,' and could hail the West as 'the second land of promise,' appreciated the resources of his Bible."[3]

A number of authors have hinted that Washington must have been a deist simply because he *never* used the word *God*. In reading the works of Christians of the same time, you will also note that they use words such as *Providence* and *Creator* very often too. Did he never use the word God? In penning Joseph Reed a letter, he said, "How it will end, God in great goodness will direct, I am thankful for his protection to this time. We are told that we shall soon get the army completed, but I have been told so many things which have never come to pass, that I distrust every thing. . . ." Yes, he could only trust his God; men had failed him and would continue to do so.

He was very sympathetic to sinners, perhaps because he felt his own need for redemption. We see he did not always trust those around him, but when it came to his own charity toward others, he was most kind. A neighbor was continually borrowing his money and then wasting it foolishly on hard liquor. But each time the army vet needed a place to rest his weary head, he could find it in George's home. Even though Washington had problems keeping himself out of debt, he often allowed people to borrow money, and he preferred to write at the bottom of the note, "to be returned or not as it suited [the individual]," instead of exacting high interest rates.

Martha's hubby heard the disturbing news from Boston in May of 1769, when he came out of the Sunday afternoon prayer meeting that he had attended like the morning service, and he considered what he should do to help these troubled Americans. The great general was to see the British pull out of Beantown a few years later, but instead of rushing into the city, which had been delivered from English rule, he quietly went to church in camp and heard the chaplain of Knox's regiment preach on Exod. 14:25: "The Egyptians said, Let us flee from the face of Israel; for the Lord fighteth for them against the Egyptians."

The following are just a sample of the times Washington referred to God in his correspondence and conversation:

1. "He was sure that Providence intervened for the affairs of men to support the righteous."
2. He was very worried about getting the reorganization completed before Boston while the enemy was only a few yards away. He wrote, "I shall most religiously believe that

the finger of Providence is in it, for surely if the enemy did not take advantage of the weakness, it must be for want of their knowing the disadvantages we labour under."

3. He worried about the British forces being able to float their men over to the peninsula outside of Boston on the next high tide, but a violent storm stopped this operation and he called it "a remarkable interposition of Providence."

4. By February 1776, he was sure that those who were under arms were fighting "the cause of virtue and mankind," which made it probable that God would not permit them to fail.

5. When the British landed on Long Island, the general sent his records to Philadelphia and penned, "I trust, through divine favor on our own exertions they will be disappointed in their views, and, at all events, any advantages they may gain will cost them dear."

6. When General Washington heard of Burgoyne's surrender, he issued the following general order: "Let every face brighten and every heart expand with grateful joy and praise to the supreme disposer of all events, who has granted us this signal success." Then he asked the chaplains to give a message of thanksgiving before the troops.

7. When France joined the Americans in an alliance against the British, Washington ordered that divine services be held and issued the following message: "It having pleased the Almighty ruler of the Universe propitiously to defend the cause of the United American States and finally, by raising us up a powerful friend among the princes of the earth, to establish our liberty and Independence up[on] lasting foundations, it becomes us to set apart a day for gratefully acknowledging the divine goodness and celebrating the important event which we owe to his benign interposition."

8. He rejoiced that they still were free outside New York while the British were bottled up in that city:

It is not a little pleasing nor less wonderful to contemplate that after two years maneuvering and undergoing the strangest vicissitudes that perhaps ever attended any one contest since the Creation, both armies are brought back to the very point they set out from, and that which was offending [offensive] party in the beginning is now reduced to the use of the spade and pickax for defense. The hand of Providence has been so conspicuous in all this that he must be worse than an infidel that lacks faith, and more than wicked that has not gratitude enough to acknowledge his obligations—but it will be time enough for me to turn preacher when my present appointment ceases, and therefore I shall add no more on the Doctrine of Providence.

9. Washington wrote the following after Arnold went over to the enemy: "In no instance since the commencement of the war has the interposition of Providence appeared more conspicuous than in the rescue of the post and garrison of West Point from Arnold's villainous perfidy."

10. After the victory at Yorktown, he urged on his troops the "gratitude of heart which the recognition of such reiterated and astonishing interpositions of Providence demand of us."

11. He could not doubt that, since national political liberty would establish international peace and happiness, fighting the American Revolution was worshiping the "Great Governor of the Universe," who would protect and reward his servants.

12. He could now look back to the night before Princeton, when he was almost trapped—had not the temperatures dropped, he would not have been able to move his cannon at night and escape the clutches of Cornwallis. But the "providential change of weather" saved them that night and throughout the war.

Washington was very interested in the piety of his men. He issued an order against swearing and asked all the officers to see to it that their men watched their language while in service. He also wrote to Acting Governor John Blair, saying, "Common decency, sir, in a camp calls for the services of the divine . . . although the world be so uncharitable as to think us void of religion and incapable of good instruction." In thinking about the joy of his soldiers, he advised attendance at religious services, which "tend to improve the morals and at the same time to increase the happiness of the soldiery and must afford the most pure and rational entertainment for every serious and well-disposed mind."

Our first president not only believed that God intervened on behalf of his fighting machine and that he should be grateful, but that there was also a need to recognize Almighty God's work for the good of the nation. He called on the Congress to look to God for a wise and meaningful Constitution, because if they looked only upon the wisdom of men, they were bound to fail.

His last day in office was a momentous occasion. In his Farewell Address, he told his listeners that "religion and morality were the two great pillars of human happiness" and "that national morality cannot prevail in exclusion of religious principle." When he resigned his commission at Annapolis, he said, "I consider it my indispensable duty to close this last solemn act of my official life by commending the interests of our dearest country to the protection of Almighty God, and those who have the superintendence of them to His holy keeping." Previously, in his swearing in ceremony as president, he vowed before God to defend the Constitution and he heard Robert R. Livingston cry, "God bless our President." He then addressed the men of both Houses, asking them to make "fervent supplications to that Almighty Being who rules over the Universe" and to realize that the "invisible hand" and the "providential agency" had been the guiding light of the United States. After he finished his address, everyone walked to Saint Paul's Chapel, where the Chaplain of Congress gave a message from the Word of God. Thus the nation began a walk of faith into the future, after meeting in divine worship before the God of Heaven.

We now move on to Thomas Jefferson, a man of learning and personal virtue. He penned from fifty to sixty volumes, and his works are probably better known than any of those by the Founding Fathers. Like Washington, he had been brought up in Virginia and owned a large plantation. Men in that station of life had to learn all sorts of things. He was interested in science, medicine, art, and universal education.

Jefferson not only developed political theory, he built up a strong political organization. While the Federalists ruled in Washington, he was pulling the political props out from under them in the various states. His ability to build a strong political party, the first of his day, made many enemies. He also took his legislation very seriously. He once suggested to a friend that they would have to pray for the death of Patrick Henry if they hoped to push laws through the legislature.

The man from Monticello penned the original draft of the Declaration of Independence, where he declared that all men were created in equality by God. He supported national freedom and liberty from British suppression, but his fight for religious freedom gave him as much personal happiness as the fame he acquired for the Declaration of Independence.

Jefferson fought hard against big government, as he feared that an energetic Congress and president would meddle in the affairs of the average man. After all of this, he felt that he was a failure when the guns of the Revolution grew silent. It wasn't until later in life, when he sat in the White House, that he discovered he would have to wield political punches if the nation was to move along a positive course.

His fight for religious freedom was not because he was rebelling against God. He knew that God ruled on high and was not blind to what was going on down on the earth. In fact, he had personally sworn before God to oppose all types of tyranny as long as he lived. He looked toward the future and he saw black clouds on the horizon. He predicted that there would be a great civil conflict unless slavery ended in the South. He said that they should tremble when they considered that God was not only just, but would punish those who committed sin against Him or against their fellowman.

Hamilton was the youngest of the Founding Fathers. He was born out of wedlock in a foreign land. He never lived down this reputation, and it made him bitter throughout his natural days on earth. Perhaps this was the reason he looked down on mobs, as they reminded him of his own poor beginnings.

As a child of fate, he was to land in the United States because of a hurricane. It ripped up the West Indies so badly that Hamilton wrote a letter to the local paper describing the terrible event, which had caused him to "see tender infancy pinched with hunger and hanging on the mother's knee for food!" This appealed to the local Presbyterian minister named Hugh Knox, and he got his friends together and asked them to donate funds to send the young genius to America to study.

In America, he worked hard and his star began to rise when he joined the American army and became an aide to Washington. His influence on the general continued while he was in the White House, as Hamilton was the most famous of Washington's cabinet ministers. As a result of his wisdom, the U.S. was able to have a firm financial foundation, and the factories began to hum, creating a new type of civilization and economy.

Even though he detested mobs, he worked hard to get the Constitution accepted. Ratification was uncertain until he collared Jefferson as the latter got off a boat from Paris. He talked Tom into throwing his political weight behind the famous document. He backed the Tories when they objected to loyalty oaths. He also defended the rights of a free press, although he was accused of wanting to control the thought processes of the nation as some other aristocrats.

Some have written that Jefferson and Hamilton were much closer to each other in political philosophy than we believe today. But surely Franklin took a very different approach to the problems of society than the young man from overseas. Hamilton seemed to have economic interests on a national scale, but Franklin was more interested in the prosperity and liberties of the common man. He was completely humanitarian in his hopes for America's future.

Franklin was a jolly individual and he loved to pull people's legs. Whether it was through pithy sayings or by writing articles for publication that had no basis of fact, he was forever stirring up society and particularly the bigwigs. This does not mean that he was always well informed about the sentiments of his people, even with all his power on the diplomatic scene. He had no idea that the Stamp Act would cause such a stir.

This well-rounded person had a great interest in practical matters. He worked out his own kind of "moral algebra" and tried to apply common sense to every area of his life. Franklin then would tell the world of his experiences so that they might profit from his victories and defeats.

He thoroughly believed that God directed the affairs of men. But he didn't express total belief in the teachings of God's word. He was trying to wing his way to heaven through personal efforts without the aid of Christ Jesus.

In the latter part of his life, he joined a society whose evangelical aim was to win Blacks to Jesus Christ.[4] The last act of his political life was to call for the complete abolition of slavery. As he had questioned the teachings of Christ and salvation, he said that he would know the truth once he stepped off into the next world—and for once he was not pulling anyone's leg.

John Adams lived longer than any other president of the United States. He passed away on July 4, 1826, along with Thomas Jefferson. James Monroe was the third member of that generation to die on Independence Day, but he outlived his political cronies by five years. Each one had played an active part in preparing the road to freedom, and each went to his grave happy that America was free. In fact, the last words of Adams were: "Independence Forever!"

Adams was called a Puritan revolutionary. He believed that it was traditional for those of the Puritan persuasion to resist governmental tyranny. The rather pessimistic approach of Puritan theology gave him a good balance in judging the world. Originally destined to become a clergyman, Adams attended Harvard College and studied for the ministry, but after teaching in a rural area, he decided to give up his vision for a career in the pulpit, and he turned to law. In reading many law books, he was soaking himself in revolutionary ideas.

He did not give up his faith in God when he switched professions. He was opposed to atheism, but he supported a positive type of Christian faith. He married a pastor's daughter and they spent a long fruitful life together. He not only penned loving thoughts to Abigail but told his children about God's loving care for them.

The self-educated lawyer loved his Bible and often saw parallels between the nation of Israel and the new, budding country in America. Even when he went abroad, he saw nothing in Paris that made him want to break with his Puritan upbringing. He described the seductive nature of the French capital, but he didn't take part in the fleshly fun. He told his wife that it was much more interesting to teach than carouse.

He boasted that America never had a king. Adams liked to see the downfall of the upper classes, as he felt that all men were basically the same under the skin. He supported the ideal of equality of all people in the sight of God and the community. From this position the next step was into the antislavery movement.

Freedom is complex. Once you start to question the rights of others to suppress the freedom of speech, the press, and assembly, you must broaden your ideas to cover the complete sphere of man's liberties. Six years before his death, Adams became very active in supporting religious toleration in his state. He took up this fight even though he was moving toward ninety and was so feeble that he could hardly hold a pen.

When they asked Adams to add something to his final two words, he refused. The two words summed up his feeling completely. In the South, there was another gentleman who had a way with words, and it was his oration in the House of Burgesses that stirred the hearts of Virginians for the rebel cause. This young man was Patrick Henry. He never seemed to be at a loss for words.

Patrick Henry's home had one book—the Bible. He was named after his uncle who was a pastor of the Anglican church. The old man would allow evangelists to fill his pulpit, although he wasn't friendly with every denomination. Henry's grandfather was much more liberal and paid a fine of twenty shillings for allowing Presbyterians to hold services in his own home while Virginia was an English colony.

Patrick heard the prince of American preachers when the evgangelists came into his area when he was young. He had become a deeply religious young gentleman. Even though he never favored book learning in his youth, he still could remember the words from the Book of Common Prayer fifty years later. The fiery figure continually read the Bible and grew in God's grace.

Henry was brought up with a Black as his close companion. They romped by the rivers and hunted in the woods together. But when he grew older, he began to consider the inconsistencies of slavery. When Patrick saw a slave auction, he was so shocked that he prayed that God might end that awful business in human flesh.

Like many people in that century, he failed at a number of jobs before he became a lawyer. He fought a famous case against the Anglican pastors to win fame in the colony, but he also used his time to protect the innocent. When he was defending an individual charged with murder, he reminded the jury that they would be guilty on the Judgment Day if they convicted an innocent man.

If Patrick Henry grew famous through the use of his golden voice, Thomas Paine won fame because of his skill with the pen. Tom also had been a failure through most of his life. He had lost two wives and every job he ever had, including that of tax collector, by the time he reached the age of thirty-seven.

He left for America, and through a kind note of Benjamin Franklin, he was accepted in the New World. As an only child, he had memorized whole passages from the Bible, and because of this he lived a very Puritan life; he was never known to swear. He worked on a magazine with the Reverend Mr. Witherspoon, and through this journal and his book, *Common Sense*, he won a famous spot in American history.

It is asserted that Paine got most of his views for his famous book through the influence of the Reverend Mr. Priestly. He even attempted to be a preacher in his younger days, but he seemed to have more ability with his pen. He also came to support the abolition of slavery in America, which was a simple extension of his vision for all mankind. Later, he would call himself a citizen of the world rather than just an American. Probably this adjustment in his thinking came about because he felt miffed that his fellowmen didn't give him more honors for his gifted pronouncements on personal liberty. He spent much of his life overseas.

Not all of those interested in freedom were deeply religious. Ethan Allen, leader of the Green Mountain Boys, seemed to take particular delight in criticizing the Christian faith. His father was anticlerical, and Allen continued the campaign against men of the cloth. He was roundly attacked by the clergy in his home area and labeled an infidel in his death. This was because he wrote an anti-Christian booklet to disprove the teachings of Christ. After his death, his daughter had a fearful vision, and she ran away to become a Catholic nun.

John Jay of New York was almost the opposite of Ethan Allen, who had several spats with the upper class of the Empire State. Jay was an aristocrat who had been raised as a French Huguenot. His family had suffered a great deal under the Catholics, and he was suspicious of anyone who followed the teachings of Rome. His wife was a pious daughter of a French Protestant pastor.

John entered King's College to prepare himself for future employment. While at the college, a student broke one of the tables, but would not give himself up to the authorities. Jay was asked by the officials if he knew who had done it, and he replied that he did. But when asked to name the culprit, he refused to inform on his friend. The leaders expelled him, but he quickly studied the rules of the college and won his case, as there certainly was no regulation demanding that students inform on others.

John's older brother, James, was an excellent student and had a fine mind. When he linked up with the Reverend Mr. Smith to raise money for King's College, he was very successful. He helped raise £10,000 but refused to hand it over until he deducted his expenses. This publicity caused John all kinds of trouble.

When the war came, John saw his brother side with the king. He himself remained true to the cause of liberty. Jay was fully convinced that he and others were making "a fight for millions yet unborn." Like many others, he came to detest the idea of slavery and felt it was ridiculous for America to claim to be fighting for true liberty, when all men in her states were not free. He wanted to abolish slavery immediately.

John Jay was a very zealous Christian. Jay worked very hard in the propagation of the Bible. Even secular writers have pointed out that his faith grew as he became older and that he became even more dedicated to the cause of Jesus.

James Madison is the fourth Virginian whom we will consider in this chapter. He was tutored by Rev. Thomas Martin and followed the "New Light" Presbyterians in his state. Seeing that the Anglican church was the most powerful denomination in his domain, he immediately became something of a rebel in the eyes of his friends and the establishment.

Even though he counseled a friend to "always keep the ministry obliquely in view," he himself became a lawyer. In considering his own outlook on the future, he turned to King Rehoboam of the Old Testament as an example to think seriously about.

Madison had a deep interest in the religious climate of Virginia. He was sure that if the Church of England had been firmly established with ruling bishops, that "slavery and subjection might and would have been insinuated among us." But the future president did not wish to see his own denomination established as the state church. He wanted to go further than George Mason, another politician, in his support of religious freedom.

The capstone of his achievement was the all-inclusive injunction of the First Amendment: "Congress shall make no law respecting the establishment of religion, or prohibiting the free exercise thereof." Virginia was organizing a formidable group of outstanding men to march for the cause of religious freedom. They were not opposed to Christianity; many were very religious, but they lived in a colony where the Established church had ruled for generations, and they wished to allow each denomination freedom to preach the Gospel and win converts.

The uncrowned heroes of the Revolution were those who signed the Declaration of Independence. Each one would dangle at the end of a rope if the rebellion was crushed. Eighteen who scratched their names on the famous document were in their thirties and three were in their twenties! Most of the signers had a lifetime to live—if the British did not annihilate their comrades in arms. "To protect them, or primarily their families scattered across the land, it was now agreed," says

T. R. Fehrenbach, "that the signatures would not be made public for six months."

Hancock said, "We must be unanimous. There must be no pulling different ways; we must all hang together." Franklin giggled and added, "Yes. We must all hang together, or most assuredly, we shall all hang separately." Benjamin Harrison, whose family tree would see two gentleman hang their hats in the White House, teased birdlike Elbridge Gerry, "With me, it will all be over in a minute. But you, you'll be dancing on air an hour after I'm gone."

It was really no joking matter. The king's forces were anxious to catch these political vagabonds, and whenever they could, they made trouble for these men of courage. They confiscated all the property of Philip Livingston, whose grandfather had been a political-religious Presbyterian emigre from Great Britain. But the first to suffer was Francis Lewis, who was the son of an Anglican clergyman. The redcoats captured his wife and locked her up in a filthy room for weeks; with no bed nor change of clothes, she finally snapped. John Hart of New Jersey was a very devout Baptist who donated land for church property. When the Hessians came to Trenton to burn his property, he had to flee to the woods and evade the enemy for many days. When he returned, his children were gone, his wife was dead and buried in a plot beside the church, and he was never able to find all his offspring before he passed into glory to meet his Jesus. Richard Stockton, "born to a family of Presbyterian gentry," had the finest library in America, but the invaders from England destroyed it completely when they attacked his home. Abraham Clark was a deeply moral man, and he would not forsake his principles when the British captured two of his sons and treated them brutally, saying that they would free them if he renounced the declaration he had signed. He stoutly refused to do so. John Morton, "a man of deep religious feeling," was rejected by his closest friends for signing the document of liberty, but on his deathbed in

1777, he said, "Tell them that they will live to see the hour when they shall acknowledge it [the signing] to have been the most glorious service that I ever rendered to my country." Dr. Benjamin Rush was perhaps the most famous physician in America. A historian wrote, "Importantly, Rush's early practice, his origins, his deep religious impressions . . . he never doubted 'the divine origin of the Bible' as he said . . . and natural instincts made him one of the earliest humanitarians in America."

These are only a handful of names of those who risked their health, homes, and happiness for the cause of liberty. The deep religious feeling that many other signers possessed kept them on the right path as they saw the fortunes of their country toss and sway. When one studies the Revolution, one realizes how much courage and faith it took to believe that things would turn out alright in the end. If their faith was built upon sand, and not upon a strong foundation, they would have given up the fight against the strongest nation on the globe.

NOTES

1. Bernard Mayo, *Myths & Men*, The Academy Library (New York: Harper & Row, Publishers, Harper Torchbooks, 1959), p. 37*
2. Thomas A. Bailey, *Presidential Greatness* (New York: Appleton-Century, 1966), pp. 5-6.
3. Richard B. Morris, *Seven Who Shaped Our Destiny* (New York: Harper & Row, Publishers, 1973), pp. 36-37.
4. Ibid., p. 19.

XX *A NEW REVOLUTION*

> *When, in an apprehensive or deploring mood . . . we should first reflect on the moral history of mankind, which can be summarized: They hang prophets—or ignore them, which hurts worse.*
>
> DR. KARL MENNINGER

Historian Howard H. Peckham said, "We continually turn back to the Revolution to renew our faith in ourselves and to resight our objectives." This faith rested in the heart, according to John Adams, when he was trying to describe the foundation of the Revolution. How else could the Americans topple the forces of oppression when the thirteen colonies entered the conflict without adequate arms, armies, or alms?

The very ideals of the American public have never tarnished

over the two-hundred-year history of this miracle state. Of all the other countries of Africa, Asia, or the Americas, only she shot forward to overtake Europe in a little more than one century. Without kings or kingpins, the rejected of Europe raised a new flag over a city that did not even exist when independence was won. In the century after 1820, some thirty-five million people entered America to make it a melting pot of the world's unfortunates. By 1972, New York City would hold more Jews than Israel, more Italians than Rome, more Irishmen than Dublin, more Blacks than any African city. The battle for these ideals continues today. A. L. Rowse wrote, "We might justly regard the main conflict raging in the world today as one between the ideals of the American Revolution and those of the Russian. For American ideals had, and have, a revolutionary appeal no less than Communist dogmas, even if their appeal is altogether more human and civilized, offering far more hope to mankind than the sinister denial of freedom from which the brutality and barbarity of communism flow."

William Appleman Williams of the New Left, would take a dim view of Mr. Rowse's article, which appeared in the *New York Times Magazine*, as he felt that the Cold War rhetoric was spoiling chances "to create a truly Christian community, devoid of strife, fear and inequality." But another historian believes that "the Revolutionary generation set a shining example to the world" as it "crumbled the Spanish Empire, inspired several national revolutions, forced liberal reforms in England, and gave hope to all repressed peoples."

Yes, the Declaration of Independence was one of the most subversive documents the world had ever seen. One could not read it but feel a stirring in the heart for all those who lived without the benefits of freedom. This slavery was preceded by sleep and a blindness to the true value of liberty. The spirit of liberty must be kept alive or it will soon be lost.

A pastor in New England believed that the reason for the

clash of arms was the sin in men's hearts. A politician agreed with him and said, "This calamity is generally owing to the DECAY OF VIRTUE." Yes, sin could bring on problems between peace-loving people, and there was enough stubbornness in both nations to raise the possibility of a fierce war. A year later, in the city of Boston, all the patriots were sure that their cause was just, and they heard their pastor warn them of overconfidence. This Puritan, in 1776, preached, "Our cause is so just and good that nothing can prevent our success but only our sins. Could I see a spirit of repentance and reformation prevail through the land, I should not have the least apprehension or fear of being brought under the iron rod of slavery, even though all the powers of the globe were combined against us."

The problem, as the preachers saw it, was that real religious faith was scarce. There might be hope for the Revolution if it could express the principles of Christ and of his kingdom. This type of Puritanism would be lost on the world, but Jean-François Revel, a left-wing radical, could still predict a new revolution would take place in America in the twentieth century that would change the world, and Black nationalist Eldridge Cleaver agreed with him. This second revolution would make America the true light of the world in the political sense, and other countries would again look to her for moral leadership and enlightenment.

The Frenchman could easily look backwards at the three most important revolutions of the last two centuries. The French Revolution and the American Revolution differed in a number of ways, but in one important feature they were similar. They both wished to throw off the power of a corrupt monarchy. But the French Revolution was offensive while the American one was basically defensive. Then, too, the Americans had nothing to destroy and the Frenchmen had nothing to preserve. Whereas the followers of Congress glorified religion and thought of it as one of the most important supports for their freedoms, many a Frenchman desecrated Catholic churches and in one case placed an unclad female on the altar, thus making an open mockery of their God.

In comparing the three revolutions, we come to some interesting conclusions. Even though the rebels in the colonies wished to throw off the yoke of an invader, they wished to retain their basic political liberties—making them conservatives at heart. In both the French and Russian Revolution, the radicals were out to destroy everything—in the name of liberalism. But what was the net result? The conservative American Revolution developed the most liberal kinds of documents, and the freedoms of its people grew as the years went by, whereas the two European revolutions brought in radical elements that swiftly wished to keep the status quo, after original upheavals had placed them in power; and as the respective regimes grew stronger, they denied more and more rights to their people.

"It may be concluded that Marxism is more revelation than theory, a surrogate faith for an age losing its religion. Marx had the self-assurance of a prophet who has talked with God, and his way of oversimplifying issues through convoluted argument befits a dogma." These are the words of Prof. Robert G. Wesson of the University of California at Santa Barbara. He is not the first one to note the similarity of Marxism and religious thought. Bertrand Russell and many others have noted the same truth. Edward J. Baccioco says that their aim has been to produce a "new man."

Arthur Koestler tells of his trip into Communism.

> I became converted because I was ripe for it and lived in a disintegrating society thirsting for faith. . . . Tired of electrons and wave mechanics, I began for the first time to read Marx, Engels and Lenin in earnest. By the time I had finished with Feuerback and *State and Revolution*, something had clicked in my brain which shook me like a mental explosion. To say that one had "seen the light" is a poor description of the mental rapture which only the convert knows. The new light seems to

pour from all directions across the skull; the whole universe falls into pattern like the stray pieces of a jigsaw puzzle assembled by magic at one stroke. There is now an answer to every question, doubts and conflicts are a matter of the tortured past—a past already remote, when one had lived in a dismal ignorance in the tasteless, colorless world of those who DON'T KNOW. Nothing henceforth can disturb the convert's inner peace and serenity—except the occasional fear of losing faith again, losing thereby what alone makes life worth living, and falling back into the outer darkness, where there is wailing and gnashing of teeth.[1]

This reverence strikes every Communist, and he becomes a messenger of faith. Bertram Wolfe speaks of a young American, John Reed, who penned *Ten Days That Shook the World,* and how he glorified the Russian Revolution. Wolfe writes, "For Reed the Revolution is holy. As a devout Christian may believe that on the night of the Savior's birth 'no spirit dares stir abroad; the nights are wholesome, then no planets strike any fairy tales, nor witch hath power to charm, so hallow'd and so gracious is the time,' so Reed writes of the night Lenin seized power: 'On that night not a single hold-up occurred, not a single robbery.' The same impression of sacredness is repeated three days later: 'Quiet the city lay, not a hold-up, not a robbery, not even a drunken fight.' "[2]

Repentance and confession have marked the path of many a believer in Marxism. Sociologist Erikson says, "In this again, as in so many other respects, the newer Puritanism of the Soviet Union seems to parallel the older Puritanism of New England." The same strictness often accompanies the walk of the Communist clerics in worker's wear. Lenin denied himself the right to listen to all types of music because of the turmoil it caused in him. But this is where the contrast ends. Adrienne Koch tells us, "The thought and character of these statesmen sharply contrast with that of the founding fathers of the Soviet Union. Lenin, Trotsky, and Stalin considered themselves to be philosopher-statesmen, but their philosophy was dialectically intolerant of any differences of thought; the differences that did arise were ultimately seen as total and therefore had to eventuate in the victory of one man, who was then deified."

Religion is based on faith and on emotions. Whereas love is the base of Christian faith, hatred is the foundation of Marxism, according to the Soviet encyclopedia. It says, "Soviet patriotism is indissolubly connected with hatred toward the enemies of the Socialist Fatherland. 'It is impossible to conquer the enemy without having learned to hate him with all the might of one's soul. . . .' The teaching of hatred toward the enemies of the toilers enriches the conception of Socialistic humanism by distinguishing it from sugary and hypocritical 'philanthropy'."

Those who would doubt the religious teachings of Communism should simply search the teachings of its own press and radio. Hung Ping-chung tells us:

> I was sent to a hospital in Peking with a cancer so big that the food I managed to swallow often went down my windpipe. I was afraid that if the cancer kept growing I would die of starvation. I was given radiotherapy. With warm class feeling the doctors and nurses showed great concern for me and advised me to study and apply Chairman Mao's works to my problem of illness. . . . I again turned to Chairman Mao's three constantly read articles, every word shines like gold. I studied the passages on life and death and his teachings that revolutionaries should be wholly dedicated to the liberation of the people and work entirely in the people's interest. One must go through many tests in order to look at life and death like a thorough-going proletarian revolutionary. . . . I was given a six and a half hour operation during which three malignant tumours which had nearly obstructed my intestine were removed. When I regained consciousness I felt an acute pain in my abdomen. At this time the image of Chairman Mao, serious, honest, and kindly, appeared before my mind's eye and filled me with warmth, and I seemed to hear his words: "In times of difficulty we must not lose sight of our achievements, must see the bright future and

must pluck up our courage." This enabled me to fight on with revolutionary optimism. My health has steadily improved. Now I can play basketball steadily for 40 minutes. Every morning I run 3,000 metres. When I feel tired I shout: "Long live Chairman Mao!" and "Be resolute, fear no sacrifice, and surmount every difficulty to win victory" (Peking Radio).

Mao also worked many more miracles; here are just three:

1. A 45-kilogram (about one hundred pounds) tumour was removed by faith in Mao (*Peking Review*).
2. Deaf mutes were healed and now 129 of the school's 168 students can cheer "Long live Chairman Mao!" and 47 can sing "The East Is Red" and other propaganda songs of China (*Peking Review*).
3. Li Shu-fang's right hand was severed in an accident, but by faith the doctors helped "restore its functions by relying on invincible Mao Tse-tung thought" (New China News Agency).

Other interesting religious ideas have made Mao another savior:

1. For a wedding present, Yin Teh-shan's daughter received a set of *Selected Works of Mao Tse-Tung*, a red-tasselled spear, and a spade (New China News Agency).
2. The Chinese press (*China Reconstructs*) had a story similar to Mary's at the time of the birth of Jesus. There was no room at the inn for a pregnant proletarian female.
3. The top Ping-Pong players won an international match by relying on the teaching of Mao found in his articles, *On Contradiction* and *On Practice* (New China News Agency).
4. Fisherman threatened by waves faced the portrait of Mao and wished the great leader a long, long life, and they were saved (Peking Radio).
5. A couple who were about to be married "studied the

teachings of the great leader Chairman Mao: 'The principle of diligence and frugality should be observed in everything' and we 'must not take a short view and indulge in wastefulness and extravagance'" (New China News Agency).

6. They were warned against unclean spirits which could destroy their fellowship (Peking Radio).

7. They glorified a martyr who had died helping to reeducate people in the country (Peking Radio).[3]

Through their faith in Mao, the Chinese also resurrected a worker from the dead! Like all other Communist regimes of the past, they deify their leaders. Robert S. Elegant writes: "Mao transcended humanity. His demi-deification followed traditional Chinese as well as new Marxist practices. The Chairman was tendered ritual forms of address and adulation prescribed for the Emperor, who had been called the Son of Heaven. Denying any power greater than man, Marxism indulged in the secular deification of its great men. Technically brilliant, though grisly, the mummification of Vladmir Ilyich Lenin and Joseph Stalin had preserved the supermen's material form. They would have been worshiped as demigods had Marxist theology permitted. In his own lifetime, Mao Tse-tung was exalted even higher."

This is why an excommunist does not defect from the faith but takes up a new belief. A Russian scholar says, "The gift of repentance, which perhaps more than anything else distinguishes man from the animal world, is particularly difficult for modern man to recover." But, he continues, "Repentance is the first bit of firm ground underfoot." Without repentance and conversion the individual cannot find the true meaning in life—it must be based on what God has done, not on what man himself can do.

Those who do not take into consideration the most important revolution in the world—the one that takes place in the heart of the new believer who accepts Christ as his personal savior—often insist that religion always supports the status quo. We have seen this definitely was not true during the Revolution, and after, when the evangelicals shook up the establishment and made America much more democratic; but what about today? Religion in general seems to be a mixed bag if we are to believe a volume published by Oxford University. "Religion has often been a force upholding the status quo, reinforcing the stability of society and enhancing political quietism. And yet, religion has also been an important force facilitating radical political and social change, providing the motivation, ideological justification, and social cohesion for rebellions and revolutions."

On the left we see believers designing new pseudo-religions with Stalin saving souls or Mao moving mountains. On the right, we see them worshiping national heroes or myths about racial or cultural superiority. I was shocked by the amount of dedication the members of Hitler Youth had to fascism. But a new, more subtle faith has risen from the ashes of World War II and the collapse of Cold War rhetoric.

Jean-François Revel, left-wing author of *Without Marx or Jesus*, believes that this new faith will bring in the multifarious millenium. He praises the likes of Abbie Hoffman, who penned *Revolution for the Hell of It*, and new organizations that have brought in a strange kind of "moral revolution," with titles like The Homosexual Community or the League of Women Homosexuals. By stressing a new kind of liberated and sensual love, they have torn at the fabric of society with the goal of a more enlightened community.

This revolution is in marked contrast to the uprisings against Marxism in Czechoslovakia and Hungary. The new generation seeks for freedom, which it feels cannot be found in the West. This attitude only confused a left-wing student in Prague. Stephen Spender tells us about this encounter as he says, "When I was in Prague, B---, one of the students, gave me a type-written copy of an essay he had written. This throws a good deal

of light on the attitude of the Czech to the western students.
B--- begins by remarking that their western colleagues sometimes reproach the Czech students for not giving more support
to the agitation of their colleagues in the west. . . . 'The fact
is,' he writes, 'that the attitude of the Czechs to the western
students is largely coloured by envy'; the conditions which
the western students take for granted appear to the Czech a
dream of bliss."

A Western leftist was chagrined by the contrast of his own
friends when he compared what had happened in Prague
during the uprising in 1968. He writes, "The observations reveal
to me a certain perversity in my own attitude. Nostalgia for
student riots, clashes with the police, and totally exposed
thighs suggests a false romanticism, an irritable desire to inflict
on an ostensibly sane society a form of chaos which, as a way
of life, is superficial and nihilistic. The manner in which the
young Czechs are conducting themselves is really a model of
civic control and enlightenment, whereas we have become
alcoholic on sensation and violence." The new attitude con-
trasts to a great degree with the confident attitude men had
in morality itself to aid humanity after World War I.

The faith in human power to build a new tower of Babel
began to topple as the 1930s appeared and even Socialists
began to look around for scapegoats for their failings. The
bitter tirade continues as followers of Herbert Marcuse call
for "the forcible suppression of false ideas." This allows them
to use a double standard in any judgment. Things they would
denounce in the West become badges of honor on the Left.

Tom Wolfe gives us a picture of these seekers as he says,
"Intellectuals are wed to a romantic dream of the past and
never want to abandon it. They have an unquenchable nostalgia
for the great scenarios of nineteenth-century Marxism such as
the Paris Commune of 1871 . . . a glorious moment! . . .
and a total failure." They immediately lose their balance so
that a splendid journal like the *New Statesman* could write

about the purges of Stalin, "A social revolution is accompanied both by violence and by idealism."

These men who claim to follow humanitarian principles would scream about the witch trials at Salem and the horrors of Puritanism, but when it comes to a few million deaths, they can be surprisingly candid. "As for the number of victims," Stuart Schram writes, "it was officially stated in October of 1951 that 800,000 cases of counter-revolutionaries had been dealt with during the first six months of 1951 by the people's courts alone. Chou En-lai later declared that 16.8 percent of the counter-revolutionaries tried had been sentenced to death, mostly prior to 1952. The combinations of those two pieces of information would give a figure of 135,000 executions during the first half of 1951. The actual number was undoubtedly much higher. Hostile estimates have ranged as high as ten or fifteen million victims. A reasonable estimate would appear to be from one to three million all told." He adds, "If we . . . figure two million victims, this [is] about 0.3 percent of the total population [150,000 Britain and France; 600,000 in the U.S.]. . . ." Another writer gleefully announces the number of people killed in the Crusades (1,000,000), the Massacre of Saint Bartholomew's Day, and the Inquisition (250,000), but never mentions the 20,000,000 murdered under Stalin.

We Christians should roundly condemn all the murders committed in the name of Jesus, although we surely had nothing to do with them ourselves. By recognizing the total legacy of our religion, we expose the blind spots in the eyes of left-wing dreamers. Sometimes they are chastened by their own members, but they seem no better than right-wingers who look the other way if freedom is being suppressed in South Africa or South Korea. Even though a number in their ranks seem to oppose the majority rule in a democracy, they do have some excellent humanitarian principles that attract the young and zealous secular do-gooder.

American youth has turned to them for two reasons. One,

they seem to stand for true equality for all men in both racial
and economic spheres. Two, they become high priests of the
intellectual community, which causes an unthinking generation
to applaud their words and deeds simply because of the position they hold in a select community.

One *must* praise their basic interest in the outer man. They
often put evangelicals to shame by their interest in the needs
of the masses, while we, like the Pharisee, walk on the other
side! But in all of this, they come up empty-handed; they say
there is no true joy in life. They are building on sand as they
aid men who can be pruned and polished but can never live
up to expectations. The New Deal, the Square Deal, and the
New Society are now tombstones engraved with the spiritual
death of their victims. The hopes of the downtrodden were
lifted in a spectacular social orbit but now lie smashed on
the sad earth. They renovated the individual but never gave
him the revolutionary heart that he desperately needed.

Walter Lippman, one of the left wing's great prophets,
understood their dilemma many years ago when he wrote *A
Preface to Morals*. In that day and age, modernism was riding
high. The fundamentalists were ridiculed and numbered only
in the hundreds. But Lippman praised the work of Prof. J.
Gresham Machen for his volume, *Christianity and Liberalism*.
Lippman not only said, "It is an admirable book," but understood what few religious leaders of that day knew—that the
liberals had blasted the bedrock out from under Christianity
and left their parishioners with dusty Bibles. Materialistic
philosophy or moral platitudes never fed the soul. Lippman
knew that "without faith man cannot please God!"

Works written about Russia just after the Russian Revolution
spoke in glowing terms of the new utopia built on a humanitarian basis of a classless society. Whereas men of the right
wince when the names of Franco or two-bit dictators are
mentioned, the left-wing youth glorifies Mao, Che, and Castro,
all of whom have fought democratic ideas tooth and nail. The
secular salvation, based on Marxist ideals but in a new setting,

has also failed to bring lasting joy, so now we turn back to the American Revolution.

America failed in two ways to continue the Revolution to this very day. The first failure involves the racial question. At the time of the Revolution, the men of means and the message saw the basic inconsistency of slavery and the cause of liberty. They struggled with this question—and lost.

The evangelicals have done the very same thing! If any group should have come to the aid of the Blacks, it was the orthodox believers in America. The fundamentalists left the Church of Christ a mighty foundation of truths, but then these men ran and hid from society. This was partially a natural reaction, as they were rejected by society and the intellectual institutions of that sad era. But another reason was the constant bickering among themselves, which caused them to pride themselves on narrow doctrinal purity, while allowing the public to go to Hades.

The call for freedom for ALL men was the never-ending ideal of the American Revolution. Whereas Communism enslaves the soul and society, Christianity should set them free. Too often the minority groups were thought of as mere numbers to be won to Christ. The orthodox believers were not interested in their whole being. They rushed to evangelize the Indians and Blacks, but they left social justice to the modernists.

America is not the only place where racism has been rampant. Ghanian students in Moscow marched on the Kremlin because of the murder of one of their own for trying to date a Russian girl. Students from Zanzibar accused the Communist Chinese of racial prejudice, as they said, "We are regarded more as animals than human beings." Eldridge Cleaver was amazed at the racial discrimination he found in Cuba. But the United States boasts of having the Statue of Liberty in New York harbor when she wears a badge of hypocrisy in Harlem and Watts!

Jefferson feared the wrath of a just God over the problem

of slavery, but he did not free his slaves! Christians have talked about love of their brothers but have not practiced what they preached. That has made America an object of ridicule, as Lincoln predicted, around the globe.

Our next failure has been our relationship to the world. Our rhetoric may be brilliant, but our practice is poor. America wisely followed a practice of no entangling alliances, but she also turned her back on the ideals she stood for. The isolationism did not just come from a conservative stance; it was rooted in "the Populist-Progressive revolt." Liberalism of the 1940s stood for "the unfettered development of the individual," but in the 1970s, it has lost this association.

The world has forgotten the realism of the Puritans, and the romantic idea that the eyes of Europe were once upon America. We Americans gave bountifully to many states after World War II, even helping our former enemies to escape starvation. But it was always gifts of money, as if we could buy their friendship and secure their joy with millions of dollars.

We also began to aid very undemocratic regimes. We seemed to be preaching the gospel of the almighty dollar and an acceptance of immorality at the same time. It is true that the Cuban Communist party supported Batista right up to the very day Castro liberated his homeland from a corrupt undemocratic government. But Communism has never respected the ideals of Christian ethics and never will. The very basis for our foreign policy should be the teachings of the Word of God and the democratic ideals of the American Revolution. If America wishes to gain respect, she must adhere to principles in her foreign policy.

The world is headed for disaster because it has rejected God, but we Christians should not rejoice and say "we told you so." Men cannot find God through reason only. Justice Holmes tells us that "life is based on imperfect knowledge." But yet, the world has often accused evangelicals of having no faith in the future. Perry Miller writes, "The most persistent misunderstanding of the Puritan mind in contemporary criticism results in the charge that it was fatalistic." He also laughed at the ridiculous charge that all the Puritans could talk about was hell.

After World War I, the leaders of the world were very confident in man's ability to direct his own fabulous future. Some even felt a little of that when the United Nations was founded after the next big bloodletting. But things have changed. Men like Russell thought that their days were numbered around the time of the Cuban Missile Crisis, and Henry Kissinger wonders if the Western world can really survive this century.

C. G. Jung was very interested in the death wish in modern literature. Socrates hinted that the true philosopher was "ever pursuing death and dying." Montaigne adds, "That to study philosophy is to learn to die." Durkheim was very pessimistic about helping prevent suicides. These doctors of the soul seem to have forgotten the one remedy of the heart—salvation through Christ.

John Donne's list of notable suicides of the classical scholars and philosophers runs for three pages, and he did not include them all. Socrates, Cordrus, Charondas, Lycurgus, Cleombrotus, Cato, Zeno, Cleanthes, Seneca, Isocrates, Demosthenes, Lucretius, Lucan, Laienus, Terence, Aristarchus, Petronius Arbiter, Hannibal, Boadicea, Brutus, and Cassius are just some of the famous people of history who despaired of all life. Historians like Toynbee also saw a very gloomy future ahead of them. Yes, men without faith face a horrible future. Historian William Appleman Williams, New Left prophet, said, "The frontier was now on the rim of hell, and the inferno was radioactive."

The world for all of its knowledge and bravado of the past has not developed a means of salvation for mankind. Some predict that the earth will destroy itself in a terrible nuclear war. Others predict that famine is just around the corner. A third group insists that pollution will grease the skids for a nightmarish hell, where civilization will collapse in a sea of gases and garbagelike existence.

Two crystal-ball-gazers have predicted an end of everything by the close of this century. While mankind careens wildly down the road of life, he seeks to drown himself in drugs, dope, and dames. Having lost all confidence in the nihilistic philosophy that has been shoved down his throat, he seeks to live out his final days in a life of wantonness and revelry.

America may have the answer for each soul in the building of a new revolution, which will set the world on fire for God. Of all the nations of the world, America seems to be the most religious—but a major problem is that much is only the froth of faith and not a bedrock foundation built securely upon the teachings of Christ.

Many youth have gobbled down Zen Buddhism without a thought. They giggle at the thought of Christ walking on the water to save his troubled friends, but these same seekers don't bat an eye when they read the Buddhist Pali Scriptures, which tell of Buddha's fast steed racing around the world in a matter of moments, or the Gautama turning himself into a snake, and of many other fantastic tales.[4]

The question whether or not God exists has troubled man since the beginning of time. Increase Mather, a sturdy Pilgrim, tells us, "Soon after my ordination I was grievously molested with temptations to atheism, whereby my spirit was much afflicted and broken. . . . The special thing that satisfied me was that I had experience of great answers of prayer, whereby I could but see that there is a God, and that he is a rewarder of them that diligently seek him." God had melted his heart. He testified, "I had rarely known any Tears, except those that were for the Joy of the Salvation of God." But now God reached out and touched his heart so tenderly that the hardness gave way to a gentle glorifying of his savior.

Immediately, people think of a church-oriented religion based not on the Bible but on a blind faithfulness to denominational ties. The old idea was that a one-church state brought peace to a nation; that sects jarred the peace of society; and that church creeds could bring a salvation of sorts to the sinner. Even a historian realized that "laws cannot succeed in rekindling the ardour of an extinguished faith."

The bewildered public scratched their heads as denominations required blind obedience and sought mindless subservience by its followers. Just as men argue about the merits of a baseball club or their choice in musical scores, individuals began to stand up for this or that group simply because of loyalty instead of a personal belief in Christ. Only evangelists could reach across religious party lines. While infidels gawked, men argued insanely about the mode of baptism or the merits of this or that rite.

Oh, if the divisions of man were broken down, what joy we would have! It must wound the heart of God to see his children wildly boast that they are Baptists, Presbyterians, or Methodists, and that their respective denominations are better than all the rest, like little children boasting about the brilliance of their own dad.

A story is told about three youngsters arguing about which father was the greatest. The lawyer's son said that his dad received $40,000 for one case. The doctor's boy laughed and said that for one operation his dad received double that. The poor lad of a pastor stared at his old dungarees and shuffled his feet nervously. Suddenly, he smiled and blurted out, "Hey, you guys, my father is so great that it takes four men to carry the money down the aisle!" They all giggled and ran home for supper.

Every Christian should be thoroughly convinced in his heart about what mode of baptism God requires, but this and other subjects should not evade the cross of Christ. Does baptism or church membership guarantee entrance into heaven?

No! One of the thieves who was crucified with Jesus turned to him in repentance and asked to be remembered by the Lord. Jesus replied, "Today you will be in Paradise!" The sinner needed no baptismal regeneration or the acceptance of any bishop to enter the pearly gates; he entered because of God's grace. Doctrinal purity is important for each group following the Lord, but acceptance by men does not mean acceptance by God.

The following are needed to enter into the rich and JOYFUL salvation that God has for everyone of us:

1. Recognition of Christ's death on the cross for salvation— John 3:16.
2. Confession of our personal sins—I John 1:8-10.
3. Repentance for our sins—Acts 2:37,38.
4. Belief in Christ to save one from his sins—John 5:24.
5. Choosing this day to receive salvation—II Cor. 6:2.

Jesus has gone to heaven to prepare a place for us (John 14:1-6), and the Puritans, Quakers, Baptists, Mennonites, Presbyterians, Methodists, and other evangelical denominations preached Christ. Paul tells us: "For it has been made clear to me, my brethren, by those of Chloe's household that there are contentions and wrangling and factions among you. What I mean is that each of you [either] says, I belong to Paul, or I belong to Apollos, or I belong to Cephas [Peter], or I belong to Christ. Is Christ, the Messiah divided into parts? Was Paul crucified on behalf of you? . . . For Christ, the Messiah, sent me out not to baptize but [to evangelize by] preaching the glad tidings [the Gospel]; and that not with verbal eloquence, lest the cross of Christ should be deprived of force and emptied of its power and rendered vain—fruitless, void of value and of no effect" (I Cor. 1:12,13, and 17—THE AMPLIFIED BIBLE).

A secular professor shows the need of people today when

he writes: "It is a centrally important fact, crucial to understanding the international student revolt, that the official institutions of the United States and other advanced Western democracies do not provide adequate outlets for these religious impulses. . . . Neither the Freudian model nor its derivatives offer, for example, a very plausible account of religion; nor for that matter do Marxian and subsequent technological-cum-economic explanations of social behavior. Is it not reasonable to assume that human beings have a basic need for something sacred, which need is quite independent of whatever sexual frustrations they may feel and whatever economic security or insecurity they may have?" Secular solutions for the sinner and his salvation will never bring him to know the PEACE (John 14:27), JOY (John 15:11), nor the SECURITY (John 10:28) God has in store for him.

But the individual must seek to find this path to God. A New England farmer tells of his seeking after the Savior. He said:

> Now it pleased God to send Mr. Whitefield into this land; and my hearing of his preaching at Philadelphia, like one of the old apostles, and many thousands flocking to hear him preach the Gospel, and the great numbers were converted to Christ, I felt the Spirit of God drawing me by conviction; I longed to see and hear him and wished he would come this way. . . . When I saw Mr. Whitefield come upon the scaffold, he looked almost angelical; a young, slim, slender youth before thousands of people with a bold undaunted contenance. And my hearing how God was with him everywhere as he came along, it solemnized my mind and put me into a trembling fear before he began to preach; for he looked as if he was clothed with authority from the Great God, and a sweet solemnity sat upon his brow, and my hearing him preach gave me a heart wound. By God's blessing, my old foundation was broken up, and I saw that my righteousness would not save me.

Historian John C. Miller continues, "These were the first pangs of the 'new birth'—a process whereby, Whitefield said,

Christians were purged of sin and otherwise prepared for their advent into Heaven."

Yes, there was a revolt against a "humanized Jesus." Christ was the very Son of God, who had come to earth to start a revolution in the hearts of men. Only he, and he alone, could cause a lasting revolution! All other revolutions in history have lasted for just a brief spell and then squandered their resources in establishing the status quo. Each one of them, whether Communist or man-made, try to protect the power of the politicians against the very wishes of the people.

What has stopped America and other countries from finding the true revelation and an abiding revolution? Mao talked about a continuous revolution but it has been more a continual violence with much shedding of blood. The problem rests with a three letter word—SIN! Men hate to think of SIN in relationship to God. They hate to think of themselves as SIN-NERS. They will admit to every other kind of illness except the one that matters most—the sickness of the heart.

Dr. Karl Menninger, a physician, points out that we have lost the sense of sin and of shame. Not since Ike has any president mentioned sin in a major message. And, then, Eisenhower borrowed the words from Abraham Lincoln: "It is the duty of nations as well as of men to own their dependence upon the overruling power of God, to confess their sins and transgressions in humble sorrow, yet with assured hope that genuine repentance will lead to mercy and pardon."

Menninger continues: "In all of the laments and reproaches made by our seers and prophets, one misses any mention of 'sin', a word which used to be a veritable watchword of prophets. It was a word once in everyone's mind, but now rarely if ever heard. Does that mean that no sin is involved in all our troubles—sin with an 'I' in the middle? Is no one any longer guilty of anything? Guilty perhaps of a sin that could be repented and repaired or atoned for?"

In his best selling book, *Whatever Became of Sin?*, Menninger points back to the central problem of mankind. No earthly revolution can answer the inner problem of man. All they can do is rearrange superficial features and, through a totalitarian system, impose a new dictatorship made by man. Jesus said: "And ye shall know the truth and the truth shall make you free" (John 8:32)!

In closing, let us consider the judgment of a legal mind in 1776 as he considered the reason for the Revolution:

> Thus, by natural causes and common effects, the American states are become dissolved from the British dominion. And is it to be wondered at that Britain has experienced the invariable fate of empire! We are not surprised when we see youth or age yield to the common lot of humanity. Nay, to repine that, in our day, America is dissolved from the British state, is impiously to question the unerring wisdom of Providence. The Almighty setteth up, and he casteth down: He breaks the sceptre, and transfers the dominion: He has made choice of the present generation to erect the American empire. Thankful as we are, and ought to be, for an appointment of the kind, the most illustrious that ever was, let each individual exert himself in this important operation directed by Jehovah himself. From a short retrospect, it is evident the work was not the present design of man.[5]

NOTES

1. Richard Crossman, ed., *The God That Failed* (New York: Bantam Books, 1950), pp. 18-19.*

2. Bertram D. Wolfe, *Strange Communists I Have Known* (New York: Bantam Books, 1965), p. 31.*

3. George Urban, *The Miracles of Chairman Mao* (Los Angeles: Nash Publishing, 1971).

4. Henry Clarke Warren, *Buddhism in Translations* (Cambridge, Mass.: Harvard University Press, 1963), pp. 65, 75, 86-87, 279, 301-303, 401-402.*

5. Hezekiah Niles, ed., *Centennial Offering—Republication of the Principles and Acts of the Revolution in America* (New York: A. S. Barnes & Co., 1876), pp. 336-37.

BIBLIOGRAPHY

Acheson, Dean. *Grapes From Thorns*. New York: W. W. Norton & Company, 1972.

Adair, Douglass and Schultz, John A., eds. *Peter Oliver's Origin & Progress of American Rebellion*. Stanford, California: Stanford University Press, 1961.

Adams, Charles Francis, ed. *The Works of John Adams, Second President of the United States*. 10 vols. Boston: Little, Brown and Company, 1850-1856.

Alvarez, A. *The Savage God*. New York: Random House, 1970.

Andre, Major John. *Major Andre's Journal*. Copyright 1904 by the Bibliographical Society.

Andrews, John. *Letters of John Andrews, Esq., of Boston, 1772-1776*. Edited by Winthrop Sargent. *Massachusetts Historical Society Proceedings*, VIII, 1866.

---

*Denotes paperback edition.

Austin, James Trecothick. *Life of Elbridge Gerry*. 2 vols. Boston: Wells, 1828-29.

Bacciocco, Edward J. *The New Left in America: Reform to Revolution 1956-1970*. Stanford, California: Hoover Institution Press, Stanford University, 1974.

Bailey, Thomas A. *Presidential Greatness*. New York: Appleton-Century, 1966.

Bakeless, Katherine and John. *Spies of the Revolution*. Philadelphia & New York: J. B. Lippincott Company, 1962.

Baldwin, Alice. *The New England Clergy and the American Revolution*. New York: Ungar Publishing Company, 1928.

Barber, James David. *The Presidential Character*. Englewood Cliffs, New Jersey: Prentice-Hall, 1972.

Barnes, G.R. and Owens, J. H., eds. *The Private Papers of John, Earl of Sandwich, First Lord of the Admiralty, 1771-1782*. Printed for the Navy Records Society, London, 1932-1938.

Bartlett, Richard A. *The New Country*. New York: Oxford University Press, 1974.

Beard, Charles A. and Mary R. *The American Spirit*. New York: Collier Books, 1942.*

Beggs, Larry. *Huckleberry's for Runaways*. New York: Ballantine Books, 1969.*

Beichman, Arnold. *Nine Lies About America*. New York: The Library Press, 1972.

Bemis, Samuel Flagg. *The Diplomacy of the American Revolution*. Bloomington, Indiana: Indiana University Press, 1967.*

Billias, George Athan, ed. *George Washington's Generals*. New York: William Morrow and Company, 1964.*

————. *George Washington's Opponents*. New York: William Morrow and Company, 1969.*

Boorstin, Daniel J. *The Americans: The Colonial Experience*. 1958. Reprint. Middlesex, England: Penguin Books, 1965.*

————. *The Americans: The Democratic Experience*. New York: Random House, 1973.

Boswell, James. *The Life of Samuel Johnson.* New York: 1872.

Boucher, Jonathan. *Reminiscences of An American Loyalist.* Boston: Houghton Mifflin Company, 1925.

Bourne, Randolph. *War and the Intellectuals.* New York: Harper & Row, Publishers, Harper Torchbooks, 1964.*

Boyd, Julian P., ed. *The Declaration of Independence.* Washington, D.C.: Library of Congress, 1943.

————. *The Papers of Thomas Jefferson.* 10 vols. Princeton, New Jersey: Princeton University Press, 1950-1954.

Brock, Peter. *Radical Pacifists in Antebellum America.* Princeton, New Jersey: Princeton University Press, 1968.*

Brown, Lloyd A. and Peckham, Howard H., eds. *Revolutionary War Journals Of Henry Dearborn 1775-1783.* New York: Da Capo Press, 1971.

Burgh, James. *Political Disquisitions.* 3 vols. New York: Da Capo Press, 1971.

Callahan, North. *Flight from the Republic.* Indianapolis, Indiana: The Bobbs-Merrill Company, 1967.

————. *Royal Raiders.* Indianapolis, Indiana: The Bobbs-Merrill Company, 1963.

Campion, Nardi Reeder. *Patrick Henry, Firebrand of the Revolution.* New York: Fawcett Publications, 1961.*

Carrol, Peter N., ed. *Religion and the Coming of the American Revolution.* Waltham, Massachusetts: Ginn-Blaisdell, 1970.

Carson, Clarence B. *The Rebirth of Liberty: The Founding of the American Republic 1760-1800.* New Rochelle, New York: Arlington House, 1973.

Chambers, Whittaker .*Witness.* New York: Random House, 1952.

Cobbett, William. *The Parliamentary History of England from the Earliest Period to the Year 1803.* 36 vols. London: Hansard, 1806-1820.

Commager, Henry Steele and Morris, Richard B., eds. *The Spirit of Seventy-Six.* New York: Harper & Row, Publishers, 1958.

Corner, George W., ed. *Autobiography of Benjamin Rush.* Princeton, New Jersey: Princeton University Press, 1948.

Covey, Cyclone. *The American Pilgrimage.* New York: Collier Books, 1961.

Crawford, Mary C. *Social Life in Old New England.* Boston: 1914.

Cremin, Lawrence A. *American Education: The Colonial Experience 1607-1783.* New York: Harper & Row, Publishers, 1970.

Crossman, Richard, ed. *The God That Failed.* New York: Bantam Books, 1950.*

Crouse, Timothy. *The Boys on the Bus.* New York: Random House, Ballantine Books, 1972.*

Cullen, Maurice R., Jr. *Battle Road.* Old Greenwich, Connecticut: The Chatham Press, Distributed by the Viking Press, 1970.*

Cunliffe, Marcus. *George Washington: Man & Monument.* New York and Toronto: The New American Library; London: The New English Library, Mentor Book, 1958.*

Davis, Burke. *The Campaign That Won America.* New York: The Dial Press, 1970.

Dawson, Henry B. *Battles of the United States by Sea and Land.* 2 vols. New York: Johnson, Fry and Company, 1858.

Deane, Charles, ed. *The Letter of Paul Revere to Dr. Belknap.* Boston. Massachusetts Historical Society, XVI, 1879.

De Crèvecoeur, J. Hector St. John. *Letters from an American Farmer.* New York: The New American Library, Signet Classic, 1963.*

De Fonblanque, Edward Barrington. *Political and Military Episodes in the Latter Half of the Eighteenth Century.* London: Macmillan, 1876.

De Tocqueville, Alexis. *Democracy in America.* 2 vols. New York: Schocken Books, 1961.*

Dickerson, Oliver Morton. *Boston Under Military Rule, 1768-1769.* New York: Da Capo Press, 1970.

Donne, W. Bodham, ed. *The Correspondence of King George the Third with Lord North 1786 to 1783.* 2 vols. New York: Da Capo Press, 1971.

Doran, John, ed. *Walpole Horace: Journal of the Reign of George the Third.* London. 1859.

Eckenrode, H. J. *Separation of Church and State in Virginia.* New York: Da Capo Press, 1971.

Elegant, Robert S. *Mao's Great Revolution.* New York: The World Publishing Company, 1971.

Erickson, Kai T. *Wayward Puritans.* New York: John Wiley & Sons, 1966.*

Fast, Howard. *Patrick Henry and the Frigate's Keel.* New York: Duell, Sloan & Pearce, 1936.*

Faust, Clarence H. and Johnson, Thomas H., eds. *Jonathan Edwards: Representative Selections.* New York: American Press, 1939.

Fehrenbach, T. R. *Greatness to Spare.* New York: D. Van Nostrand Company, 1968.

Filler, Louis. *The Crusade Against Slavery 1830-1860.* New York: Harper & Row, Publishers, The University Library, Harper Torchbooks, 1960.

Fitzpatrick, John C., ed. *The Writings of George Washington—From the Original Manuscript Sources, 1745-1799.* 39 vols. Washington, D.C.: U. S. Government Printing Office, 1931-1944.

Fitzsimons, Raymund. *Barnum in London.* New York: St. Martin's Press, 1970.

Flexner, James Thomas. *George Washington: The Forge of Experience.* Boston: Little, Brown and Company, 1965.

————. *George Washington: In the American Revolution.* Boston: Little, Brown and Company, 1967.

————. *George Washington: And the New Nation.* Boston: Little, Brown and Company, 1969.

————. *George Washington: Anguish and Farewell.* Boston: Little, Brown and Company, 1969.

————. *The Traitor and the Spy.* Boston: Little, Brown and Company, 1953.

Force, Peter, ed. *American Archives.* Fourth and Fifth Series. 6 vols., 1837-1846; 3 vols., 1948-1853. Washington.

Ford, Paul Leicester, ed. *The Life and Writings of John Dickinson.* Vol. I. Philadelphia, Pennsylvania: The Historical Society of Pennsylvania, 1895.

————. *The Writings of Thomas Jefferson.* 10 vols. New York: G. P. Putnam's Sons 1892-99.

Ford, Worthington Chauncey, ed. *Letters of William Lee, 1766-1783.* 2 vols. Brooklyn, New York: Historical Printing Club, 1892.

Franklin, Benjamin. *The Autobiography of Benjamin Franklin.* New York: Washington Square Press, 1955.*

Franklin, John Hope. *From Slavery to Freedom.* New York: Random House, Vintage Book, 1969.*

Frazier, E. Franklin. *The Negro Church in America.* New York: Schocken Books, 1964.*

Freeman, Douglas Southall. *Washington.* Vol. 7. Abridged. New York: Charles Scribner's Sons, 1968.

French, Allen. *The First Year of the American Revolution.* Boston: Houghton Mifflin Company, 1934.

Furnas, J. C. *The Americans: A Social History of the United States 1587-1914.* New York: G. P. Putnam's Sons, 1969.

Gaer, Joseph and Siegel, Ben. *The Puritan Heritage. America's Roots in the Bible.* New York: The New American Library, Mentor Book, 1964.*

Gentz, Friedrich and Possony, Stefan T. *Three Revolutions.* Gateway edition. Chicago: Henry Regnery Company, 1959.*

Gershen, Martin. *Destroy or Die.* New Rochelle, New York: Arlington House, 1971.

Gipson, Lawrence Henry. *The Coming of the Revolution.* Harper

& Row, Publishers, The University Library, Harper Torch-books, 1954.*

Golden, Harry. *Mr. Kennedy and the Negroes.* Crest reprint. New York: Fawcett Publications, 1964.*

Graham, James. *The Homosexual Kings of England.* London: Tandem, 1968.*

Great Britain Historical Manuscripts Commission. *The Manuscript of the Earl of Carlisle; Preserved at Castle Howard, Fifteenth Report, Appendix, Part IV.* London: Eyre & Spotiswoode, 1897.

Gruver, Rebecca Brooks. *American Nationalism.* New York: G. P. Putnam's Sons, 1970.

Hadley, Arthur Twining. *The Moral Basis of Democracy.* New Haven, Connecticut: Yale University Press, 1919.

Halle, Louis J. *The Cold War as History.* New York: Harper & Row, Publishers, 1967.

Handlin, Oscar. *Immigration.* Englewood Cliffs, New Jersey: Prentice-Hall, 1959.*

Hansen, Chadwick. *Witchcraft At Salem.* New York: George Braziller, 1969.

Hardie, Frank. *The Political Influence of the British Monarchy 1868-1952.* New York: Harper & Row, Publishers, 1970.

Harris, Louis. *The Anguish of Change.* New York: W. W. Norton & Company, 1973.

Hartmann, Frederick H. *Relations of Nations.* New York: Macmillan, 1957.

Hawke, David Freeman. *Paine.* New York: Harper & Row, Publishers, 1974.

Hawks. *Contributions to the Ecclesiastical History of the United States.* Virginia.

Higginbotham, Don. *The War of American Independence.* New York: Macmillan Company, 1971.

Hofstadter, Richard. *Anti-Intellectualism in American Life.* New York: Alfred A. Knopf, 1970.

Holbrook, Stewart H. *Ethan Allen.* New York: Macmillan, 1940.*

Holliday, Carl. *The Wit and Humor of Colonial Days.* New York. 1960.

Hughes, Emmet John. *The Living Presidency.* New York: Coward, McCann & Geoghegan, 1972.

Hunt, Gaillard, ed. *Journals of the Continental Congress, 1774-1789.* Washington: U.S. Government Printing Office, 1904-1937.

Janowitz, Morris. *The Professional Soldier.* New York: Collier-Macmillan, The Free Press, 1960.*

Kelley, Dean M. *Why Conservative Churches Are Growing.* New York: Harper & Row, Publishers, 1972.

Kennedy, John F. *The Strategy of Peace.* New York: Popular Library, 1960.

Ketchum, Richard M. *The Winter Soldiers.* Garden City, New York: Doubleday & Company, 1973.

Kittredge, George Lyman. *Witchcraft in Old and New England.* Cambridge, Massachusetts. 1929.

Koch, Adrienne. *Power, Morals and the Founding Fathers.* Ithaca, New York: Cornell University Press, Cornell Paperbacks, 1961.*

Kohn, Richard H. *Eagle and Sword.* New York: Macmillan, The Free Press, 1975.

Knollenberg, Bernhard. *Origin of the American Revolution.* 2d ed., rev. New York: Collier-Macmillan, Free Press, 1960.*

Lacy, Dan. *The Meaning of the American Revolution.* New York: The New American Library, Mentor Book, 1964.

Lankford, John. *Captain John Smith's America.* New York: Harper & Row, Publishers, The University Library, Harper Torchbooks, 1967.

Leder, Lawrence H. *The Meaning of the American Revolution.* Chicago: Quadrangle Books, New York Times Book, 1969.

Lenin. V. I. *Lenin: Selected Works.* 3 vols. Moscow: Foreign Languages Publishing House, 1961.

Lewy, Guenter. *Religion and Revolution.* New York: Oxford University Press, 1974.

Lippman, Walter. *A Preface to Morals.* London: George Allen & Unwin, Ruskin House, 1929.

Lipset, Seymour Martin. *Political Man: The Social Bases of Politics.* Garden City, New York: Doubleday & Company, Anchor Books, 1960.*

Lubell, Samuel. *The Future While It Happened.* New York: W. W. Norton & Company, 1973.

Maddox, Robert James. *The New Left and the Origins of the Cold War.* Princeton, New Jersey: Princeton University Press, 1973.

Malone, Dumas. *Jefferson the Virginian.* Boston: Little, Brown and Company, 1948.

Martin, Ingsley. *Editor.* Middlesex, England: Penguin Books, 1969.

Mayo, Bernard. *Myths & Men.* New York: Harper & Row, Publishers, The Academy Library, Harper Torchbooks, 1959.

McKitrick, Eric L., ed. *Slavery Defended: The Views of the Old South.* Englewood Cliffs, New Jersey: Prentice-Hall, Spectrum Book, 1963.*

Mellon, Matthew T. *Early American Views on Negro Slavery.* New York: The New American Library, Mentor Books, 1934.*

Menniger, Dr. Karl. *Whatever Became of Sin?* New York: Hawthorn Books, 1973.*

Miller, John C. *The First Frontier: Life in Colonial America.* New York: Dell Publishing Company, Laurel Edition, 1966.*

Miller, Perry and Johnson, Thomas. *The Puritans.* 2 vols. 2d ed., rev. New York: Harper & Row, Publishers, The Academy Library, Harper Torchbooks, 1938.*

Moore, Frank, ed. *Diary of the American Revolution.* 2 vols. New York: Charles Scribner's Sons, 1860.

Morgan, Edmund S. *American Slavery American Freedom.* New York: W. W. Norton & Company, 1975.

————. *The Puritan Dilemma: The Story of John Winthrop.* Boston: Little, Brown and Company 1958.

————. *The Puritan Family.* New York: Harper & Row, Publishers, The Academy Library, Harper Torchbooks, 1944.*

Morgan, Edmund S. and Helen M. *The Stamp Act Crisis.* London: Collier-Macmillan, Collier Books, 1953.*

Morison, Samuel Eliot. *The Oxford History of the American People.* New York: Oxford University Press, 1965.

Morris, Richard B. *Seven Who Shaped Our Destiny.* New York: Harper & Row, Publishers, 1973.

Newell, Timothy. *A Journal Kept During the Time That Boston Was Shut Up in 1775-76.* Massachusetts Historical Society Collections. Fourth series, vol. I. 1852.

Niles, Hezekiah, ed. *Centennial Offering—Republication of the Principles and Acts of the Revolution in America.* New York: A. S. Barnes & Co., 1876.

Nobile, Philip. *Intellectual Skywriting.* New York: Charterhouse, 1974.

Norton, Mary Beth. *The British-Americans.* Boston: Little, Brown and Company, 1972.

Pearce, Roy Harvey, ed. *Colonial American Writing.* New York: Rinehart Editions, 1950.

Peckham, H. H. *The War for Independence: A Military History.* Chicago: University of Chicago Press, 1968.*

Penn, William. *Sandy Foundations Shaken.*

Phillips, Kevin. *Mediacracy.* Garden City, New York: Doubleday & Company, 1975.

Price, Richard. *Observations on the Nature of Civil Liberty, the Principles of Government, and the Justice and Policy of the War with America.* 1776. Reprint. New York: S. Loudon, 1776.

Ramsey, David. *History of the American Revolution.* 2 vols. London: John Stockdale, 1793.

Reed, Joseph. *Remarks on Governor Johnstone's Speech in Parliament.* Philadelphia: Francis Barley, 1779.

Revel, Jean-Francois. *Without Marx or Jesus*. London: Paladin, 1972.*

Rives, W. C. *Life & Times of James Madison*.

Ryerson, A. E. *The Loyalists of America and Their Times*. Toronto. 1880.

Salisbury, Harrison E. *War Between Russia & China*. New York: W. W. Norton & Company, 1969.*

Scammon, Richard M. and Wattenberg, Ben J. *The Real Majority*. New York: Coward-McCann, 1970.

Schlesinger, Arthur M., Jr. *The Crisis of Confidence*. New York: Bantam Books, 1969.*

Selsam, J. Paul. *The Pennsylvania Constitution of 1776*. Philadelphia: University of Pennsylvania Press, 1936.

Sewall, Samuel. *Letter-Box*. 2 vols. Boston: Massachusetts Historical Society, Sixth series. 1886.

Shaw, Bernard. *The Political Madhouse in America and Nearer Home*. London: Constable & Company, 1933.

Shepard, James. *The Tories of Connecticut*. Connecticut Quarterly, 1898, vol. IV.

Shirer, William L. *End of A Berlin Diary*. New York: Alfred A. Knopf, 1947.

————. *Midcentury Journey*. New York: Farrar, Straus & Young, 1952.

————. *The Rise & Fall of the Third Reich*. New York: Simon & Schuster, 1960.

Shy, John. *Toward Lexington*. Princeton, New Jersey: Princeton University Press, 1965.*

Singer, Kurt. *Spies Who Changed History*. New York: Ace Books, 1960.*

Siracusa, Joseph M. *New Left Diplomatic Histories and Historians*. Port Washington, New York: Kennikat Press, 1973.

Smith, Gerberding. *The Radical Left: The Abuse of Discontent*. Boston: Houghton Mifflin Company, 1970.*

Smith, Paul H. *Loyalists & Redcoats*. Chapel Hill, North Carolina: University of North Carolina Press, 1964.*

Solzhenitsyn, Alexander, et al. *From Under the Rubble*. Boston: Little, Brown and Company, 1974.

Stark, James H. *Loyalists of Massachusetts*. Boston. 1910.

Stone, William L., translator. *Letters of Brunswick and Hessian Officers During the American Revolution*. Albany: Joel Munsell's Sons, Publishers, 1891.

Storms, J. C. *Origin of the Jackson Whites of the Ramapo Mountains*. Park Ridge, New Jersey. 1936.

Stryker, William S. *The Battles of Trenton and Princeton*. Boston: Houghton Mifflin Company, 1898.

Sydnor, Charles S. *American Revolutionaries in the Making*. New York: Collier-Macmillan, The Free Press, 1952.

Taylor, Tim. *The Book of Presidents*. New York: Arno Press, 1972.

Tebbel, John. *The Media in America*. New York: Thomas Y. Crowell Company, 1974.

Thomas, John L., ed. *Slavery Attacked: The Abolitionist Crusade*. Englewood Cliffs, New Jersey: Prentice-Hall, Spectrum Book, 1965.*

Thornton, John Wingate. *The Pulpit of the American Revolution*. New York: Da Capo Press, 1970.

Tomilson, Abraham. *The Military Journals of Two Private Soldiers, 1758-1775*. New York: Da Capo Press, 1971.

Tower, Charlemagne. *The Marquis de Lafayette in the American Revolution*. 2 vols. New York: Da Capo Press, 1970.

Urban, George. *The Miracles of Chairman Mao*. Los Angeles: Nash Publishing, 1971.

Vogelgesang, Sandy. *The Long Dark Night of the Soul*. New York: Harper & Row, Publishers, 1974.

Walton, Richard J. *Cold War and Counter-Revolution*. New York: The Viking Press, 1972.

Ward, Barbara. *Nationalism & Ideology*. New York: W. W. Norton & Company, 1966.*

Warren, Henry Clarke. *Buddhism in Translations*. New York: Atheneum Publishers, 1963.*

Wattenberg, Ben J. *The Real America*. Garden City, New York: Doubleday & Company, 1974.

Wertenbaker, Thomas Jefferson. *The Puritan Oligarchy*. New York: Charles Scribner's Sons, 1947.

Werth, Alexander. *Russia At War 1941-1945*. London: Barrie Books, Pan Books, 1965.*

Wesson, Robert G. *Why Marxism?* New York: Basic Books, 1975.

Wheatley, Henry B., ed. *The Historical and the Posthumous Memoirs of Sir Nathaniel Wraxall, 1772-1784*. 5 vols. New York: Scribner and Welford, 1884.

White, Theodore H. *Breach of Faith*. New York, Atheneum Publishers, Reader's Digest Press, 1975.

————. *The Making of the President 1960*. New York: Atheneum Publishers, 1961.*

————. *The Making of the President 1964*. New York: Atheneum Publishers, 1965.*

Wildes, Harry Emmerson. *William Penn*. New York: Macmillan, 1974.

Willard, Margaret Wheeler, ed. *Letters on the American Revolution, 1774-1776*. Boston: Houghton Mifflin Company, 1925.

Wilson, Woodrow. *George Washington*. New York: Schocken Books, 1896.*

Wolfe, Bertram D. *Strange Communists I Have Known*. New York: Bantam Books, 1965.*

————. *Three Who Made a Revolution*. 1948. Reprint. Middlesex, England: Penquin Books, 1966.*

Wolfe, Tom. *Radical Chic & Mau-Mauing the Flak Catchers*. London: Michael Joseph, 1971.

Wolff, Robert Paul. *The Ideal of the University*. Boston: Beacon Press, 1969.

Woodmason, Charles. *The Carolina Backcountry on the Eve of the Revolution*. Chapel Hill, North Carolina: University of North Carolina Press, 1953.*

Worcester, J. H., Jr. *The Life of David Livingstone*. Chicago: Moody Press.

Wright, Louis B. *Gold, Glory and the Gospel.* New York: Atheneum Publishers, 1970.

Wyatt-Brown, Bertram. *Lewis Tappan and the Evangelical War Against Slavery.* Cleveland: The Press of Case Western Reserve University, 1969.

Young, Alexander. *Chronicles of the Pilgrim Fathers of the Colony of Plymouth 1602-1625.* New York: Da Capo Press, 1971.

Zobel, Hiller B. *The Boston Massacre.* New York: W. W. Norton & Company, 1976.